ROGER EATWELL
AND MATTHEW GOODWIN

National Populism
The Revolt Against Liberal Democracy

A PELICAN BOOK

PELICAN
an imprint of
PENGUIN BOOKS

PELICAN BOOKS

UK | USA | Canada | Ireland | Australia
India | New Zealand | South Africa

Penguin Books is part of the Penguin Random House
group of companies whose addresses can be found at
global.penguinrandomhouse.com.

Penguin
Random House
UK

First published in 2018
002

Copyright © Roger Eatwell and Matthew Goodwin, 2018

The moral rights of the authors have been asserted

Book design by Matthew Young
Set in 10/14.664 pt FreightText Pro
Typeset by Jouve (UK), Milton Keynes
Printed and bound in Great Britain by Clays Ltd, Elcograf S.p.A.

A CIP catalogue record for this book is available from the British Library

ISBN: 978-0-241-31200-1

Contents

PREFACE

Across much of the West, especially in Europe and the US, national populism is now a serious force. Our argument in this book is that to really make sense of this movement we need to take a step back and look at the deep, long-term trends that have been reshaping our societies over decades, if not longer.

We are academics who have researched this topic for many years. Roger Eatwell specializes in political parties, traditions and ideas, including fascism, which, for reasons that we will show, is different from national populism. Matt Goodwin is a political sociologist who looks at why growing numbers of people across the West are abandoning the mainstream for national populism. We hope to offer readers a unique insight into what has become, in only a short period, one of the most controversial yet misunderstood movements of our times.

Many people have worked or talked with us about these issues. They are too numerous to name individually, but we would particularly like to thank: Noah Atkinson, Jonathan Boyd, Bobby Duffy, Harold Clarke, Stefan Cornibert, David Cutts, James Dennison, James Eatwell, Judith Eatwell, Jane Farrant, Robert Ford, Craig Fowlie, David Goodhart, Oliver

Heath, Simon Hix, Eric Kaufmann, Marta Lorimer, Nonna Mayer, Fiona McAdoo, Caitlin Milazzo, Michael Minkenberg, Brian Neve, Mark Pickup, Jon Portes, Jacob Poushter, Jens Rydgren, Thomas Raines, Bruce Stokes and Paul Whiteley.

Last, but by no means least, we would like to thank our literary agent, Charlie Brotherstone of Brotherstone Creative Management, for his helpful comments and encouragement, Chloe Currens, our editor at Penguin Books, who provided us with an extremely helpful set of comments on an earlier draft, Linden Lawson, our proactive copy editor and Penguin's helpful marketeers Isabel Blake and Julie Woon.

Any errors or faults which remain are entirely our own.

R. E. and M. G. July 2018

INTRODUCTION

This book is about 'national populism', a movement that in the early years of the twenty-first century is increasingly challenging mainstream politics in the West. National populists prioritize the culture and interests of the nation, and promise to give voice to a people who feel that they have been neglected, even held in contempt, by distant and often corrupt elites.

It is an ideology rooted in very deep and long-term currents that have been swirling beneath our democracies and gaining strength over many decades. In this book we explore these currents, setting out an overview of how politics is changing in Europe and the US. Our broad argument is that national populism is here to stay.

We decided to write this book in 2016 amid two moments that shocked the West: when the billionaire and celebrity businessman Donald Trump was officially nominated as the Republican presidential candidate and then defeated Hillary Clinton in the race to the White House; and when more than half of Britain's voters stunned the world by voting for 'Brexit', choosing to withdraw their country from the European Union (EU), an organization it had joined in the 1970s.

Few pundits saw these results coming. Only two weeks

before the 2016 presidential election, the *New York Times*'s election forecast confidently told readers that Hillary Clinton had a 93 per cent chance of winning the presidency. Others put it at 99 per cent and pondered whether she might even turn Texas blue on her way to the White House.

In Britain, more than 300 scholars, journalists and pollsters were asked to predict what would happen at the 2016 referendum and 90 per cent thought that British voters would choose to remain in the EU. Gambling on politics is legal in Britain, and so, had you bet £100 on Brexit on the day of the referendum, you would have made a £300 profit in the morning and £900 in the evening. The groupthink was certain that Remain would win, even though many of the online polls were suggesting the opposite.

The American engineer W. Edwards Deming once said: 'In God we trust; all others bring data.' Yet though we live in an era when we have more data than ever before, hardly anyone successfully read the public mood. We think this is because too many people are focusing too much on the short term and failing to take into account the historic shifts in politics, culture and economics that are now having profound effects on the outcome of our elections.

National populists emerged long before the financial crisis that erupted in 2008 and the Great Recession that followed. Their supporters are more diverse than the stereotypical 'angry old white men' who, we are frequently told, will soon be replaced by a new generation of tolerant Millennials. Brexit and Trump actually followed the much longer rise of national populists across Europe, like Marine Le Pen in France, Matteo Salvini in Italy and Viktor Orbán in Hungary.

They are part of a growing revolt against mainstream politics and liberal values.

This challenge to the liberal mainstream is in general not anti-democratic. Rather, national populists are opposed to certain *aspects* of liberal democracy as it has evolved in the West. Contrary to some of the hysterical reactions that greeted Trump and Brexit, those who support these movements are not fascists who want to tear down our core political institutions. A small minority do, but most have understandable concerns about the fact that these institutions are not representative of society as a whole and, if anything, are becoming ever more cut adrift from the average citizen.

Shortly before Trump won the White House, more than half of white Americans without degrees felt that Washington did not represent people like them, while just prior to the Brexit victory nearly one in two of Britain's workers felt that 'people like them' no longer had a voice in the national conversation.[1] Against the backdrop of major scandals over lobbying, 'dark money', the abuse of parliamentary expenses, lucrative speeches for major banks and 'revolving-door politics', when former politicians exploit their contacts to finance private deals, is it any wonder that large numbers of citizens today are openly questioning the trustworthiness of their representatives?

Some national-populist leaders, like Hungary's Viktor Orbán, speak of creating a new form of 'illiberal democracy' that raises worrying issues about democratic rights and the demonization of immigrants. However, most national-populist voters want *more* democracy – *more* referendums and *more* empathetic and listening politicians that give *more* power to the people and less power to established economic and political elites. This 'direct' conception of democracy differs from the 'liberal' one that has flourished across the West following the defeat of fascism and which, as we discuss in Chapter 3, has gradually become more elitist in character.

National populism also raises legitimate democratic issues that millions of people want to discuss and address. They question the way in which elites have become more and more insulated from the lives and concerns of ordinary people. They question the erosion of the nation state, which they see as the only construct that has proven capable of organizing our political and social lives. They question the capacity of Western societies to rapidly absorb rates of immigration and 'hyper ethnic change' that are largely unprecedented in the history of modern civilization. They question why the West's current economic settlement is creating highly unequal societies and leaving swathes of people behind, and whether the state should accord priority in employment and welfare to people who have spent their lives paying into the national pot. They question cosmopolitan and globalizing agendas, asking where these are taking us and what kind of societies they will create. And some of them ask whether all religions support key aspects of modern life in the West, such as equality and respect for women and LGBT communities. There is absolutely no doubt that some national populists veer into racism and xenophobia, especially towards Muslims. But this should not distract us from the fact that they also tap into widespread and legitimate public anxieties across a range of different areas.

This movement needs to be explored as a whole because it is international in character. Many of our debates about politics are very insular: we focus on our own countries in isolation. Americans often interpret Trump solely from the perspective of American politics. But they can learn much from Europe, as their national populists are already doing. This is why, in 2018, Trump's former chief strategist Steve Bannon went on a tour of Europe and met with several leading national populists, including Marine Le Pen in France, in countries that have been grappling with national populists for some time. Well before this, Trump himself had close ties to the Brexiteer Nigel Farage, the former leader of the United Kingdom Independence Party (UKIP), who in turn has links to populists in Europe, such as the Alternative for Germany, which broke through in 2017 and shattered the old myth that populism could never succeed in the country that had given the world National Socialism.[2]

Other controversial populist figures frequently visit the US, such as Geert Wilders in the Netherlands, who infamously alleges that Europe is being 'Islamified' and has garnered the support of Republican members of Congress like Steve King, while members of the Le Pen dynasty in France have journeyed to the US Conservative Political Action Conference. In the EU, a broad alliance named the 'Europe of Nations and Freedom' brings together national populists from an array of countries including Austria, Belgium, Britain, France, Germany, Italy, the Netherlands and Poland. If you looked only at Trump or Brexit, then you would miss the broader trends.

Why Is this Book Necessary?

Trump, Brexit and rebellions in Europe have fuelled an explosion of interest in populism – what it is, who votes for it and why it matters. In the years to come there will be countless books, articles and no doubt movies about these political crusades that are being waged in the name of the people – what Trump calls the 'silent majority', Farage 'the people's army' and Le Pen 'the forgotten France'.

Yet we see problems in this debate as it is currently unfolding. It is often distorted by flawed assumptions, bias and an overwhelming obsession with the short term – with the here and now. Much that is written embraces misleading claims about national populism's roots and supporters, such as the idea that this turbulence is merely a passing protest in response to the financial crisis that erupted in 2008, the austerity that followed, or the refugee crisis that has swept through Europe since 2014. These are comforting ideas for people who cling to the belief that 'normal business' will soon resume once economic growth returns and the flow of refugees slows or stops altogether. But these ideas are wrong.

Many writers who claim to be impartial also find it hard to avoid being influenced by their own sympathy for liberal and left-wing politics (in the US, 'liberal' is often used as a synonym for 'left-wing', rather than in its historic sense of defending individual freedom and rights, which Americans refer to as 'libertarianism'). This is not to say that *everybody* who writes about populism is biased. There have been important contributions. Scholars who might not be familiar to some readers, like Piero Ignazi and Jens Rydgren, point-ed out how these revolts in Europe were a long time in the making. Thinkers like Margaret Canovan have shown how populism is an alternative form of democratic politics, and will be with us for as long as we have democracy. But many are too quick to condemn rather than reflect, buying into stereotypes that correspond with their own outlook rather than challenging claims by consulting the actual evidence.

Consider a couple of common reactions to the election of Trump. David Frum, a former speechwriter for George W. Bush, has written about 'Trumpocracy', which he sees as an authoritarian threat to liberal democracy and world peace, led by a president who accused Hillary Clinton and the 'Washington swamp' of endemic corruption before es-tablishing his own kleptocratic and nepotistic White House.[3] Or the professional psychologists who came forward to diag-nose Trump's behaviour – in spite of the American Psychi-atric Association's prohibition of diagnosing politicians they have never personally evaluated – as being symptomatic of fundamental problems like anger, malignant narcissism and an impulsiveness which raise major questions about his abil-ity to govern and safeguard world peace.[4] While there are good reasons to be concerned about Trump, focusing on his personality brings us no closer to understanding the popu-lar roots of the revolt that have nurtured his rise, and that of others like him in Europe.

Although most national populists in Europe do not hold office, they are subjected to much the same treatment. They are dismissed as extremists whose authoritarian and racist politics pose a serious threat to liberal democracy and minorities. More damningly still, they are alleged by many to be 'fascists' - harbingers of a dangerous revival of dictatorship. Shortly before the 2017 presidential election in France, the American magazine *Vanity Fair* asked: 'Can Marine Le Pen make fascism mainstream?', while a prominent French intellectual, Bernard-Henri Lévy, countered that 'France is not ready for a fascist regime today', implying that it could be soon.[5]

In popular debates the term 'fascist' has degenerated into little more than a term of abuse. But concerns about Trump have meant that dropping the 'f-bomb' has extended even to historians who are specialists in the turbulent inter-war years. The Yale historian Timothy Snyder has warned about the onset of tyranny, comparing Trump's choreographed, macho and narcissistic 2016 campaign meetings with Nazi rallies, adding that his lying 'post-truth is pre-fascism'. The New York University historian Ruth Ben-Ghiat claimed that Trump's attacks on key aspects of liberal democracy, such as judicial and media freedom, mean that Americans 'cannot exclude an intention to carry out a type of coup', and that his aggressive 'blitzkrieg . . . forces us to take sides'. Others point to the risk of creeping authoritarianism through policies such as conservative court appointments, which is more plausible, though it is a view based largely on polemical speculation rather than careful analysis.[6] Too often the focus is on what *could* happen rather than what is *actually* happening.

Meanwhile, those who vote for national populists are ridiculed and dismissed as 'hillbillies', 'rednecks', 'chavs' or 'Little Englanders'. Hillary Clinton described half of Trump's supporters as a 'basket of deplorables', people whose views were 'racist, sexist, homophobic, xenophobic, Islamophobic, you name it'. In Britain, Prime Minister David Cameron derided those who favoured Brexit as a bunch of 'fruitcakes, loonies and closet racists', while leading newspaper columnists urged established politicians in Westminster to turn their backs on the struggling areas in England that were about to break for Brexit. Today we live in an era in which more people than ever before campaign to ensure that rights, dignity and respect are granted to all in society, yet it is hard to imagine any other group being treated with as much contempt.

Our collective obsession with the short term is holding back our thinking. Why was Trump elected? Why did people vote for Brexit? Why are millions of people in Europe casting their votes for national populists? Answers to these questions routinely fail to appreciate the deeper currents that have been swirling beneath our democracies.

Trump's victory has been widely attributed to a host of factors in the 'here and now': the influence of Steve Bannon during the closing stages of the 2016 presidential race, who advocated a more populist and patriarchal appeal; allegations that Trump's victory was helped by collusion with Russia; and Russia-backed manipulation of social media like Facebook and Twitter. Regardless of the truth of these claims, the obsession with the short term tells us nothing about why so many Americans felt so alienated from the mainstream or why, as research has shown, white Americans without degrees were defecting to the Republicans long before Trump even announced his candidacy.

Similarly, ever since the Brexit victory, 'Remainers' who wanted Britain to remain in the EU have suggested that old white workers who live away from cosmopolitan London were too stupid to recognize the wonders of European integration and immigration. Some argue that Brexit only won because Russia used online 'bots' to manipulate social media, or that during the campaign Brexiteers 'lied' by claiming that Brexit would allow up to £350 million per week of EU payments to be redirected to Britain's struggling National Health Service. Again, irrespective of the validity of these claims, to focus on the short term diverts us from stepping back to appreciate the broader trends that made this radical political moment possible.

Brexit and Trump were quickly lumped together in international debates about a 'white working-class backlash'. But a closer look at the evidence, as we will see in the next chapter, reveals how these simplistic conclusions are wide of the mark. Writers across the West are now making sweeping claims about the people who vote for national populists, yet hardly any of them scrutinize the large body of evidence that has been built up in the social sciences over the past forty years. Brief journalistic visits to the Rust Belt or some of England's deteriorating coastal towns result in the portrayal of crude bigots and old white men. But many Trump voters were relatively affluent, while in Europe lots of those lining up behind national populists are neither ignorant racists nor particularly old. Some are even pro-LGBT, but at the same time deeply suspicious of the ability of Islam to conform to liberal democracy.

The search for 'one type' of supporter and 'one motive'

is also unhelpful. Trump and Brexit appealed to a broad and loose alliance of middle-class social conservatives and blue-collar workers who together rejected the advice of global elites represented by private-school- and Oxford-educated David Cameron and by Barack Obama, who had been to two Ivy League universities and spoke with the clean accent and fluency of an East Coast law professor.

Trump pulled in not only manual workers who were worried about immigration, but also fairly affluent mainstream Republicans, as well as around one in three Latino men and notable support from specific minorities like Cuban Americans. Brexit not only won the day in 140 heavily working-class districts that historically voted for the left-wing Labour Party, but was also endorsed by one in three of Britain's black and ethnic-minority voters and around half of those in Britain aged between thirty-five and forty-four.

The desire to pull Britain out of the EU was a majority view not only in largely white and prosperous conservative counties like Hampshire but also ethnically diverse areas like Birmingham, Luton and Slough. In these communities, settled minorities saw immigrant workers from other EU member states not only as a threat to their own position but also as beneficiaries of preferential treatment over their own relatives and friends who wished to come from outside Europe. Headlines that scream 'Angry white working-class backlash' miss these nuances.

There will always be intriguing questions about what *could* have been. Had Hillary Clinton fought a less hubristic campaign, had she inspired more Millennial graduates and African Americans to vote, had she invested more effort in the 209 counties that voted twice for Obama before switching to Trump, had she launched a more meaningful dialogue with whites without degrees in the key Rust Belt states who easily outnumber degree-holders, then things might have been different.

In Britain, had Boris Johnson, the charismatic Conservative politician and admirer of Winston Churchill, not made a late decision to campaign for Brexit, had Brexit not received a surprise boost from around 2 million 'non-voters' who tended to shun politics, and had the pro-EU Remain strategists not made a conscious decision to completely ignore the issue of immigration, the top concern for Leavers, then Britain might have stayed in the EU.

In politics there will always be 'what ifs'. But this kind of speculation is unhelpful because it prevents us from forming a deeper, more sophisticated understanding of exactly *why* our political world is in so much flux. Even if things had turned out differently, support for Brexit and Trump would still have been strong. Marine Le Pen was written off when she failed to become President of France, but we still need to make sense of why she attracted one in three French voters, including lots of under-forties – and why in recent years movements from the League in Italy to the Freedom Parties in Austria and the Netherlands have enjoyed rapidly rising and often record levels of support.

To really get our heads around what is happening we must trace the origins of these populist revolts much further back. Rather than examine individual movements and leaders, in this book we will focus on the bigger picture and make two broad arguments.

The 'Four Ds'

We cannot make sense of these revolts without understanding how longer-term trends have been reshaping politics in the West for decades. National populism revolves around a set of four deep-rooted societal changes which are cause for growing concern among millions of people in the West. We refer to these four historic shifts as the 'Four Ds'. These are often based on legitimate grievances and are unlikely to fade in the near future.

The first is the way in which the elitist nature of liberal democracy has promoted *distrust* of politicians and institutions and fuelled a sense among large numbers of citizens that they no longer have a voice in their national conversation. Liberal democracy always sought to minimize the participation of the masses. But in recent years, politicians' growing distance from ordinary citizens has led to a rising tide of distrust, not just of mainstream parties but also of institutions like the US Congress and the European Union, a trend clearly mapped by surveys and other data. There was never a golden era when political systems represented everybody in society, and in recent years important steps have been taken to ensure that historically marginalized groups like women and ethnic minorities have a louder voice in legislatures. But at the same time many political systems have become less representative of key groups, leading many to conclude that they are voiceless, and driving the national populist turn.

The second is how immigration and hyper ethnic change

are cultivating strong fears about the possible *destruction* of the national group's historic identity and established ways of life. These fears are wrapped up in a belief that culturally liberal politicians, transnational organizations and global finance are eroding the nation by encouraging further mass immigration, while 'politically correct' agendas seek to silence any opposition. These concerns are not always grounded in objective reality – as is reflected by the fact that they are manifest not only in democracies that have experienced rapid and profound ethnic shifts like Britain, but also in those that have much lower levels of immigration like Hungary and Poland. They are nonetheless potent and will become more so as ethnic and cultural change continues to sweep across the West in the coming years.

The third is the way in which neoliberal globalized economics has stoked strong feelings of what psychologists call relative *deprivation* as a result of rising inequalities of income and wealth in the West and a loss of faith in a better future. Though many people who support national populism have jobs and live on average or above-average incomes (even if many of these jobs are insecure), the West's economic transformation has fuelled a strong sense of 'relative' *deprivation* – a belief among certain groups that they are losing out *relative to others*. This means they are very fearful about the future and what lies ahead for themselves and their children. This profound sense of loss is intimately entwined with the way in which people think through issues like immigration and identity.

Today there are millions of voters who are convinced that the past was better than the present and that the present, however bleak, is still better than the future. They are not part of the jobless white underclass or welfare-takers. If national populism depended for its support on the unemployed, then dealing with it would be easier – it would be about creating jobs, especially ones with long-term security and decent wages. But most of the people in this category are not on the bottom rung of the ladder; they do, however, share a strong belief that the current settlement no longer works for them and that others are being prioritized.

National-populist leaders feed on this deep dissatisfaction, but their path into the mainstream has also been cleared by a fourth trend: the weakening bonds between the traditional mainstream parties and the people, or what we refer to as *de-alignment*. The classic era of liberal democracy was characterized by relatively stable politics, strong mainstream parties and loyal voters; we have seen it now come to an end. Many people are no longer strongly aligned to the mainstream. The bonds are breaking. This de-alignment is making political systems across the West far more volatile, fragmented and unpredictable than at any point in the history of mass democracy. Politics today feels more chaotic and less predictable than in the past because it is. This trend too was a long time coming, and it still has a long way to run.

Together, the 'Four Ds' have carved out considerable room for national populists, or what we call the 'pool of potential' – large numbers of people who feel that they no longer have a voice in politics, that rising immigration and rapid ethnic change threaten their national group, culture and ways of life, that the neoliberal economic system is leaving them behind relative to others in society, and who no longer identify with established politicians.

These trends need to be analysed together, not presented as competing approaches. We say this because, unfortunately, across the West there is an unhelpful debate about populism that pits factors against each other as though they are mutually exclusive. Is it economics, or is it culture? Is it about jobs, or is it about immigrants? Is it austerity, or is it nationalism?

The reality, of course, is that no one factor can explain the rise of what are highly complex movements. Nonetheless, some, like the journalist John Judis, argue that all of this change is about 'economics and not culture', while others, like the scholars Ronald Inglehart and Pippa Norris, contend that it is 'culture and not economics'.[7] The first approach contends that people's worries about issues like immigration are really just a by-product of their economic distress. The second holds that people's worries about issues of identity operate independently of their economic environment, as can be seen from the fact that many people who feel concerned about immigration are not poor, and that many of those who vote for national populists are in work and often skilled.

But this binary debate is extremely unhelpful: real life never really works like this. It is far too simplistic and glosses over the way in which concerns about culture and economics can, and often do, interact. The longer-term approach that we take is also very different to popular arguments that draw a straight line from the political turmoil to the financial crisis, Great Recession and sovereign debt crisis in Europe.

Many on the liberal left like that argument because it puts economics centre-stage, presenting Trump as a by-product of crisis-led inequality, or the rise of populists in Europe as a reaction to the harsh austerity that was imposed on democracies after pressure from non-elected transnational institutions like the European Central Bank and International Monetary Fund (IMF).

There is no doubt – as we will see – that the seismic events of the crisis and the subsequent fallout exacerbated the deep cultural and economic divides in the West that underpin national populism. But these divides began well before the collapse of Lehman Brothers. Financial analysts would do well to look at the life cycle of national populism, as we will in the next chapter. As the Austrians, British, Bulgarians, Danish, Dutch, French, Hungarians, Italians, Norwegians, Poles and Swiss will tell you, national populism was a serious force long before the Great Recession. And even had it never happened, we would still have national populists to contend with.

The Arrival of a Serious Revolt

Our second broad argument is that national populism has serious long-term potential.

One interesting macro question is whether political shocks like Brexit and Trump signal that the West is nearing the *end* of a period of political volatility, or instead is closer to the *beginning* of a new period of great change. The former is premised on the idea that, as countries leave the financial crisis and return to growth, people will flock back to the traditional parties. It is also shaped by thinking about generational change.

One very popular argument is that national populism represents one 'last howl of rage' from old white men soon be replaced by tolerant Millennials, who were born between the 1980s and 2000s, and who, we are told, feel far more at ease with immigration, refugees, ethnic change and open borders.

Progressive liberals are fond of this argument because it chimes with their own identification not as nationalists but as internationalists or 'citizens of the world', and their firm belief that the West is on a conveyor belt towards a far more liberal future. They point to how only one in four Millennials approved of Trump's first year in office, compared to one in two of the much older Silent Generation, the members of which were born between the 1920s and 1940s. They point to the sweeping victory of young liberal centrist Emmanuel Macron in France in 2017. And they point to the fact that Brexit was endorsed by two in three pensioners, but only one in four of those aged between eighteen and twenty-four.

Such findings also reflect the differing priorities of different generations. Whereas in many established economies Millennials are the first modern generation to be financially worse off than their parents, even after accounting for their greater ethnic diversity they are still far more liberal than older generations. In major democracies like the US, Britain and Germany, Millennials are far more accepting of homosexuality and same-sex marriage, feel less concerned about and more positive towards immigration, are more supportive than older generations of relationships and marriages between members of different racial groups and are more opposed to the death penalty, which is a touchstone for the definition of holding liberal values.[8]

With the arrival of President Trump, these generational differences have become even sharper. Millennials in the US are even more likely than older generations to oppose the building of a wall on the border with Mexico, to reject the idea that Islam promotes violence more than other religions, and to welcome immigration, agreeing with the notion that 'America's openness to people from all over the world is essential to who we are as a nation'. On each of these points there are substantial differences between the young and old, as there are in many other Western democracies.[9] National populists won battles in the form of Brexit and Trump, so the argument goes, but in the long term they will lose the war.

This is certainly a seductive argument, especially if you already have a liberal outlook. But there is a competing view, namely that rather than nearing the end we are closer to the beginning of a new era of political fragmentation, volatility and disruption. Seen from this perspective, national populism is only just getting going as the bonds between the people and the traditional parties fray and unprecedented ethnic change and rising inequality continue to gain pace.

Those who hold this view point to a shopping list of big changes in the West that have the potential radically to overturn the status quo: rising public concern over immigration and rapid ethnic change, neither of which will slow in the coming years due to ongoing migration and comparatively low birth rates in the West; fundamental divides in Europe and the West about the refugee crisis and how to deal with it; the emergence of Islamist terror and the much-publicized fact that the intelligence services are monitoring tens of thousands of suspected radicalized Muslims in the West; the collapse of public support for centre-left social-democratic parties in Europe; stubbornly persistent and rising inequality; the ongoing and largely unpredictable effects of automation; a new culture conflict focused on competing sets of values among different groups of voters; the way in which national populists are pulling some 'non-voters' back into politics; and the fact that many Millennials and other young voters today are much less likely than older generations to feel a strong, tribal allegiance to the mainstream parties. Advocates of this view also point to the fact that, while there are big generational and value divides in the West, these are partly shaped by the experience of college education, which is still beyond the grasp of many.

While many in Europe saw the election of Emmanuel Macron in 2017 as marking the beginning of the end for populism, within months national populists had staged their first major breakthrough in Germany, returned to government in Austria, were re-elected in Hungary and, in 2018, joined a coalition government in Italy, where they took control of the Interior Ministry.

And when you look at the age of the national populists' followers, as we will in the next chapter, it becomes clear that the argument about generational change is not as convincing as it first appears. In very broad terms, the young are more tolerant than their parents and grandparents, but national populists are nonetheless forging ties with significant numbers of young people who today feel left behind in their own way.

As Lao-Tzu, the ancient Chinese philosopher, once said, those who have knowledge don't predict and those who predict don't have knowledge. In politics especially, many will think that trying to predict what will happen in the coming years is a game for fools. This is why we should be sceptical of the fashionable claim that 'populism has peaked', that these revolts are on their way out rather than just getting started. We do not share this view: the evidence that we have points in a different direction. National populism is not a flash protest. After reading this book you might find it difficult to avoid the conclusion that it looks set to remain on the radar for years to come. Stepping back and taking in the broader view allows us to see that, contrary to popular claims, national-populist movements have won over fairly loyal support from people who share coherent, deeply felt and in some cases legitimate concerns about how their nations and the West more generally are changing.

Towards Post-Populism

The rise of national populism is part of a broader challenge to liberalism. Critics argue that liberals have prioritized individuals at the expense of community, have focused too heavily on dry, transactional and technocratic debates and have lost sight of national allegiances while obsessing over transnational ones. For these reasons, unless it proves able to revitalize itself, the liberal mainstream will continually struggle to contain these movements. But we suggest that another debate will become increasingly important, and this centres on what we call 'post-populism' – namely the dawning of an era in which people will be able to evaluate whether or not voting for populists has made a tangible difference to their lives, and whether they even care.

What happens if Trump does not restore a large number of relatively well-paying, secure and meaningful jobs and greater border protection in a way that satisfies his core supporters? What if his protectionist measures start an international trade war? What happens if Brexit does not reform Britain's unpopular liberal immigration system or bring greater economic equality in areas that have long felt excluded from the benefits that go to London and the university towns? How will Marine Le Pen's voters in France respond in towns where her party's elected mayors fail to deliver on their promises to curb the influence of Islam and crack down on Islamist terrorism? What happens if the entrance of national populists into governing coalitions in democracies like Austria does not produce sharp reductions in immigration? And in Eastern Europe what happens if populists like Viktor Orbán, who call Muslim refugees 'invaders', are unable to halt the flow, or if *they* widely become seen as the new corrupt elite who have used their position in government to feather their own nests?

Conversely, what happens if these parties *do* enact meaningful change – if they *are* able to point to 'successes' like creating new good-quality jobs, new infrastructure, the building of stronger borders, or significantly limiting unskilled immigration from Muslim states? For example, plans by the Austrian government in 2018 to restrict welfare and child allowances for people who do not speak the language may broaden their appeal to potential voters who want radical action in other areas, like rolling back further elite-driven agendas, such as rising inequality. Although national populists often think differently from one another on economics, a growing number in Europe advocate aspects of traditionally left-wing policies, including expanding the state and promoting welfare for those born in their country, while excluding immigrants. This is making it even harder for centre-left social democrats to win back their voters.

The stock answer to the failure scenario is that those who vote for populists are mainly protestors who will inevitably drift back to the mainstream, but this seems unlikely. Furthermore, and as we will see in Chapter 6, it ignores the way in which national populism is *already* having a clear impact by dragging the West's political systems further to the right. Paradoxically, if national populism fails electorally it could be because it has succeeded in broader terms. In Britain, Nigel Farage and UKIP slumped in 2017, but only after they had got what they wanted – a Brexit referendum victory and a Conservative prime minister who promised to pull Britain out of the EU and overhaul the country's immigration system. Populists might 'lose' elections, but the mainstream increasingly looks and sounds like them, becoming in the process 'national populism-lite'.

Against the backdrop of a Western liberal hegemony which stresses individual rights over communal obligations and solidarity, which concurs with ever more ethnic change and which supports economic and political globalization, those who vote for national populists want to push the pendulum in the other direction. They are not transactional voters who weigh up the costs and benefits of policies like an accountant and fixate on the detail of policy – who is delivering what, how and when. Rather, they are driven by a deeper desire to bring a broader set of values back onto the agenda and to regain their voice: to reassert the primacy of the nation over distant and unaccountable international organizations; to reassert cherished and rooted national identities over rootless and diffuse transnational ones; to reassert the importance of stability and conformity over the never-ending and disruptive instability that flows from globalization and rapid ethnic change; and to reassert the will of the people over those of elitist liberal democrats who appear increasingly detached from the life experiences and outlooks of the average citizen. Just as many liberals saw their values reflected in the remarkable rise of Barack Obama in the US and Emmanuel Macron in France, many others in society see their values now reflected in national populism. And now many of them feel for the first time in a long while that they can finally have their say and effect change.

CHAPTER 1

Myths

There are many myths about national populism. From the US to Europe, national-populist movements are seen as a refuge for irrational bigots, jobless losers, Rust Belt rejects, voters who were hit hard by the Great Recession and angry old white men who will soon die and be replaced by tolerant Millennials. In the shadow of Trump, Brexit and the rise of national populism in Europe, countless writers drew a straight line to an alienated white underclass in America's industrial heartlands, angry pensioners in England's fading seaside resorts and the unemployed in Europe's wastelands.

People tend to reduce highly complex movements to 'one type' of voter or to 'one cause' because they want simple and straightforward explanations. But when more than 62 million voted for Trump, more than 17 million for Brexit, more than 10 million for Marine Le Pen and nearly 6 million for the Alternative for Germany, the idea that national-populist movements can be reduced to simplistic stereotypes is ridiculous. It also has real implications: misdiagnosing the roots of their support will in the long run make it harder for their opponents to get back into the game.

Misleading Claims and the Life Cycle

Myths are flourishing. Foremost is the idea that national populism is almost exclusively powered by the unemployed and
people on low incomes or in poverty. But while there is variation from country to country, it has cast its nets surprisingly
widely across society, scooping up votes from full-time workers, middle-class conservatives, the self-employed, people on
average or high incomes and even the young.

The tendency to portray Trump as a refuge for poverty-
stricken whites, for instance, is deeply problematic. During
the US primaries, the median household income of a Trump
voter was $72,000, compared to $61,000 for supporters of
Hillary Clinton and Bernie Sanders and $56,000 for the aver-
age person. In states like Connecticut, Florida, Illinois, New
York and Texas, the average Trump voter earned $20,000
more per annum than average, reflecting how Republican
and primary voters tend to be better off. The idea that it was
poor whites who came out in droves for Trump is also undermined by the finding that economic hardship was actually a
stronger predictor of support for Hillary Clinton.[1]

Indeed, in the spring of 2018 the political scientist Matt
Grossmann reviewed nearly every study that had so far been
done on Trump's electorate. While he found plenty of disa-
greements, he also noted how the dominant findings were
clear: attitudes to race, gender and cultural change played a
big role, while objective economic circumstances played only
a limited role. Similarly, the influential scholar Diana Mutz
found that changes in people's financial well-being actually

were insignificant in explaining support for Trump. They paled in comparison to people's worries over the rise of a 'majority-minority America', which they saw as a threat to their group's dominant position. 'Those who felt that the hierarchy was being upended – with whites discriminated against more than blacks, Christians discriminated against more than Muslims, and men discriminated against more than women – were most likely to support Trump.'[2]

Or look at Brexit. Some traced the shock result to dire macroeconomic conditions, despite the fact that the vote occurred as Britain's unemployment neared its lowest rate since the 1970s. The idea of ending Britain's EU membership was certainly popular among people on low incomes, but even among those who lived on average or just-above-average incomes support for Brexit was 51 per cent. Britain's departure was cheered on in struggling industrial towns, but it was also celebrated in affluent Conservative counties.[3]

Another popular myth is that all this turbulence is rooted in the global financial crisis that erupted in 2008, the Great Recession and the austerity that was subsequently imposed on democracies in Europe. Seen from this point of view, national populism is driven by the financially disadvantaged who were battered by the post-2008 economic storm. In the aftermath of Trump and Brexit, the *Financial Times* columnist Martin Wolf argued that the financial crisis 'opened the door to a populist surge'. Nor was he alone. Economists traced what they called the 'Brexit-Trump Syndrome' to unregulated markets, harsh public-spending cuts and a loss of faith in economic orthodoxy. In their words: 'It's the economics, stupid.'[4]

This 'crisis narrative' has been strongly influenced by the experience of inter-war Europe and the rise of Nazism which followed the Wall Street Crash in 1929 and the Great Depression. That Mussolini and Italy's Fascists took power eleven years earlier is ignored, as is the fact that similarly dire economic conditions in other European states did not trigger the rise of fascism. The crisis narrative has also been encouraged by more recent events such as the sudden breakthrough of a neo-Nazi movement in Greece called Golden Dawn. In 2012, amid a near-total financial collapse, a party that organized 'Greek-only' food banks and torch-lit processions, and demanded that businesses replace foreign workers with ethnic Greeks, won its first seats in the Greek parliament. To many observers the event confirmed the hypothesis that 'economic crises equal political extremism'. So too did the arrival of national populism in the wake of the financial crisis in democracies that were once thought to be immune to this force, such as Finland, Germany and Sweden.

There is no doubt that the financial crisis did create more room for national populists. Aside from exacerbating existing divides among voters, it contributed to a loss of support for traditional parties and record levels of political volatility in Europe, where people became much more willing to switch their allegiance from one election to the next, as we examine in Chapter 6. So the crisis is important. But the notion that it is the primary cause is not convincing at all. If all you needed was a crisis, then why did past crises, like the oil-price shocks of the 1970s, not produce a similar reaction? Why have democracies that were hit hardest by the Great Recession, such as Ireland, Portugal or Spain, not seen successful national-populist uprisings? Conversely, why have some of the most successful national-populist movements emerged in strong and expanding economies with low unemployment like Austria, the Netherlands or Switzerland? And if the financial crisis really is to blame, how can we explain the fact that this revolt against liberal democracy began long before the collapse of Lehman Brothers?

Tracking the life cycle of national populism is important because it challenges the idea that what we are witnessing is new and reminds us that we need to take deep and long-term change seriously. As readers with long memories will know, it was actually in the 1980s when the most significant national populists in post-war Europe showed up. They included people like Jean-Marie Le Pen in France and Jörg Haider in Austria, who emerged while promising to slash immigration, strengthen law and order and take on a 'corrupt' establishment. And they turned out to be far more durable than many pundits predicted, building their support over different economic cycles and cultivating a strong relationship with key groups in society. They laid the foundation for what we are witnessing in much of Europe today.

It was in 1988, the same year that George H. W. Bush was elected President of the US, that Jean-Marie Le Pen stunned the French by taking 14 per cent of the vote at a presidential election; his slogan was simply 'Le Pen, le peuple' (Le Pen, the people). As leader of the National Front (now called National Rally) he stayed firmly on the landscape and fourteen years later, in 2002, shocked the world by making it into the final round of the presidential contest. Le Pen lost that election, but it was still a major shock. Strongly attacking the mainstream parties, he presented the National Front as the only party which could solve the country's socio-economic divisions, stop immigration, build 200,000 more prison cells, reintroduce the death penalty to combat rising crime, use import duties to protect French jobs, scrap the Euro single currency and pull France out of the EU.

There were soon others. During the 1990s and 2000s an array of national populists emerged in Western countries. One major study of seventeen democracies in Europe found that national populism experienced the bulk of its growth *before* the financial crisis and then often enjoyed its largest gains in areas that escaped the worst effects of the meltdown.[5] In Britain, although many writers would later trace Brexit to post-crisis austerity, they forget that it was back in 2004 when Nigel Farage and UKIP enjoyed their first major success, which came after forty-eight consecutive quarters of economic expansion. Farage, like others, won votes not only from an employed yet precarious working class but also relatively affluent middle-class conservatives. National-populist movements arose in other countries too: the League in Italy, the Progress Party in Norway, Law and Justice in Poland, the People's Parties in Denmark and Switzerland and Viktor Orbán's Fidesz in Hungary. By the early twenty-first century some were so successful that they had entered government, either outright or as part of a coalition. Many were well under way long before the crisis and President Trump.

Angry Old White Men?

The second prevailing myth is that national-populist support comes entirely from old white men who will soon die. This is a comfortable narrative for liberals because it implies that they do not need to engage with any of the *ideas* of national populism, such as the importance of community and the desire to be listened to rather than ignored or despised. Rather, they just need to wait for pensioners to slip over the horizon, at which point socially liberal Millennials will take over, while the West's populations become ever more ethnically and culturally diverse. This view has won support from, among others, the *Financial Times* columnist Janan Ganesh, who argued that Brexit was 'as good as things will get for traditional conservatives' because over time their support will be eroded by generational change.[6]

Such voices point to big differences in outlook between the young and old. In 2018, for example, the British were asked whether the Brexit vote had been right or wrong: while 65 per cent of pensioners thought it had been the right decision, 68 per cent of those aged eighteen to twenty-four thought it had been wrong. One writer even worked out that if you assume that birth and death rates in Britain remain constant and that the young will remain far more supportive of the EU, then 'Remainers' will have a commanding majority in 2022! But liberals routinely exaggerate both the pace and scale of generational change. They gloss over the fact that while the young generally tend to be less racist, quite a few of them are instinctively receptive to national populism.

Consider the US. No less than 41 per cent of white Millennials turned out for Trump; they tended to lack college degrees, worked full-time and were actually *less* likely than those who did not back Trump to be on low incomes. Contrary to the claim that the young are not bothered about issues like immigration, these younger Americans were especially anxious about 'white vulnerability' – the perception that whites, through no fault of their own, are losing ground to others in society, a view that was intimately bound up with their resentment of other racial groups. As the authors of one study noted: 'Many white Americans are uneasy with what they see as their future, surrounded as they are by growing racial and cultural diversity in mainstream media, politics, entertainment and music. White millennials are part of the US's most diverse generation . . . but not all of them are comfortable with it.'[7]

Or consider Britain. It is certainly true that national populists like Nigel Farage, who called on the people to 'Say no' to mass immigration, the EU and the established politicians in Westminster, relied heavily on pensioners for votes. Only one in ten of his supporters were under thirty-five, whereas since the Brexit vote seven in ten of those aged between eighteen and twenty-four have supported the culturally liberal and radical left-wing leader of the Labour Party, Jeremy Corbyn, whom many compare with Bernie Sanders.

These different generations have had profoundly different life experiences. The older voters who supported Farage came of age amid a very different era, when Britain was heavily white and racist views were commonplace, collective memories of Empire and victory in the Second World War

were strong, university education was rare, abortion and homosexuality were illegal and the death penalty was still used
until the 1960s. In sharp contrast, the young Millennials who
support Jeremy Corbyn were born between the 1980s and early
2000s: they have only ever known a Britain that is in the EU,
has high rates of immigration, where heading off to university is commonplace and where most politicians subscribe to
a liberal consensus that supports immigration and the EU.[8]

Yet this binary 'young versus old' debate oversimplifies a
complex picture. Beneath these broad brushstrokes lies the
fact that Brexit was endorsed by one in four British graduates, one in two women, one in two people from urban areas,
around two-fifths of those aged between eighteen and thirty-
four and half of those aged between thirty-five and forty-
four. Had these voters, who are routinely left out of debates
about populism, not cast their pro-Brexit vote, then Britain
would still be in the EU. Simply to dismiss national-populist
movements as a final resting place for old men is incredibly
misleading.

It also falls into the trap of assuming that their supporters
are exclusively white. While this is more true in Europe, it ignores important findings. Despite portraying immigrants as
drug dealers and rapists, Trump still won around 28 per cent
of the Latino vote, while Clinton underperformed among
this group relative to Obama. Trump also won more than
half of the Cuban-American vote in the key state of Florida
(though in the longer term this group appears to be drifting
towards the Democrats).

Brexit was dismissed by senior liberal politicians like
Vince Cable as a vote by old people who longed for a world

where 'faces were white' and the map of the world was 'coloured imperial pink', as it was during the era of Britain's Empire. But this caricature does not sit easily with the fact that Brexit was supported by one in three black and ethnic-minority voters, some of whom felt that Britain's liberal immigration policy was giving preferential treatment to immigrants from inside Europe at the expense of those from outside Europe, or who themselves felt anxious about the historically unprecedented rates of immigration that had taken place in the decade before the referendum. This non-white support was visible in cities and towns like Birmingham, Bradford, Luton and Slough, which have large ethnic-minority communities that originate in South Asia.

The age profile of these supporters also pushes back strongly against the narrative of angry old men. In many of Europe's democracies national populism polls strongly among the under-forties. Let's look at a few examples. In Italy the national-populist League movement has drawn its support fairly evenly across the generations, including young Italians who felt anxious over immigration (in fact, those aged between eighteen and forty-nine were more likely than pensioners to see this is a key issue facing their country). In France, when Marine Le Pen ran unsuccessfully for the presidency she still won over more people aged between eighteen and thirty-four in the first round than any other candidate. In Austria, more than half of men aged between eighteen and twenty-nine voted for the Freedom Party's presidential candidate, whose leader was fond of rapping and campaigning in nightclubs for youth support. In Germany, the Alternative for Germany appeals most strongly not to old pensioners with distant memories of Nazism but to people aged between twenty-five and fifty, who have no direct connection with that period of history.[9] And ahead of an election in Sweden in 2018 the national-populist Sweden Democrats were the second most popular party among eighteen to thirty-four-year-olds and the most popular party among those aged between thirty-five and fifty-four.

In Greece, too, the neo-Nazi Golden Dawn won most of its support from young men, people with only high-school education who felt that their position in society had deteriorated relative to others, while in Hungary, where national populists are strong, the Jobbik movement (a play on *jobb*, which can mean 'better' and 'right') is popular among young men who are hostile towards the minority Roma community and also Jews. And while UKIP relied on the support of older men, the average age of Leavers at the Brexit referendum was fifty-two – hardly people who are about to kick the bucket!

We should also not lose sight of the broader picture. In the US, as Trump celebrated the end of his first year in the White House, the Pew Research Center found that while in recent decades Millennials have become more liberal, still 43 per cent hold clearly conservative or mixed values while only 25 per cent could be described as 'consistently liberal'.[10] Research on young Americans of the more recent 'iGen' generation, who were born between 1995 and 2012, suggests that the share of high-school seniors who identify as conservative has increased to nearly 30 per cent, making them more conservative than the 'Gen X' teens during the Reagan era. Raised amid the Great Recession, rampant inequality and hyper ethnic change, some of these young Americans talked openly of their anxiety about immigration. Others went further, like the one in six white eighteen-year-olds who told researchers they felt it would be best if their daily lives did not involve close contact with other races. Or look at Britain. In the spring of 2018, 41 per cent of eighteen- to twenty-four-year-olds and 58 per cent of twenty-five- to forty-nine-year-olds felt that immigration into the country was 'too high'.[11]

The point is that we often talk about generational change in sweeping terms, but if you look more closely you find a picture that is far more varied than headlines suggest. The idea that the West is on a one-way journey to a liberal future is also challenged by other research on how ageing affects our political outlook. In Britain, Professor James Tilley at the University of Oxford tracked the same people over a long period of time and found that as each year passed there was a 0.38 per cent increase in support for the right-wing Conservative Party. Now this might not sound like much, but over the course of a lifetime it adds up and accounts for most if not all of the gap in support for the Conservative Party between the young and old. As Tilley points out, as we all age and assume more responsibility in life we become instinctively more receptive to parties that want to preserve the status quo. Furthermore, populations in the West are not only getting older, but older voters are more likely to vote, which means that in the longer term right-wing conservatives should not worry too much about their supporters dying off.[12]

Populists are also often portrayed as appealing only to men, but a closer look at gender reveals a different picture.

Hillary Clinton won women overall, but an estimated 53 per cent of *white* women backed Trump, who had made various derogatory statements about them. Clinton would later suggest that these women were pressured by their husbands or partners into switching to Trump or not voting at all, downplaying the possibility that they had made up their own minds. In Britain, men and women alike were just as likely to back Brexit; and while national populists in Europe draw more votes from men, some of them, like Marine Le Pen, who specifically reached out to women, have recently closed the 'gender gap'. Between 1988 and 2017, the percentage of French women aged between eighteen and twenty-six who were first-time voters and decided to support the national-populist Le Pen family in France's presidential elections soared from 9 to 32 per cent. In fact, in 2017 these young women and women aged between forty-seven and sixty-six were markedly more likely than men to do so. This is not to say that, overall in Europe, women are significantly more likely to vote for national populists than men – they are not – but there are cases where the evidence runs counter to the stereotypes.[13]

There are also good reasons to predict that the narrative about old white men might lead to further polarization and make things even worse for the liberal mainstream. In the US, it seems likely that Trump was helped by the popular claim among Democrats that he *simply could not win* because of how America was rapidly becoming more ethnically and culturally diverse. These arguments were pushed by people like the Democrat pollster Stan Greenberg in his book *America Ascendant*, which hints loudly that the future belongs to

Democrats because of the way America is becoming more educated and ethnically diverse.[14] A 'newly ascendant' coalition of Millennial graduates, cultural liberals and minorities will propel Democrat after Democrat into the White House, so the thinking went.

But people often overstate the case. Across the West, and as we discuss in Chapter 3, non-graduates continue to outnumber graduates by a wide margin, as they did in America's key Rust Belt states, which partly explains Trump's success. Furthermore, at crunch elections when the stakes have been high – like the 2016 US presidential election and the Brexit referendum – key groups in the supposedly ascendant coalition failed to mobilize en masse.

Hillary Clinton was damaged by lower than expected turnout rates among African Americans, young minorities and Millennial students. In Britain, the Remain camp struggled as turnout rates in the more culturally liberal university towns and hipster districts of London failed to match those in blue-collar districts where Brexit supporters were more determined to have their say. Ironically, when a petition to overturn the referendum result was launched, it attracted large numbers of signatures in hipster districts like Camden, Hackney and Shoreditch, where turnout had been lower than expected when it really mattered. These differences in turnout were likely encouraged by the narrative of an inevitable liberal future. Prophecies about a rapidly changing nation alarmed the already alarmed, stoking fears about future ethnic change and entrenching a belief that this really was their 'last chance' to push their concerns onto the table before it was too late.

A Diverse Alliance

Misleading narratives distract us from the fact that in reality national populism appeals to a broad alliance of different groups in society. While it is routinely portrayed as a refuge for only one type of voter, in reality it appeals strongly to a coalition of key groups, albeit with white workers at their core. Both Trump and Brexit were nudged over the winning line by a loose but committed coalition of voters who often came from different walks in life but were united by their shared values and concerns.

Now, it must be acknowledged that Trump is certainly not a national populist in the way that similar figures in Europe are. Nigel Farage in Britain and Marine Le Pen in France are genuine outsiders who have never been accepted by the mainstream. They are leaders of their own parties. Trump, in contrast, effectively took over the mainstream Republican Party and was then eventually embraced by it. He captured the White House not only by mobilizing Americans in swing states but also by retaining the vast majority of mainstream Republicans who had voted for Mitt Romney in 2012.

Nor was Brexit a typical national-populist revolt. While the shock vote to pull Britain out of the EU was presented as part of the populist wave, there were some unique factors at play. The Brexit vote did not arise through a normal election but by a binary 'Remain or Leave' referendum that saw turnout hit 72 per cent, the highest in a national election for a quarter-century. Just as Trump cannot be fully understood without reference to America's long populist heritage, which we will discuss later, Brexit cannot be fully understood without reference to a decades-old tradition in Britain (or, more accurately, England) of strong public suspicion of the idea of integrating the country politically with Europe. This latent hostility has ebbed and flowed through the mainstream Conservative Party, which saw the EU as a threat to national sovereignty, and also worries some in the Labour Party who are concerned that the EU undermines workers' rights and is a vehicle for free-marketeer capitalists and furthering America's interests.

That said, these movements did share common threads. The tendency to view Trump's electorate as a homogenous bloc of poor whites is misleading. He not *only* appealed to an impoverished white underclass of the sort described in the bestselling book *Hillbilly Elegy*.[15] In reality, he captured the White House by attracting a broad alliance of whites without college degrees and traditional social conservatives who typically voted Republican.

Contrary to popular belief, many of Trump's supporters were not on the bottom rung of the economic ladder. As the analyst Emily Ekins has shown, his message resonated among several distinct groups. One of the most important were those she calls *Staunch Conservatives*, a group of steadfast fiscal conservatives, moral traditionalists and loyal Republicans who were often middle-class, moderately educated, interested in politics and who backed Trump from the primaries. A second and also large group were the *Free Marketeers*: small-government fiscal conservatives and passionate free traders who loathed Clinton, were middle-aged, on high incomes, and who usually owned their own homes. Combined, these two groups that identified as Republican and conservative comprised more than half of the Trump electorate; without these fairly middle-of-the-road Republicans, who often lived on good incomes, he would never have won.[16]

However, Trump did also draw strongly on a few core groups of voters who more closely approximate the profile of national-populist voters in Europe. His most loyal supporters were the *Preservationists*. These fiercely pro-Trump voters usually had only some high-school education and lived in low-income households that earned less than $50,000 each year. They had much in common with two other elements that were key to his victory – the *Anti-Elites*, who tended to be better off but were profoundly unhappy with the status quo, and the *Disengaged*, a smaller demographic that knew little about politics but turned out just so they could vote for Trump. It was the combination of these five quite different groups that rallied to the call to 'Make America Great Again' and propelled Trump into the White House (and who will probably still be receptive to the call to 'Keep America Great', should Trump run again in 2020).

What most Trump supporters had in common was their fairly mainstream Republican views. Compared to Americans who did not back him, they were more likely to oppose gay marriage, to be pro-life rather than pro-choice, to believe that women who complain about harassment cause more problems than they solve, to support the death penalty, to describe themselves as traditional, to believe that life in America today is worse than it was fifty years ago and to oppose affirmative action for women and minorities. With the exception of the *Free Marketeers*, they were also more

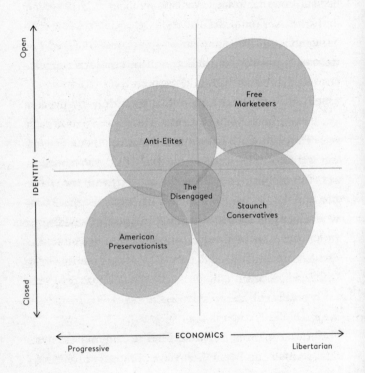

Figure 1.1
Comparing Trump voters on a political map.
Axes approximate the median Trump voter.

likely than other voters to feel that it is more important for a child to be obedient rather than self-reliant, an outlook that reflects their traditional values which prioritize order, stability and group conformity. And most of them voted *for* Trump rather than *against* Clinton. While they often held different views about the economy, many shared similar outlooks on cultural issues like immigration, although these chiefly dominated the thinking of his core supporters.

Brexit, too, was delivered by a patchwork of different groups with shared values. As in America, people were quick to push simplistic stereotypes. Attempts to explain the vote quickly zoomed in on the white working class. While 52 per cent of voters overall backed Brexit, the figure rose to 60 per cent among the working class and 70 per cent among working-class pensioners. One tweet that went viral after the result portrayed 'Leavers' as being almost exclusively white and elderly. One was an old man who, readers were told, lived in an all-white village where he never met immigrants. Another was an old lady who 'died of old age two days after the vote'.

Yet, as with Trump, in reality there were several elements that led to Brexit. It was delivered not by one group but by a diverse alliance of people who shared a few intensely held concerns. Three groups were key. *Affluent Eurosceptics* were people who supported the Conservative Party and were generally well off. Around half of them identified as working-class, but fewer than one in eight said they were struggling financially. The *older working-class* were people who also leaned towards the Conservative Party: they saw themselves as more strongly working-class, were aspirational, held socially conservative views, were patriotic and would no doubt have liked Margaret Thatcher very much. They also tended not to be struggling financially: only one in four said they were finding it hard to get by. The third and smaller demographic were the *economically deprived*, people who tended to completely reject mainstream politics, who had often voted for Nigel Farage in the past, identified very strongly as working-class and who *were* struggling financially. These people were also especially anxious about the specific issue of immigration, though all three groups held similar views on this issue, as we will see.[17]

When it comes to national populists in Europe, the picture is slightly different. Trump and Brexit were broad and successful campaigns that cast their nets widely across society. National populists in Europe have generally been less successful, though they have assembled a coalition of supporters in their own right that has much in common with Brexit and Trump.

Especially since the 1990s, the likes of the National Front in France and the Freedom Parties in Austria and the Netherlands have won much of their support not from people on the very bottom rung of the economic ladder but skilled and semi-skilled workers, some of whom have specialized skills, like mechanics or factory workers. Whereas the unemployed and those on welfare often avoid voting altogether, manual workers find themselves sandwiched between the middle-class on one side and, on the other, those out of work.[18] They are especially likely to feel as though they are losing out relative to others in society, or that some groups are getting unfair advantages, and they are fearful about the future.

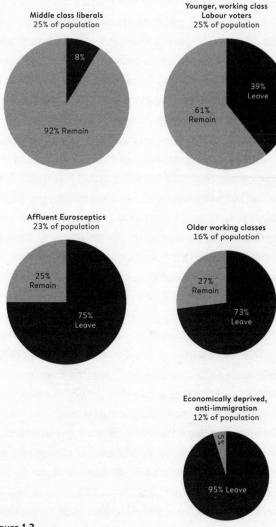

Figure 1.2
How different demographics
voted in the EU Referendum.

Much like the Democrats, who watched many of their traditional working-class supporters defect to Trump in key states like Michigan, which the Democrats had won consistently since 1992, over the past three decades in Europe centre-left social democrats have seen their traditional working-class voters in historic bastions drift over to national populism (although not all of these working-class voters came from the left). This was a long time in the making.

It was actually way back in 1995 when national populists like Jean-Marie Le Pen emerged as the most popular choice among workers, especially in areas that had historically been controlled by the socialists or communists. Nearly a quarter of a century later, in 2017, the only group in French society that gave his daughter majority support in her final-round clash with Emmanuel Macron was the working class. And this strong appeal to the working class holds true across much of Europe. Even before the financial crisis, the scholar Daniel Oesch found that working-class voters were twice as likely as their middle-class counterparts to vote for national populists in Austria, three times as likely in Belgium and France, and four times as likely in Norway. Though workers made up around half of these electorates, they delivered around two-thirds of the votes going to the national populists.

While workers form their core, Europe's populist movements have also recruited support from social conservatives who share many of their traditional values and strong concerns about issues like immigration, border security and law and order. Some of the more successful national populists have also won over small-business owners, the self-employed and people from the lower-middle class. But, as with Brexit and Trump, they have consistently struggled with college-educated middle-class professionals, particularly those in the education, health, welfare, culture and media sectors.

The Key Fault Lines

This brings us to one of the major fault lines that runs beneath national populism across the West – the educational divide. Debates about it often focus heavily on income and jobs, but education is actually far more important.

It is also an issue that needs to be discussed carefully. It is neither accurate nor fair to portray the people who support national populism as 'uneducated' and 'thick'. These crude stereotypes are misleading and will only entrench polarization, so we must begin by clarifying that many of them finished high school, and a far from trivial number went to college, like those one in four Brexit voters who had a degree. In the US, the Voter Study Group estimates that slightly more than one-third of Trump's support during the primaries and more than two-fifths during the 2016 presidential election came from whites who had degrees. Clearly, Trump did not appeal strongly to graduates; but it is inaccurate to argue that Trump appealed only to the uneducated.

Supporters of national populism might also have decided to pursue their education through other channels, outside the (increasingly expensive) college system, such as technical training, or by their own learning. And while many commentators portray the absence of a college degree as a symbol of failure, it should be remembered that many of these supporters are on decent incomes, have full-time jobs and enjoy a comparatively good standard of living. Only a minority of the pro-Trump *Free Marketeers* had been to college, yet on average they earned far more than Democrats. Trump drew significant levels of support from Americans who earned at least $70,000 per year.

Yet people without degrees are notably more likely to cast a vote for populists. White non-college voters comprised around two-thirds of Trump's base in the primaries and around three-fifths in his election battle with Clinton. If you look at Trump's most loyal voters, the *Preservationists*, six in ten had left the education system during or after high school while only around one in eight had gone to college. Democrat voters were about twice as likely as this group to have graduated and nearly five times as likely to have pursued postgraduate study.

This divide was crucial for Trump. In 2012, Obama had lost whites without degrees by twenty-five points. Yet four years later Clinton did even worse, losing them by an estimated thirty-one points, while the swing against her among this group in the Rust Belt states was often double the average. These losses put key states beyond her grasp. They were so important that some suggest that, even had Clinton managed to replicate Obama's levels of turnout among African Americans, she would *still* have lost the election.[19] Clinton and her team should have seen this coming. Trump's appeal to non-degree holders had been visible early on. During the primaries, he had won all but a handful of the more than 150 counties where at least eight in ten people were white without a college degree.

Clinton and her strategists could also have taken more

from Brexit, which only five months earlier had clearly demonstrated populism's strong appeal to non-degree holders. Remarkably, support for Brexit among people without any educational qualifications had averaged 74 per cent. Crucially, this educational divide was also greater than divides by social class, income or age, showing that it is often education which plays the dominant background role.

Look at the interaction between age and education. Whereas 80 per cent of Brits aged under thirty-four with a degree voted for Britain to remain in the EU, only 37 per cent of their peers without a degree did the same.[20] Elsewhere in Europe, national populism similarly appeals most strongly not to the uneducated but to the middle-educated, people who have finished high school and sometimes pursued some further education, but who have typically not graduated from college. At the presidential election in France in 2017, whereas the most highly educated broke for Macron over Marine Le Pen by a staggering ratio of 83:17, his winning margin among the least educated was only 54:46.[21]

The educational divide is also one reason why so few people saw Trump coming. Whites without degrees were under-represented in the opinion polls, as they were in some of the polls in Britain. This was especially true in the key Rust Belt states like Michigan, Ohio, Pennsylvania and Wisconsin, where whites without degrees easily outnumber their degree-holding counterparts. This is why one obvious response to the Brexit and Trump shocks is to ensure that polling samples capture this critical group.[22]

The educational divide is also key because it has been shown to have a very strong influence on our values and the way in which we interpret the world around us. Those who have gone to college tend to have a culturally liberal mindset that puts a premium on the tolerance of difference, has little time for social hierarchies and prioritizes individual rights above group identities. In contrast, those who have not gone to college lean towards a more socially conservative outlook which places more value on preserving social hierarchies, stability, maintaining order and tradition and ensuring that people conform to the wider group.

Scholars continue to debate why this link exists, but many have shown that it is the experience of college education itself that really matters. Having to leave home and attend college comes at a formative point in our lives, when we are usually young and impressionable adults who are still making up our minds about how we see the world. Socializing, debating and sharing life experiences in an environment that is filled with liberal students and teachers who come from different backgrounds encourages many young people to absorb a more culturally liberal outlook, which continues to influence their thinking long after they have left college.[23]

Of course, college education does not explain everything. Some people pass through higher education while holding on to their more socially conservative values. Others grew up in an era when college education was still restricted to a privileged few. But this general picture does help to explain why some citizens are more instinctively receptive to national populism than others. Because of their educational background and closely associated values, they share core concerns about how their communities, nations and the West more generally are changing. As we will see in this chapter and those that follow, they think in profoundly different ways from graduates and more liberally minded voters on a whole range of issues – such as who truly belongs to the national community, how immigration is changing their country, whether or not Islam is compatible with the West, the position of their wider group relative to other groups in society, the extent to which political and economic institutions can be trusted, and whether they feel they have a say.

Drilling Down to the Core Concerns

We will explore these concerns throughout this book, but we can begin to tease them out by considering another popular myth, which is that the people who support Trump, Brexit or the likes of Le Pen are voting *against* the system rather than *for* the national populists.

This 'protest theory' is popular because many writers, particularly those on the liberal left, struggle with the idea that people might actually want things like lower immigration, stronger borders, fewer welfare benefits for recent immigrants who have not paid tax over the years, and more powers returned from distant transnational institutions to the nation state. Yet when eight in ten of Trump's voters supported his idea of building a wall on America's border with Mexico, or when three in four voters in Britain, worried about how immigration was changing their country, voted for the Brexit offer to 'Take Back Control', it is hard to accept that they did not know what they were voting for, or that they were just protesting against the establishment. Certainly, many loathe established politicians, but they are also endorsing the message – they are voting for it because they want it.

This leads us to a further point on which those who campaign against national populists often go wrong. Their supporters are not driven simply by individual self-interest, nor is their vote chiefly rooted in objective economic concerns. Yet Democrats in the US, the Remain campaign in Britain and many social democrats in Europe often talk only and very narrowly to these voters about their jobs and income – as was reflected in the 2016 warning in Britain that if people voted for Brexit their personal household would be £4,300 worse off every year. This pitch to individual economic self-interest has been outflanked by national populists, whose appeal to voters is rooted in the Four Ds.

The first is strong *distrust* of established political and economic elites and a belief that ordinary people no longer have a meaningful voice. Contrary to hysterical claims that emerged in the aftermath of Brexit and Trump, most people in the West are actually not giving up on democracy, although many are open to more 'direct' forms of democracy that would give people a greater say in the decisions that affect their daily lives.

But there is clear and overwhelming evidence of a rising tide of distrust and a strong belief among many voters that they are no longer even in the conversation. While key groups in Trump's electorate agreed with large numbers of Democrats that America's economic system is biased towards the wealthy, his most loyal supporters were *more* likely than

Democrats to feel that 'people like me don't have any say in what the government does': seven in ten felt this way. These voters would have much in common with Leavers in Britain, who reached the same conclusion – that they no longer have a voice. Among Brits who felt they *were* being listened to, the vote for Brexit was only 37 per cent; but among those who felt that politicians 'do not listen to people like me' it spiralled to 58 per cent. Many of these Trump and Brexit supporters saw an opportunity to get back into a national discussion from which they felt they had been shut out long ago, and they seized it with both hands.[24]

Both campaigns also tapped into a second concern about relative *deprivation* – a sense that the wider group, whether white Americans or native Brits, is being left behind relative to others in society, while culturally liberal politicians, media and celebrities devote far more attention and status to immigrants, ethnic minorities and other newcomers.

Trump appealed strongly to people who were absolutely convinced that white Americans are losing out relative to others: 90 per cent of his core supporters believed that discrimination against whites is now a major problem in America, while less than 10 per cent of Democrats shared this view. In fact, white Americans who felt there was a great deal of discrimination against their group were nearly forty points more likely to back Trump than those who did not see this discrimination. Similarly, people who believed that whites could no longer get jobs because businesses were giving them to minorities were fifty points more likely to turn out for Trump. Given these views, it is unsurprising to find that large numbers of them also strongly opposed affirmative action programmes and felt deeply anxious about political correctness, views that we will explore later in the book.[25]

In Britain, many Leavers shared this intense anger about how in their eyes their wider group is being treated relative to others. Brexit appealed not simply to those on the lowest economic level but also to people who worked full-time yet who believed that both they and their group were being left behind. The people who had first started to vote for Nigel Farage and UKIP before later endorsing Brexit were twenty points more likely than average to believe that government authorities allow immigrants to jump the queue for social housing (nearly eight in ten thought so). When the crunch referendum arrived, support for Brexit averaged only 25 per cent among people who felt things for them were 'a lot better compared to other people'. But among those who felt things had 'got a lot worse for me compared to other people' the figure soared to 76 per cent.[26]

This sense of relative deprivation is absolutely central to national populism. It acts as a bridge between culture and economics. It is intimately bound up with people's worries about the broader economic and social position of their wider group and how this compares to others in society. But it is also linked closely to people's specific concerns about how they feel that immigrants, ethnic minorities and rapid ethnic change are threatening their group, not only economically but also socially and culturally. These feelings of loss and worries about ethnic change fuel an animosity towards established politicians, who either failed to prevent this from happening or, even worse, actively encouraged it, leading to strong fears about the future: will their national group, identity and ways of life fall further behind and perhaps eventually be destroyed for ever? This is the third concern, which focuses on *destruction*.

Such fears are not always grounded in objective reality, but they are still potent. This is especially true in America, where non-whites are projected to be the majority of the nation's children by 2020, while large parts of Europe are also witnessing major shifts, as we outline in Chapter 4. For those who support national populists these trends are deeply alarming and stoke major worries about what kind of future awaits them and their children.

Trump tapped directly into these fears of cultural displacement, which lay at the heart of his vote: white Americans who said they often felt like strangers in their own country and believed that the US needs protecting from foreign influence were nearly four times more likely to back Trump than Americans who did not share these worries. Another study found that when you reminded white Americans who identified strongly with their group that non-whites will outnumber whites in the US by 2042, this not only led them to become far more concerned about the declining status and influence of white Americans but also to be more supportive of Trump, and more opposed to political correctness. Indeed, a growing pile of studies now show that Trump benefited much more from public fears over immigration, ethnic change and Muslims than did Republican candidates in the past such as John McCain and Mitt Romney.[27]

Serious concerns about ethnic change and its effect on white Americans were shared by many of Trump's most loyal voters. Aside from believing that discrimination against whites is a major problem, they were far more likely than other Americans to express strong opposition to illegal immigrants, to want to make it harder for foreigners and Muslims to enter the US, to see immigration as a major issue, to support Trump's travel ban, to believe that Islam encourages terrorism, and to openly admit to holding negative views of Muslims. At the heart of these attitudes were intense fears about how ongoing immigration and ethnic change in America will impact on white Americans. Of the nearly 40 per cent of Republican voters who felt it is bad for America that over the next twenty-five to thirty years ethnic minorities will become the majority, most of them liked Trump.[28]

This anxiety about ethnic and cultural change also helps to explain why some of Obama's supporters defected to Trump. Hillary Clinton held on to nearly all of Obama's white voters who felt positively about immigration, but she lost one in three who were anxious about it. Nor was this a small group. Lurking in Obama's electorate were white voters who thought illegal immigrants were a drain on America and who wanted to make it harder for foreigners to emigrate to the US, many of whom switched to Trump. Just as national populists in Europe are pulling in white workers from centre-left social democrats, Trump attracted some white Democrats who felt anxious about how America was being radically ethnically transformed, although this trend began long before he and his wife descended the escalator in Trump Tower, as we discuss later.

Trump's shock victory, therefore, was partly a symptom of much deeper divides over the ethnic transformation of

America. As the scholar John Sides and his colleagues observe: 'As the United States changes demographically, socially, and culturally, Americans' political identities are increasingly driven by competing understandings of what their country is and ought to be – a multicultural society that welcomes newcomers and embraces its growing diversity, or a more provincial place that recalls an earlier era of traditional gender roles and white Christian dominance in economic and cultural life.'[29] But these divides are by no means restricted to America.

In Britain, many Leavers similarly saw the Brexit referendum as a prime opportunity to voice their strong concerns about how immigration was changing the nation – concerns which had increased with the historically unprecedented flows of immigrants into Britain from the early 2000s onwards. Nigel Farage stepped into this toxic climate by claiming that the immigrants settling in Britain from elsewhere in Europe were taking jobs away from British workers, empathizing with people who no longer heard the English language being spoken on public transport and arguing that Britain had reached 'breaking point'. Most Leavers shared his concerns: 64 per cent believed that immigration had been bad for the economy, 72 per cent thought that it had undermined British culture and 80 per cent saw it as a burden on welfare. If people felt anxious about immigration in Britain they were not only more likely to vote Leave, they were also more likely to bother to turn out and vote, and to reject the idea that Brexit was a risk. Remainers were talking endlessly about economic risks while Leavers were chiefly concerned about perceived threats to their identity and national group.

So strong was the desire among Leavers to chart a different path that six in ten said that significant damage to the British economy would be a 'price worth paying for Brexit', while four in ten were willing to see their own relatives lose their jobs if it meant that Brexit was delivered.[30] The anti-Brexit Remain strategists handled this badly. By deciding to completely avoid the immigration issue they sent voters a signal that 'the elite' had no real interest in taking their concerns seriously.

The same potent cocktail is on display in Europe, where national populism has been propelled by intense public angst over immigration and ethnic change. One major study of five democracies found that workers who voted for Marine Le Pen in France or Geert Wilders in the Netherlands were driven by a desire both to reduce the influence of immigration on their culture and to voice their disapproval of established politicians. Workers who felt anxious about immigration were seven times more likely than those who did not feel anxious about this issue to defect to national populists. Other studies likewise show how these voters were driven not by protest but a belief that their wider group was under threat from immigration and Muslims, and that mainstream politicians could not be trusted to deal with the problem.[31]

Look at Sweden, which was always thought to be immune to national populism because of its very tolerant culture, the strong relationship between workers and the main parties, and the fact that immigration was not high on the agenda. But while national populists have been active for years, over the past decade they enjoyed a major breakthrough by wrapping their opposition to immigration and Islam in apocalyptic-style claims about the destruction of native Swedes and their way of life. The campaign video of the national-populist Sweden Democrats, which was banned on television, showed an elderly lady hobbling towards her pension, only to be overtaken by a crowd of burqa-clad women (it was watched more than a million times on YouTube). Ahead of an election in 2018 their leader told voters: 'You have created a Sweden where families are forced to move because they no longer feel safe in their own neighbourhoods. A Sweden where the welfare is collapsing, where friends and family die waiting for medical care. A Sweden where women are raped, gang-raped, girls are mutilated and married off against their will.'

The national populists' narrative focuses less on the detail of policy and far more on claims about national decline and destruction, which they link not only to immigration and ethnic change but also to what they see as culturally incompatible Muslims and refugees. This is blamed too on an established political class that is in cahoots with capitalists to put profits before the people, encouraging endless flows of low-skilled or unskilled workers to satisfy the neoliberal economic system and 'betray' the nation (in Eastern Europe more extreme movements link these changes to Jews). It is primarily a narrative rooted in fears of destruction – in Hungary, Viktor Orbán presents refugees as 'a Muslim invasion force'; in France Marine Le Pen warns that 'the whole of France will become a gigantic no-go zone'; in Austria Heinz-Christian Strache tells voters that unless they end the policy of 'Islamization' Europeans 'will come to an abrupt end'; in the Netherlands Geert Wilders warns that Europe will 'cease to exist' if it does not slow the growth of Islam; and in Italy the leader of the Italian League Matteo Salvini warns that centuries of Europe's history are at risk of disappearing 'if Islamization, which up until now has been underestimated, gains the upper hand'.

Ordinarily, were we still in an era when their bonds with the people remained strong and robust, the traditional parties might have been able to fend off these challenges. But the classic era of the early-to-mid twentieth century, when political allegiances were more stable and the dividing lines of politics fixed, has ended. The old bonds between the people and the traditional parties have started to break down, a process that we call *de-alignment*. Because larger numbers of people, including many of the young, are now less willing than in the past to bear allegiance to the traditional parties, the path for national populists has been cleared further. Many political systems in the West today are characterized by record volatility, whereby people are not only less trusting of politics than before but are more willing to switch their votes from one election to the next. This has been central to the collapse of movements that have played a key role in the evolution of post-war Europe, such as social democracy, and has provided a further opening for national populism, which we explore in Chapter 6.

Trump, Brexit and national populists in Europe are by no means identical. There will always be differences from one country to another, as there are in all 'political families'. But in this chapter we have stepped back to look at the broad landscape, to point to some of the misleading myths that have become entrenched in wider debates and to identify some of the common threads that tie these national-populist rebellions together. We have seen how they have won over support from a fairly broad alliance of people without degrees and social conservatives who share traditional values and a cluster of core concerns about their lack of voice, the position of their group relative to others, and in particular immigration and ethnic change.

One point that has recurred throughout is that people who support national populism are not merely protesting: they are choosing to endorse views that appeal to them. So we need to look more closely at the promises that are being made by these politicians and examine whether, contrary to the popular claim that it is a new form of fascism, national populism strives towards a new form of democracy in which the interests and voices of ordinary people feature far more prominently.

CHAPTER 2

Promises

What do we mean by 'populism'? And to what extent is it fair – if at all – to lump populists in with fascists or the far right?

Populism is routinely portrayed as a home for extreme nationalists, often a dangerous step on the slippery slope to fascism. During a recent world tour, the global pop star Madonna projected a picture of Marine Le Pen with a swastika superimposed over it. The Dutch philosopher Rob Riemen posted an essay to all members of parliament warning them that the rise of Geert Wilders and his Party for Freedom represented the return of historic fascism.

In the US, the neoconservative writer Robert Kagan captured the mood when he argued that Trump's campaign to win the White House displayed 'an aura of crude strength and machismo, a boasting disrespect for the niceties of the democratic culture that he claims, and his followers believe, has produced national weakness and incompetence . . . This is how fascism comes to America, not with jackboots and salutes . . . but with a television huckster, a phony billionaire, a textbook egomaniac "tapping into" popular resentments and insecurities.'[1]

A year later, the Nobel Prize-winning economist Joseph Stiglitz stated that Trump 'certainly' has 'fascist' tendencies.

Shortly afterwards, the eminent American-Canadian social theorist Henry Giroux blogged: 'Fascist thought is on the rise all over the world, but its most blatant and dangerous manifestation has emerged in the Trump administration.'[2]

These arguments reflect how many people are quick to lump national populism in with extreme ideologies like Nazism. This in turn reflects a serious problem about how we think about populism.

The Populist Style

The equation of populism with fascism typically focuses on style more than content. Many critics reject the idea that populism is a serious ideology, comprising a body of policies and views about politics and society. Rather, it is seen as a way of competing for power, a way of *doing* politics.[3]

National-populist leaders are routinely presented as lacking any programme beyond diatribes against immigrants, minorities, established politicians, the media and miscellaneous other 'enemies of the people'. Their critics focus mainly on the face they present to the world while downplaying the ideas and values that unite them and the promises they are making to people. Populism is seen as a movement that is typically defined by a charismatic or demagogic leader who claims to speak on behalf of the masses. Populist leaders often use common and even coarse language to demonstrate their affinity with the 'true', 'pure' or 'real' people; they seek to cement their bond with them and reinforce their status as outsiders through 'us versus them' or 'good versus evil' terminology.

Another common concern among critics is that populism

is linked to a belief in conspiracy theories about dark forces that are allegedly at work in society, shadowy organizations that collude behind closed doors to undermine 'the people' and dismantle the nation. Donald Trump regularly attacks the 'Washington swamp', which encompasses the 'deep state' – a supposed network of government bureaucrats and linked interests who conspire behind the scenes to undermine presidential actions and, by extension, the will of the people. Some of those around Trump link this to what they see as a broader threat to the West from 'cultural Marxists', an amorphous alliance inspired by the Marxist thinker Antonio Gramsci who are seeking to spread liberal and left-wing values through the media, universities and other civic institutions.[4]

Similar ideas have been voiced in Britain. Trump's ally Nigel Farage lampoons what he calls 'global elites' who, he argues, not only failed to listen to the people before the Brexit referendum but have since sought to overturn it. Others also nod to the same 'deep-state' thesis, arguing that 'Establishment' civil servants in Westminster are seeking to soften, even reverse Brexit, while scholars and think tanks are allegedly turning university students into pro-EU automatons.

Elsewhere in Europe, national populists like Hungary's Viktor Orbán argue that liberal politicians within the EU, along with the billionaire Hungarian-Jewish financier George Soros, are engaged in a plot to flood Hungary and 'Christian' Europe with Muslim immigrants and refugees, which they see as part of a quest to dismantle Western nations and usher in a borderless world that is subservient to capitalism. Especially in Eastern Europe, anti-Semitic conspiracy theory as well as prejudice is very much alive and kicking.

This emphasis on conspiracy theory is not new. As long ago as the 1960s the historian Richard Hofstadter wrote influentially about the 'paranoid style' of populism, highlighting traits that he saw as characteristic of all populist movements. 'The paranoid spokesman', wrote Hofstadter, 'sees the fate of conspiracy in apocalyptic terms – he traffics in the birth and death of whole worlds, whole political orders, whole systems of human values . . . Like religious millennialists he expresses the anxiety of those who are living through the last days and he is sometimes disposed to set a date for the apocalypse.'[5]

National populists today share these ideas, but it is also worth noting that some of their claims are not entirely without credence. For example, Soros *does* invest heavily in civil-society campaigns that tend to be pro-EU and anti-Brexit, while financiers in the City of London *did* line up to fund anti-Brexit campaigns and issued dubious economic forecasts about the short-term impact of the vote for Brexit, many of which were wide of the mark. Trump's attacks on plots against him by the 'deep state' partly reflect the fact that there *have* been serious leaks from intelligence and other agencies, such as the wiretap which led to the resignation of the National Security Adviser Michael Flynn.

Moreover, the heavy focus on national-populist leaders and their style glosses over the extent to which they are united by core values. In recent years a growing number of scholars have been willing to see populism as a 'thin ideology', albeit one that needs to be combined with another ideology if it is to develop a full range of policies, especially in the economic sphere.[6] This means that the populist 'party family' can take on left- and right-wing forms.

Both left-wing and right-wing populists promise to give a voice to ordinary people and curb powerful elites who threaten their interests. But whereas the promises of left-wing populists, like Bernie Sanders in the US or Podemos in Spain, focus on limiting socio-economic inequalities, right-wing populists stress the need to limit immigration and preserve national identity. But as we will see later on, it is not always easy to attach neat labels to 'right-wing' populists, who increasingly share concerns about socio-economic inequalities, but in particular how they apply to whites. This point is frequently overlooked by critics, who only stress populism's desire to exclude immigrants rather than include what they see as the neglected and voiceless people.[7]

Many also see fascism as a style rather than ideology, focusing on its taste for authoritarian racist leaders, paramilitarism and choreographed rallies. However, a growing number of scholars have accepted that fascism too can be seen as offering a potentially appealing 'ideology' in its own right that demarcates it from other 'isms'.[8]

These debates about labels are not just a scholarly game. The term 'fascism' sends a message that certain people are beyond the pale. For the populists, those who damn them as 'fascist' are working to a 'politically correct' agenda that suppresses legitimate questions about issues like immigration, Islam and unresponsive elites.[9] Critics who mis-label them are fanning a populist fire.

We do not see leaders like Trump, Le Pen or Wilders as fascist. Rather, we hold that they are 'national populists' who represent a distinct tradition of thought in the West. And we think that this body of thought needs to be taken seriously.

National populism is an ideology which prioritizes the culture and interests of the nation, and which promises to give voice to a people who feel that they have been neglected, even held in contempt, by distant and often corrupt elites.

Far from being anti-democratic, populism – as scholars like Margaret Canovan argue – is a response to contradictions within liberal democracy, which on the one hand promises 'redemptive' rule by the people, but which in practice is increasingly based on 'pragmatic' and technocratic competing elites whose values are fundamentally different from many of those they govern, as we will explore in the next chapter. While the 'pragmatic' vision views democracy as an elitist system of institutions and rules to cope peacefully with conflicts, the 'redemptive' approach sees democracy as delivering 'salvation' through more direct forms of politics, identifying the people as the only source of legitimate authority. This is why, for Canovan, as long as we have liberal democracy we will have populism, which will continue to follow our democratic systems around 'like a shadow'.[10]

The Ideological Foundations of Populism

Although there were 'populares' (from the Latin '*populus*'), Senators in ancient Rome who courted the people, most historians trace the origins of populist movements to the nineteenth century. Many see the first as the Russian 'Narodniks', educated proselytizers who sought 'to go to the people' in the countryside. They campaigned for the liberalization of the autocratic Tsarist regime and celebrated simple rural life and authentic values. But they made little headway among an illiterate and superstitious peasantry, so many of them turned to revolutionary socialism.

The rise of populism is better understood as a response to the spread of liberal democracy during the nineteenth century. This was a period of growing literacy in the West, the extension of the franchise and the introduction of the secret ballot. Moreover, politics at this time was becoming influenced by new forms of communication, especially the popular press, which conveyed messages direct to voters. Terms like 'people' and 'popular sovereignty' were potentially powerful rhetorical tools, challenging the way in which political and economic power rested in the hands of elites.

Although the elitist enemies of early populists varied and were often deliberately vague, they included the parties that were increasingly dominating political power and a new capitalist economic class, which in countries like the US was characterized by immense wealth and divorced from the concerns and lifestyles of ordinary people. These elites were portrayed as small but inter-connected, highly powerful and a dominant force in national decision-making. The media (and later universities and 'experts') were also included in the 'elite' when populists sought to point to those who influenced public opinion or were regarded as part of secretive conspiracies against the nation. Populists were not necessarily opposed to all elites, however: their targets were leaders and powers that allegedly neglected the people's interests and views. We can tease out these themes by looking at some of the most significant populist movements in America and France.

America has a long and entrenched tradition of populism.

Echoing the 'Right of the People' to rule that was enshrined in the Declaration of Independence in 1776, a succession of populist movements have since claimed to speak on behalf of the people against corrupt, self-serving and out-of-touch elites. A key American harbinger was the humble-born slave owner and national military hero Andrew Jackson (President 1829–37), whose portrait hangs in Trump's Oval Office. Jackson lauded the virtues of the productive common white man against the idle rich, including bankers, and portrayed America as a unique self-governing republic. Another important early example was the American Party of the 1850s, formerly a secret society whose members were commonly called the 'Know Nothings' (because when asked about the movement they would respond 'I know nothing'). They sought to defend America's Protestant historic stock from new Catholic immigrants, who they feared were part of a papist conspiracy to rule America.

Then came a series of other movements that also helped to mould the populist tradition. The People's Party of the 1890s, which many see as the first 'major' populist party, briefly attracted a significant following. 'Radio Priest' Father Coughlin and Senator Huey Long's 'Share Our Wealth' movement in the 1930s, and the anti-communist campaigns led by Senator Joseph McCarthy in the 1950s, though very different, also attracted many supporters. Others followed, including the blatantly racist Governor George Wallace, who after an early defeat in Alabama notoriously announced that he was never going to be 'out-niggered' again. Wallace ran as the American Independent Party candidate for the presidency in 1968, attacking 'pointy-headed' intellectuals and 'bearded beatnik bureaucrats' in Washington. In the 1990s, Pat Buchanan ran for the presidency on a mix of hostility to economic elites and sympathy for hard-working ordinary people, combined with an 'America First' nationalism which was notably out of keeping with Republican globalism, though his social views were more in line with the conservative right. The billionaire Ross Perot ran as a third-party presidential candidate, gaining almost 19 per cent of the vote in 1992, attacking corruption in Washington, the North American Free Trade Area proposal and other policies which anticipated Trump. More recently, the Tea Party, which began as a campaign against 'big-government' bailouts following the 2008 financial crash interests, developed into an eclectic revolt against Barack Obama and immigration and in favour of socially traditional values, often linked to evangelical Christianity.

Populism spread in other countries too, especially in France, where the 'sovereignty of the people' had been a rallying call for Revolutionaries during the eighteenth century. The most important early movement was known as 'Boulangism', named after the former War Minister General Georges Boulanger. During the 1880s Boulangists combined attacks on condescending and corrupt parliamentary elites with calls for a war of revenge against Germany, which in 1870 had inflicted a humiliating defeat on France. However, Boulangism collapsed when its leader fled after being charged with treason, later committing suicide on his mistress's grave.

In the aftermath of the Second World War, when European populism was supposed to be dead and buried, Poujadism suddenly emerged in 1950s France. This was named after a shopkeeper called Pierre Poujade, who founded a movement for artisans and small-business owners who were protesting against an unfair tax system. But it soon broadened into a nationalist attack on parliamentary elites and the defence of 'l'Algérie française' (French Algeria, a colony whose Arab nationalists would win independence in 1962). One of these activists was Jean-Marie Le Pen, a paratrooper who had fought in Algeria and who, as we know, would go on to lead the National Front, one of the most important national-populist movements in Europe; it was founded in 1972 and led by Le Pen until 2011, when he was succeeded by his daughter Marine. By this time his granddaughter, Marion Maréchal-Le Pen, was also involved and the Le Pens would develop links to allies of Trump.

But what exactly connects these disparate leaders and movements? For their critics, the short answer lies in nationalism, racism and even fascism, which we are told is preached by unstable demagogues who exploit social tensions and a yearning for the things that people with traditional values prioritize such as stability, respect for authority and conformity to the wider group. Moreover, these movements' conception of the 'people' that they represent is seen as narrow, exclusionary and predicated on an outright rejection of the legitimacy of alternative views and social groups.

There is certainly a dark side to national populism. But to focus unduly on this aspect diverts attention from the way in which populists also raise sometimes uncomfortable but legitimate issues that would otherwise remain unaddressed. Today, and often for legitimate reasons, populists attack the elitist nature of liberal-democratic politics, the scale and pace of ethnic change and the increasingly unequal economic settlement – three broad challenges that we explore later.

Populists also attack those in society who have failed to address these challenges or, worse, encouraged them in the first place. While populists raise questions about how to overhaul or radically reform the existing settlement, they simultaneously argue that the established politicians and other influential people such as journalists, scholars and financiers are far too uncritical of the status quo. Populists routinely criticize more culturally liberal politicians and opinion formers, whom they regard as having neglected or opposed public concerns about the nation and national identity.

These points can be seen clearly by probing the three core themes that underpinned the important People's Party in the US, the first movement to call itself 'populist'. This was a coalition of agrarian workers in the South and plains states and urban industrial workers and peaked in the late nineteenth century. Revealingly, some contemporary liberal critics of populism refuse to term the People's Party 'populist' as it does not fit neatly into their hostile model, which sees populism as a form of 'anti-pluralist' politics that dangerously homogenizes the 'people' and promotes charismatic anti-democratic leadership.[11] But by promising to reform democracy around the notion of *popular will*, to defend *plain, ordinary people* and replace what it saw as *corrupt and distant elites*, the People's Party was a classic early example of what would later emerge in many Western democracies. Crucially, and like many subsequent populist movements, it accepted that society is legitimately made up of different groups. Its objective was to redress the balance of discussion towards the 'voiceless', not to install a proto-fascist-style dictatorship.

1. POPULAR WILL
Populists Promise To Reform Democracy So That
The Popular Will Is Heard And Acted Upon

The People's Party's Omaha Platform of 1892 proclaimed: 'We seek to restore the government of the Republic to the hands of the "plain people".' It set out a number of proposals for putting the plain people back into the heart of decision-making. These included the direct election of the president (rather than an electoral college of 'notables'), introducing direct election to the Senate, the regular use of referendums and the secret ballot.[12] Far from despising knowledge (a charge that has often been thrown at populists), the party had a strong educational wing and envisaged government being guided by experts rather than corrupt mainstream parties.

As a result, the party was divided over whether to collaborate with others. Its poorly funded candidate, James B. Weaver, carried four states in the 1892 presidential elections. But with no hope of capturing the presidency, the People's Party backed the 1896 Democrat candidate, William Jennings Bryan. The victor, William McKinley, used the first professional consultant to run his campaign, starting a trend of hiring teams of experts, thus introducing another barrier to poor insurgent third parties that were already hampered in districts using the simple majority election system.[13] Moreover, the People's Party was plagued by another problem that would continue to afflict populist parties, namely Democratic and Republican 'progressives' adopting and adapting aspects of their fight for greater democracy, including the war against corporate and personal greed – a strategy that would be familiar to contemporary centre-right politicians, especially in Europe, who often try to use 'national-populist-lite' policies to defuse their new challengers, a point we develop in the final chapter.

2. PLAIN, ORDINARY PEOPLE

Populists Promise To Defend Them, Always Portraying Distant Elites As Enemies But Also Targeting Others Such As Immigrants

One of the most important national populists to emerge in post-war Europe was Jean-Marie Le Pen, who used to claim that he 'said out loud what the people are thinking inside'. In Austria Jörg Haider used to say something similar: 'They hate me because I am with you.' Both of these national populists would have had much in common with the People's Party.

The People's Party often identified the people with a 'heartland', a culture that is viewed as being authentic, hard-working and endowed with common sense.[14] Although this can privilege a specific group, the Omaha Platform argued that 'the interests of rural and civic labour are the same', and the party had links with sections of the industrial labour movement as well as its strong rural base. The People's Party, therefore, sought a major rebalancing of power in favour of a broadly conceived protean American people, not a return to an idealized rural past in the face of rapid industrialization. Nor did many of its leaders defend patriarchy, often supporting the extension of the franchise to women, many of whom were active in the movement.

While the People's Party sought to ban Asian immigrants who, it believed, lowered wages and lacked a democratic culture, it is important to note that such views were widespread at the time. The party certainly did not see the people in terms of a nativist founding stock like the earlier Know Nothings. Indeed, many Catholics and other new immigrants were active within the party, and leaders supported alliances with poor African Americans. However, their Southern Democrat opponents played the race card, and by 1900 the leadership had turned on African American and Jewish communities in the hope of restoring the party's flagging fortunes. This anticipated the way in which later populists would use ethnic and racial conceptions, linked to national identity as well as democracy, as a means of rallying support.

3. CORRUPT AND DISTANT ELITES
Populists Promise To Replace Self-Serving Elites,
Though Their Agenda Is Moral Rather Than
A Physical Call To Arms

Anticipating contemporary arguments about the role of 'dark money' in politics, there was some truth in the People's Party's claim that wealthy interests had bought off Democrat and Republican politicians, much of the press and even judges. Its moral fire was directed especially at a new plutocratic elite, which was described as 'unprecedented in the history of mankind'. One of the People's Party leaders, Mary Lease, summed up a widespread feeling when she adapted Abraham Lincoln's Gettysburg Address (1863) to argue that, behind the façade,

American 'democracy' was the government 'of Wall Street, by Wall Street and for Wall Street'.

These early populists were especially hostile to the owners of banks that refused to tide farmers through the hard times following the 1870s 'Long Depression'. They also targeted railroads that had hiked prices for small producers, profit-oriented carriers which had prospered from massive government aid as they drove their tracks west to the Pacific, and whose owners lived in grand mansions rather than shacks. The People's Party argued that the state should be given control of monopolies, sought to link dollar convertibility to silver as well as the much scarcer gold (to allow more money to be coined in order to reflate the economy), and a graduated income tax. They were not socialists as they were strong defenders of honest private enterprise and individual initiative. But they wanted the state to re-establish a fair and level playing field for independent producers, whom they saw as the backbone of the nation.

The Ideological Foundations of Fascism

How do these core themes of populism, as embodied in the People's Party, compare to those of fascism? Although we can trace aspects of fascist ideology back to before the First World War, it was only after those traumatic years, including the game-changing Russian Revolution, that it took on an identifiable form against a background of division and economic and political instability across much of Europe.[15]

Benito Mussolini, a former leading Italian socialist,

founded the first self-styled 'Fascist' movement in 1919. The concept of *Fasci*, meaning 'union' in a political context, had previously been used by both the left and the right, and the movement's symbol became the ancient Roman *fasces*, an axe that is bound in rods symbolizing unity and authority. Extreme nationalism lay at Fascism's core, but its first programme also included policies that overlapped with those of the left, including the eight-hour working day, progressive taxation on capital and the seizure of Church possessions.

Adolf Hitler's German National Socialist Party is seen as the other major 'fascist' movement, though it never used the term as a self-reference. Most inter-war 'fascist' movements – like the Arrow Cross in Hungary, Falange in Spain and Iron Guard in Romania – stressed their national roots and had their own idiosyncrasies. Indeed, some historians hold that Nazism was unique to Germany, emphasizing a 'blood' conception of the nation and a rabid hatred of Jews, both of which were embedded in a longer tradition of German nationalism.

So what exactly links 'fascists'? The historian Richard Bessel brands the Nazis 'a band of political gangsters, inspired by a crude racist ideology'.[16] But critics' focus on racism and paramilitary violence makes it difficult to understand why it attracted major intellectuals like the elite theory sociologist Robert Michels, the philosopher of the 'ethical' state Giovanni Gentile, his fellow philosopher Martin Heidegger, whose ideas focused on authentic 'being', and the legal-political philosopher Carl Schmitt, who argued that liberalism was divisive and that dictatorship was necessary both at times of crisis and in order to achieve radical change. Although some intellectuals only turned to fascism after it came to power, few were driven by pure opportunism. To appreciate its intellectual appeal, we need to identify its three core themes.

1. HOLISTIC NATION
Fascists Promise To Forge A Spiritual Community That Demands Total Loyalty And Devotion To Its Interests

Most people think of nationalism as an all-embracing ideology, but in fact there are radically different strands. Liberal 'civic nationalism' is consistent with democracy and an open conception of citizenship. But 'holistic nationalism' typically holds that the nation has a closed and ethnically pure foundation. This holistic nationalism was also wrapped in 'authoritarian' policies, like a strong stance on law and order, stability and group conformity, which would be used to defend the interests of the whole nation, an approach that appealed to many people from different social classes who lived in highly divided societies which in the inter-war years had only a weak tradition of democratic rule.

The Nazis held that the roots of the German nation were deep and had a specific view of the ethnically defined national group. It was linked to the Caucasian-Mongoloid-Negroid racial typology first set out in the nineteenth century by the French thinker Arthur de Gobineau, in which Nordic Caucasians were the 'purest of the pure', a view reinforced by later 'racial science' (which in America legitimized immigration quotas and policies like compulsory sterilization, studied by the Nazis).[17]

Nationalism in Italy was based more on a sense of a common culture and history, though one that the Fascists argued had been weakened by centuries of division. Indeed, the proto-fascist writer Giovanni Papini wrote on the eve of the First World War that Italy was 'made up of shit, dragged kicking and screaming into a new state by a daring elite, and shit it has remained for the last fifty years'. Some of its supporters were Jewish and Mussolini had a Jewish intellectual mistress, though Fascism became anti-Semitic after Mussolini fell under Hitler's influence. However, this is not to say that Italian Fascists were not racist: they believed that they had the right to conquer *spazio vitale* (living space) in areas of the world that were inhabited by what they saw as inferior races, like Slavs and Africans, which led to brutal expansionism.

This new imperialism was underpinned by the growth of geopolitical thought, which portrayed the world as divided into natural spheres that needed to be controlled and exploited by great powers. Hitler's conception of *Lebensraum* held that the Volga was 'our Mississippi', though he sought to enslave the racially inferior Slavs rather than exterminate them, the fate of the 'scheming' 'Eternal Jew'.[18] For the Nazis the conquest of the Soviet Union was further linked to a crusade against 'Jewish' Bolshevism, which was seen as one side of a two-pronged attack on the health of nations (the other was 'Jewish' capitalism). The holistic nation was, therefore, a community of destiny, a force that would reshape the world into great power fiefdoms.

2. NEW MAN

Fascists Promise To Create A Communal And Spiritual
'New Man' Under The Direction Of Dynamic New Leaders

After the First World War Mussolini, who like Hitler had seen active service, called on a dynamic and young 'trenchocracy' to replace what he saw as divisive and weak conservative and liberal elites in the main parties who were incapable of uniting the nation. Inter-war fascists sought to build mass movements, but they did not believe that the people were capable of ruling. Only a vanguard, with a great leader, would be capable of driving the nation forward and creating a new social order.

Hitler wrote in *Mein Kampf* (1925) that the 'mob' needed a decisive leader to make them understand a great alternative 'idea' to Marxism's divisive and materialist promises. After the failure of the Nazis' violent Munich *Putsch* in 1923, Hitler decided that the modern state was too strong to attack head on, and instead placed his faith in his ability to mobilize widespread support through the ballot box. He proclaimed himself as the widely longed-for great *Führer* (leader), a messianic figure who had been sent by destiny to unify and restore the great German nation. This image was cultivated during election campaigns, orchestrated by Joseph Goebbels, that saw Hitler criss-cross the country in aeroplanes so that he not only looked modern but could also descend from the clouds to the cheering masses below. The Nazis built up their organization and targeted violence at their opponents rather than at the state, a tactic that encouraged sympathy from certain members of the German establishment who were extremely fearful of the rise of the communist left.

Central to this fascist thinking about the new man was a focus on 'decadence', a strong belief that society was decaying from within due to materialistic individualism. It was a view encapsulated in the French proto-fascist claim that on the tombstone of 'bourgeois man' should be carved the epitaph 'Born a man: died a grocer'. A sense of the idealized holistic new man can be gained from Mussolini's claim that 'he is political, he is economic, he is religious, he is saint, he is warrior'. Feminism was damned and traditional roles like motherhood and home-making were celebrated, but space was accorded for women to be active in their own fascist organizations (a formula which helps to explain why over half the Nazis' vote came from women by 1932).[19]

3. AN AUTHORITARIAN THIRD WAY
Fascism Promises To Create An Authoritarian State-Led Socio-Economic Third Way Between Capitalism And Socialism

Among leading fascists, there was a clear desire to create a new order that combined social unity with economic development, and which avoided capitalism's periodic slumps like the one which overwhelmed Germany after 1929. The 'socialist' wing of the Nazis, associated with the Strasser brothers, was of marginal importance as most leading Nazis courted industrialists and big business before coming to power and held entrepreneurs in high regard. Nevertheless, these were expected to work in the national interest and the Nazi state oversaw the establishment of full employment, welfare schemes and benefits like cheap holidays.[20] Fascists also rejected the supposed benefits of international free trade. They instead sought a self-sufficient economy within an 'autarchic' geopolitical framework. Nazi planners even developed the idea of a co-ordinated European economy; although the wartime reality was German exploitation, fascists in countries like France and Hungary welcomed this vision of the future.

Fascism is often classified as 'totalitarian', a term that was first coined by its opponents (and later popularized by liberal academics to highlight similarities between Soviet communism and Nazism such as leader worship, the police state and the destruction of civil society). Fascist intellectuals like Giovanni Gentile picked up the term, arguing that a single-party 'ethical state' could achieve goals that liberal democracies, divided by party politics, could not. In practice the Catholic Church retained a major influence in Italy, while opposition from the party, army and business led to Mussolini's arrest in 1943 (though he was liberated by SS commandos and installed in the puppet Salò Republic). Fascism, therefore, is a hybrid 'authoritarian regime' which destroyed liberal democracy but which was less pervasive than the 'totalitarian model'.[21]

While the Nazis did not speak of 'totalitarianism', they sought a radical breakdown of the private sphere, and dissent was stamped upon ruthlessly. The role of terror, however, has been overstated: many Germans were only too happy to denounce enemies of the nation, and Hitler attracted wide support by the late 1930s following successes such as full employment and the reoccupation of the demilitarized Rhineland in 1936.[22] Thus while the Nazi state was totalitarian, it should not be seen simply in terms of top-down control.

Figure 2.1
Populist and fascist core themes summary

A New Fascism or Far Right?

When you consider the foundations of fascism and populism, it is clear that the likes of Trump, Le Pen and Wilders do not signal a return to fascism but stand in the populist tradition.

This makes them different from, say, the Italian Social Movement, which was founded in 1946 and whose symbol was an Italian tricolour-hued flame rising from Mussolini's coffin, or the present-day CasaPound group in Italy, named after the American modernist poet and supporter of fascism Ezra Pound, which acknowledges the inspiration of the allegedly left-fascism of the Salò Republic.

The promises made by Trump, Le Pen and others also differ notably from those values. Outside Eastern Europe, they operate within mature, advanced and well-established democratic systems that have a strong and tested framework of checks and balances (systems that are also supported by most of their voters, as we will see in the next chapter). They do not advocate an end to free and fair elections. Nor do they talk about wanting to concentrate power in the hands of a dictator. Rather, many speak positively about wanting to give *more* power back to the people through a 'Swiss-style' model of democracy, a system of popular initiatives and referendums linked to representative government.

There are other important differences. After announcing that he would run for the Republican nomination in 2015, Trump, with his 'Make America Great Again' slogan, reflected the nationalist appeal that lay at the heart of his campaign and base of popular support. But while he held that America was ailing, Trump clearly did not, and does not, seek to forge a 'holistic nation', let alone a radically 'new man' in a country whose culture is characterized by rugged and self-confident individualism. Although Trump's statements have given succour to racists, his views are a far cry from fascist racism, let alone Nazi anti-Semitism.

The historical provenance of Trump's appeal is, rather, 'American exceptionalism', the belief that America is a unique nation based on democratic values and hard-working individuals, combined with the allure of contemporary celebrity culture, meaning that ordinary people were not offended by his great personal wealth. In the economic sphere, the Trump campaign was critical of globalization, called for the repatriation of jobs and the replacement of 'Obamacare' medical insurance with an alternative system, and supported the need for extensive public works. While unusual in a Republican Party that strongly endorses neoliberal economics, this constitutes nothing like a fascist third way.

It is important to acknowledge that Trump does play the strongman, that he has criticized key aspects of liberal democracy, including the 'fake-news' free media and judiciary, and that he has made use of executive orders to curb immigration, end the Trans-Pacific Partnership and impose tariffs and other policies. But whilst his actions are often ill-considered, this is far from an attempt to establish an authoritarian state in a stable country with strong democratic values.

Or take the French National Front, which grew out of a 1970s alliance between neo-fascists and hard-line nationalists. Its long-time leader, Jean-Marie Le Pen, who came from the nationalist wing, was rightly accused of extremism, not least following a string of derogatory comments about Jews. But after replacing her father as leader in 2011, Marine Le Pen sought to detoxify the party's image. She expelled her father for his renewed extremism, reached out to women and LGBT communities, who were included among her close advisers, promised referendums, which could be triggered by the collection of at least 500,000 signatures, including one on France's membership of the EU, and dropped the party's name from publicity for the 2017 presidential elections in favour of just 'Marine. Présidente'; her party is now returning to a stronger focus on nation and immigration. There is no serious evidence that party policy is being driven by neo-fascists, even if some remain on its fringes. Indeed, the change of party name to National Rally in 2018 was aimed at facilitating alliances with the mainstream right.

National Populism

So, if they are not 'fascist', how should this 'family' be labelled? One common approach is to call them 'far-right', on the grounds that the term covers all those movements that focus on immigration and ethnic change as threatening the nation. But 'far-right' is very broad. It includes violent fascists who want to overturn democracy, in addition to those who play by the democratic rules. It also encompasses blatant racists as well as those whose views on immigration are not significantly different to the mainstream right.

The latter point is especially important, given the extent to which many figures in the political mainstream are borrowing language from the 'far right' in an attempt to defuse it, such as the Interior Minister of Germany, Horst Seehofer, who in 2018 suggested: 'Islam does not belong in Germany.' The national-populist Alternative for Germany could not have put it better.

This is partly why some thinkers split the 'far right' into two groupings – the 'extreme right' and the 'radical right'. 'Radical-right' parties can effectively make the same distinction when they refuse to associate with 'extremists'. Many national populists in Europe distance themselves from openly neo-Nazi and extremist movements like Golden Dawn in Greece. In the Netherlands during the 2002 French presidential elections, the gay national populist Pim Fortuyn criticized Islam's ability to adapt to liberal freedoms while at the same time denouncing Jean-Marie Le Pen as a 'racist'. Mainstream parties too can make this distinction, accepting the radical right as coalition partners in countries like Austria, Italy and Switzerland, where the Swiss People's Party forms the largest grouping. Although in countries such as France and Germany the mainstream parties have refused to work with these parties, in Sweden the centre-right recently said it is open to co-operation with the once-extremist Sweden Democrats.

By this approach, the 'extreme right' is characterized by a rejection of democracy and comprises 'authoritarians' who do not tolerate the 'marketplace of ideas' where people broker and compromise, the essence of liberal-democratic life. Instead, extremists want to shut the marketplace down and divide the nation into an 'us versus them' situation.[23]

This is why some democracies like Germany actively seek to ban organizations that they consider 'extremist'.

The extreme right also includes terrorists like Anders Breivik, who murdered seventy-seven mainly young left-wing activists in bombings and shootings in Norway in 2011, in what he saw as part of a broader mission to prevent the 'Islamicization' of Europe and to fight back against the influence of 'cultural Marxism'.

The 'radical right', on the other hand, is typically used to describe groups that are critical of *certain aspects* of liberal democracy but which do not seek to overthrow democracy and are open to alternative forms of 'rule by the people', as we discuss in the next chapter. The 'radical right' encompasses large movements like the National Front in France, the Freedom Parties in Austria and the Netherlands, the Italian League and the Alternative for Germany.

These parties advocate 'authoritarian' social policies, like a tough stance on law and order, but also call for the greater use of referendums to strengthen the link between the rulers and the ruled. They also want to reclaim national sovereignty from distant transnational organizations such as the EU. This argument is often linked back to immigration by pointing the finger at the 'freedom of movement' principle in the EU, which allows people to travel and work freely in its member states. This, in turn, is often linked to security issues. National populists often argue that the EU does not adequately police its external and internal borders, an omission which, particularly since the start of the refugee crisis, has enabled Islamist terrorists to cross borders and commit atrocities.

However, the term 'radical right' is also problematic. Confusingly, in the US it can be used to refer to a variety of groups, including anti big-government conservatives and the motley group of racists that make up the 'Alt-Right', who vociferously supported Trump in 2016. Moreover, it makes it more difficult to perceive how they have attracted different 'constituencies', including people who used to vote for the left, and younger voters from historically left-wing areas. Calling them 'radical right' also distracts us from appreciating how some of these movements are shifting in important ways.

So, there is no misunderstanding: we do not challenge the fact that these politicians are, broadly speaking, right-wing. But we must also acknowledge that they have adopted policies that often do not fit neatly into the classic 'left versus right' division. This first emerged during the French Revolution, which began in 1789, the 'right' referring to those who supported the divine right of kings and the 'left' to advocates of progressive ideas, including the equal political 'rights of man'.[24] Increasingly during the nineteenth century, the 'left' became associated with achieving economic as well as political equality. Parallel to this development, a sociological understanding of the left-right spectrum emerged in which the left stood for the working class and the right for the interests of the privileged and wealthy (though by the turn of the twentieth century the right in some countries, such as Britain and Germany, offered welfare programmes to help defuse the rise of socialism).

In the late twentieth century, many mainstream parties, including social democrats, adopted key aspects of the neoliberal economic settlement, leading to rising inequality in the West, as we discuss in Chapter 5. This paved the way for parties like the National Front in France, which adopted 'statist' policies that had previously been offered by the left, including 're-industrialization' and 'intelligent protectionism'. While these parties had already started to outflank the left on immigration, some of them now also began to meet the left's demands for greater protections for workers and to act against the negative effects of unbridled globalization.

In 2017, Marine Le Pen campaigned on the slogan 'Neither right nor left', attacking globalization and stating that 'Our leaders chose globalization, which they wanted to be a happy thing. It turned out to be a horrible thing.' Where Le Pen diverges from the historic left is in how this critique of globalization is infused with strident opposition to immigration. In her words, 'economic globalization, which refuses any regulation . . . sets the conditions for another form of globalization: Islamist fundamentalism'.[25] She is by no means the only politician to appeal in this way.

The Danish People's Party calls itself the 'real social democrats', pointing not only to its sensitivity to working-class concerns about immigration, but also its desire to protect welfare benefits for the native group while restricting them for recent immigrants and refugees. The leader of the Sweden Democrats has said to voters simply: 'The election is a choice between mass immigration and welfare. You choose.' Even parties that are broadly sympathetic to the free market, like the Austrian and Dutch Freedom Parties, have strongly defended generous welfare for the national group and look with increasing suspicion at the broader impact of globalization.[26]

There are undoubtedly big variations in radical-right

policies towards cultural norms. Some, like Viktor Orbán's governing Fidesz in Hungary or the Law and Justice party in Poland, are clearly right-wing socially, arguing that rampant liberals have been obsessed with expanding the rights of minority groups and promoting multiculturalism, placing the nation's religious values and traditional family life under threat. Given that Orbán has also attacked key groups such as the judiciary and free media as part of his attempt to create an 'illiberal democracy', it is hardly surprising that many commentators are worried that this form of politics may presage the collapse of liberal-democratic freedoms and rights, especially after the legitimacy given him by his renewed mandate in 2018.[27]

In contrast, while Western European national populists usually share an open hostility towards Islam and rapidly growing Muslim communities, they increasingly anchor this in a defence of women's and LGBT rights, an outlook that is shared by some of their voters. In France Marine Le Pen actively presented herself as a twice-divorced single mother who was successful in her own right as a lawyer. But she also argued that the creeping influence of 'Islamic fundamentalism' is 'rolling back women's rights' and voiced her worry that the refugee crisis that has swept through Europe since 2015 will trigger 'social regression' and could signal 'the beginning of the end of women's rights', arguments that were inspired by Pim Fortuyn in the Netherlands.

National-populist ideas are also often linked to an emphasis on what are portrayed as 'European' values stretching back to Classical Greek democracy and based on the Judeo-Christian tradition. Whereas the Bible teaches us to 'Render to Caesar the things that are Caesar's; and to God the things that are God's', Islam is portrayed as lacking a secularized version of itself which distinguishes between the autonomous public and private religious spheres.

However, this line of argument does not represent an attempt on the part of most national populists to promote religious beliefs: its main aim is to attack Islam as a highly repressive form of what the likes of Geert Wilders call 'totalitarianism' or 'Islamofascism'. At the same time, today many Western European radical-right leaders court Jewish votes. Wilders in the Netherlands and Heinz-Christian Strache in Austria both supported Trump's decision to move the American embassy in Israel to Jerusalem. While this is partly strategic, there is no doubt that the views of these parties are today very different from the openly racist and anti-Semitic ones which have typically characterized extreme-right parties.

These points are central to the debate about national populism and racism, a term that has suffered 'mission creep' in recent years due to the growing influence of anti-racist groups. Blatant expressions of old-style racism and prejudice involving hierarchical and antagonistic characterization have broadly vanished from daily life in much of the West. They have increasingly been rejected since the end of the Second World War, the dismantling of Empire, the achievement of Civil Rights in the US, the opening up of access to education and the spread of liberal values.

In their place, recent decades have seen the emergence of what has been called the 'new racism', which focuses on 'cultural threats' to national identity – the idea that immigration and ethnic change present an imminent risk to the cultural

73

distinctiveness of the national group, to national values, identity and ways of life.[28] Islam has become the main target in this broader shift to cultural rather than racial arguments, largely because it is seen by many on the right as culturally incompatible with the West, due to its religious beliefs and attitudes towards key aspects of Western life (fears which have been reinforced by Islamist terrorism and home-grown killers in countries like Britain, France and the US).

Many scholars also identify other forms of new racism that do not involve conscious labelling. Institutional racism refers to the failure of organizations to offer fair treatment of ethnic minorities, as found in policing. Psychologists also talk of 'implicit bias', namely the way in which even people who genuinely think of themselves as non-racist can have prejudices that are unknown to themselves.

However, clumsily applied, these approaches can designate large numbers of white people and social institutions as 'racist', a charge which clearly alienates, even angers people. They can also stifle important debates around immigration and Islam. For example, should economic immigration be closely linked to the receiving country's economic needs, or should such immigrants have immediate access to benefits on the same terms as native people? Turning to Islam, should what many see as symbols of women's oppression like the niqab be banned in public, and Muslim schools be expected to teach Western values openly and fairly?

We use 'racism' to refer to the erroneous and dangerous belief that the world is divided into hierarchically ordered races, to anti-Semitism which plays more on conspiracy theory, and to violence and aggressive attitudes towards others based on their ethnicity. Where the disparagement and fear of different cultural groups is not linked to this form of systematic thinking we prefer the term 'xenophobia', which denotes a distrust and rejection of that which is perceived to be foreign and threatening. We do not think that the term 'racism' should be applied solely because people seek to retain the broad parameters of the ethnic base of a country and its national identity, even though this can involve discriminating against outsider groups (see also Chapter 4).

In this regard, we broadly agree with the Oxford philosopher David Miller, who has defended the right of states to control their borders and exclude immigrants on the basis of community goals and preferences. Critics claim that immigration controls reinforce global inequalities, while policies like fences and militarized borders lead to inhuman exclusion and the death of those trying to evade them. It is certainly impossible for reasonable people not to be deeply saddened by events such as drownings in the Mediterranean as unseaworthy boats succumb on the crossing to Europe. However, Miller argues that the basic responsibility of government is to maximize the welfare of its citizens and listen to their wishes. He adds that states have an obligation to do their fair share to protect refugees, but argues that valid reasons for rejecting immigration include the cost of integrating hyper-diverse groups and the threat to national cultures if this is not achieved. He adds that immigrants who are admitted have a responsibility to integrate into their adopted countries.[29]

Using this approach, most national-populist leaders and parties today are not properly 'racist', though there are undoubtedly exceptions. Roberto Calderoli of the Italian League took a leaf from classic racist texts when in 2013 he stated that the country's first black government minister had the features of an orang-utan. Many also call Trump racist, including the commentator Ta-Nehisi Coates who has described him as 'the first white president', referring to what he sees as his overt and long-running white-supremacist views, including his 'birther' attacks which claimed that Barack Obama was not born in the US and was thus ineligible to be President, in contrast to the older dog-whistle racism of Republican elites.[30] However, while we agree that Trump advocates discriminatory immigration policies and is deeply xenophobic, as evidenced in a host of provocative statements about Mexican 'rapists', Muslim 'terrorists' and 'shithole' countries, he does not fit the systematically racist mould, though his language is hardly that of the presidential moral high ground in a country still troubled by racial divisions.

Partly to avoid the baggage surrounding the term 'racism', some scholars prefer to call national populists 'nativist', a term which refers to the belief that a country should be inhabited exclusively by members of the native group, and that others are threatening.[31] However, few are nativist in the sense of the US nineteenth-century Know Nothings, who as we have seen defined the people on a narrow Protestant ethnic basis. Although there is a widespread desire to reduce immigration, and especially stem the major flows of refugees and economic immigrants, few advocate a totally closed conception of the nation either ethnically or in terms of new immigration.

Poland's Law and Justice party certainly seeks to maintain the country's exceptionally high level of ethnic homogeneity, whereby 97 per cent of the population is Polish. Together with Hungary, Poland has led resistance to an EU redistribution of refugees after 2015. Viktor Orbán even ordered the building of a fence on the Hungarian-Serbian border to halt the flow, though many were heading for Germany. Strong opposition to the EU's handling of the ongoing refugee crisis has also come from Matteo Salvini and the Italian League, who threatened in 2018 to kick out 500,000 recent immigrants who had made the sea crossing from North Africa.

On the other hand, the Swiss People's Party accepts that its country has a high need for immigrant labour, though it seeks to cap numbers and citizenship is difficult to obtain. For the Dutch People's Party the core issue is to exclude Muslims and immigrants who they believe cannot be assimilated and who have few, if any, desirable skills. While Geert Wilders holds xenophobic views about new Muslim immigration, his party has never agitated against Chinese or Vietnamese minorities, or those from the former colonies Surinam and Indonesia. The Austrian Freedom Party has similar views about new immigration, but its programme states that the country's historic ethnic minorities 'both enrich and are an integral part of the nation'. And while Nigel Farage and UKIP firmly opposed the arrival of low-skilled workers into Britain from Central and Eastern Europe, Farage took to the stage flanked by ethnic-minority supporters to proclaim that his party 'was not racist', and praised the contributions of immigrants from Britain's Commonwealth nations.

A clear thread running throughout this book is that we

need to understand national-populist voters better, not simply denounce them. But while a minority of national-populist supporters wear the 'racist' badge with pride, the vast majority are offended and even angered by this charge. When we look carefully at what national populists propose, it becomes much easier to see why many of them do not see themselves as racist.

Given the problems with alternative terms, the two most appropriate labels for leaders and parties like Donald Trump, Marine Le Pen and Geert Wilders are 'national-populist' or 'populist-nationalist', which combine the 'isms' that most accurately describe the promises they are making.

Although populism is often dismissed as merely a style, we have argued that it is a thin ideology in its own right, based on three core values: 1) an attempt to make the popular will heard and acted on; 2) the call to defend the interests of the plain, ordinary people; and 3) the desire to replace corrupt and distant elites. As these can be found in different forms of populism, for example Bernie Sanders' left-wing campaign for the US presidency in 2016, we need to add the term 'nationalism' to clarify what kind of populists people like Trump or Le Pen really are.

By nationalism we refer to a way of thinking which is more than a patriotic love of one's country or nativist boundary-setting. Nationalism refers to the belief that you are part of a group of people who share a common sense of history and identity and who are linked by a sense of mission or project. Many people in the West readily express nationalist beliefs, as we discuss in Chapter 4.[32] This is not necessarily based on ethnicity, as multi-ethnic nations like the US show. But it is territorially bounded, which differentiates a nation from ethnic or religious groups, like Muslims or white people, that are often spread across nations. Nationalism involves more than simply a love of one's homeland, which is often referred to as 'patriotism'. Although nationalism is consistent with having diverse identities, such as those of class, region or sexual orientation, it involves a strong desire to preserve national identity from radical change, and to promote the national interest.

'Populist nationalism' puts the emphasis on nationalism, which is unquestionably an important perspective of these parties. However, in general they are not insular, as they accept various forms of international links and obligations, including in many cases membership of the EU, even if they oppose further integration. As Trump told the 2018 Davos World Economic Forum, 'America First does not mean America alone'. Trump's goal in terms of trade is to promote what he sees as 'fair trade', not to create fortress America, to attack policies such as the way in which US business can be undercut through foreign government subsidies or work practices like child labour and lack of adequate safety precautions. He believes that important aspects of neoliberal economics have not worked in the American interest and has questioned the belief that free trade is always a positive for domestic workers. While a trade war would undoubtedly harm the US, he does rightly highlight issues that most politicians and economists ignore (see Chapter 5).

Nationalism, moreover, can encompass a *very* broad range of politics. 'Populist nationalism' could in theory include movements like the Scottish National Party, whose policies in general are left of centre and which in 2014 fought unsuccessfully to achieve independence from what it argues is a distant and exploitative English-dominated Britain via a referendum. The Scottish Nationalists would thus find themselves in the same camp as the Hungarian Jobbik movement, which is strongly hostile to minorities and for a time even had a paramilitary-style wing that was eventually banned (although it has recently moderated its policies in order to attack the governing national-populist Fidesz Party for corruption and other crimes against the people). Thus 'populist nationalism' could stretch from left to right, including both liberal democrats and supporters of authoritarian government.

'National populism' is the better shorthand form of reference. While we must not ignore the possibility that leaders and parties hide their true beliefs from voters, there is no question that their agenda is ultimately a populist one and that even their strong emphasis on immigration and ethnic change has to be understood in this light.

As we will see, the intense anxieties that national-populist voters express about how their nations are changing are both real and legitimate. They are not simply by-products of other forces. But these worries also encompass a host of concerns about the cosmopolitan and uncaring elites who allowed immigrants and other minorities into their country in the first place, as well as broader feelings of social and cultural loss which are also partly linked to ethnic change. By putting the emphasis more on populism, we highlight the way in which people want to be heard, rather than ignored or treated with contempt.

CHAPTER 3

Distrust

Liberal democracy has only existed in a fully developed form for about 100 years; human civilization as we know it has existed for around 6,000. Sometimes we forget how young our democracies are.

Liberal democracy is a system in which we all participate by voting for a representative who usually comes from a political party, and where the scope of government is limited by liberal freedoms and the rule of law. It was not until the final decades of the twentieth century that a great wave of liberal-democratic optimism spread across the West. This optimism coincided with the 'third wave' of democratization that saw dozens of countries around the globe throw off their authoritarian chains, most dramatically the Soviet Union in the early 1990s. Francis Fukuyama's much-cited claim that the world was nearing the 'end of history' caught the *Zeitgeist*.[1]

Fukuyama, who at the time was an analyst at the US State Department, argued that liberal democracy and its associated capitalist economic system would become dominant because of two factors. The first was 'the struggle for recognition': humans want to live in a system that allows them to freely choose their beliefs and way of life. The second was the dynamism and efficiency of capitalism, which had given the West a winning edge in the Cold War, both in living standards and high-tech weaponry. Because of these, Fukuyama famously predicted 'the end point of mankind's ideological evolution and the universalization of Western liberal democracy as the final form of human government'. The idea that liberal democracy was now the only game in town swept throughout the West.

But history had not read the script. The continuing power of ethnic nationalism was reflected in war and genocide in the Balkans, while influential thinkers like Fareed Zakaria were soon pointing to the growth of 'illiberal democracies'. These included many former communist states where power was concentrated in the hands of strongmen who claimed to speak for the entire nation, appointed Cabinets of cronies and went unchecked. By the twenty-first century, even in developed democracies scholars like Colin Crouch argued that an age of 'post-democracy' had arrived, where power has shifted to small circles of elites who operate behind a democratic façade.[2]

Today, liberal democracy is still being challenged. According to Freedom House, an independent watchdog, 2018 was the twelfth year in a row that the number of democracies suffering setbacks outnumbered those that had made gains by increasing freedoms and bolstering the rule of law. Of particular concern was the rise of national populism in Europe, the Trump presidency and the contested claim that young people 'may be losing faith and interest in the democratic project'.[3]

To fully understand this challenge we need to step back and explore how Western political thought and democratic practice have evolved over the long term. Looking at today's democracies from a wider perspective allows us to make several points which shed light on the foundations of national populism.

Ever since the age of 'direct democracy' in ancient Greece most thinkers in the West have been wary of people power, a view that continued after the seventeenth century when major debates about democracy re-emerged and there was a clear desire to marginalize the masses. This long tradition of a more 'elitist' conception of democracy has, for many decades now, created room for populists who promise to speak on behalf of people who have been neglected, even held in contempt, by increasingly distant and technocratic political and economic elites.

In recent years this tension has been compounded by a growing disconnect between the rulers and the ruled. Across the West, liberal democracies are increasingly dominated by highly educated and liberal elites whose backgrounds and outlook differ fundamentally from those of the average citizen, a development that has been exacerbated by the rise of a new 'governance elite', connected through informal and formal networks that cut across elected national governments. Linked to this has been the growth of 'politically correct' agendas, driven by degree-holding liberals and the young, which are especially focused on identity issues. These points lead to our overarching argument that national populism partly reflects a deep-rooted *distrust* of elites that can be traced back over decades and is now mirrored in a rising tide of public discontent with the current political settlement.

It is not true that people are giving up on democracy.

Large majorities remain supportive of democracy as a system of governing their societies. But many do have strong concerns about how their democracies are functioning and are receptive to a different, 'direct' concept of democracy. Large numbers no longer believe that 'people like them' have a voice and they reject the idea that their elected representatives share their concerns about new issues that have risen up the agenda. This distrust has accelerated in recent years and will remain evident for many years to come.

Direct and Liberal Democracy

Critics of national populism argue that it threatens liberal democracy's celebration of diversity and its ability to broker compromise between different groups. Combative populists like Trump are alleged to be attracting people looking for fascist-style strongmen rather than a new form of democracy. However, to attack populists as the cause of the challenge facing liberal democracy puts the cart before the donkey: large numbers of people were politically disillusioned long before the populists turned up.

To begin to understand how we got here, let's recall how democracy began and developed. Although some see democratic practices in several early civilizations, the term 'democracy' derives from the Greek words *demos* and *kratos*, meaning rule by the people, and it was in ancient Greece that the first serious thinking about people power took place.

DIRECT DEMOCRACY

Classical Athenian democracy was far more 'direct' than the democracies that we have today. It was based on three key principles. The first involved the right of all freeborn adult male 'citizens' to participate in the Assembly. Women, slaves and foreigners were excluded. Their participation was intended to develop their political education and encourage their support for the often difficult decisions that were made about public life. Second, this involvement in politics was intended to promote political equality. To achieve this and to prevent a permanent elite from emerging, many official positions in politics were chosen by lot and rotated on a regular basis. And third, the system required a relatively small city-state 'polity' in order to allow a sufficient degree of direct participation. Although in practice it was often unequal, as the most highly educated and the rich tended to be more eloquent and had more time to discuss politics, the system did encourage a sense of respect and worth among all, which as we will see is certainly not the case today.

Yet many Greek thinkers were also suspicious of this model of 'direct' democracy that gave significant power to the people. The philosopher Plato believed that 'A good decision is based on knowledge and not on number.' He feared that the majority would make poor decisions and could easily be swayed by demagogues. In *The Republic* (360 BC) he argued that tyranny 'naturally arises out of democracy', and contrasted it with rule by an ascetic elite of 'philosopher kings' who were trained to promote the communal good. This was a form of thinking which the philosopher Karl Popper later controversially identified as the origins of communist and fascist authoritarian elitism and their threat to the 'open society' in which political freedoms, human rights and a plurality of different ideas are allowed to flourish.[4]

Aristotle, who was a pupil of Plato, believed there were problems with all existing forms of government. *Monarchy*, rule by a single person, tended to mean autocracy; *aristocracy*, rule by the best, turned into an oligarchy of the richest; and *democracy*, rule by the people, meant that the poorest could turn their vengeance on the rich. Instead, Aristotle advocated a mixed system that would combine leadership with the participation of the masses, and which would protect against the dangers of an irrational or vengeful majority. To achieve this, he also believed that a relatively high degree of economic equality would be necessary in order to build consensus and stability, a point we will return to when exploring today's rampant inequalities in Chapter 5.

LIBERAL DEMOCRACY

How has our thinking about democracy evolved since ancient Greece? Although some discern aspects of democracy in places such as Italy's city states in the Middle Ages, serious thinking about new forms of democratic rule remained dormant until the seventeenth century. Though feted as an early harbinger of modern democracy, the English *Magna Carta* of 1215 was an attempt to settle a dispute between King John and his barons. Similarly, the rise of Parliament owed less to grand design than to circumstance, although the introduction of local representatives was later key to adapting democracy to large states.

Far more important was the English Civil War (1642–51),

a direct challenge to the doctrine of the divine right of kings. While the most radical proposals, like universal adult male suffrage, were rejected, by the time of the Bill of Rights in 1689 England had become a constitutional monarchy with an independent judiciary, freedom of speech and regular free elections to Parliament, though only those who owned property were allowed to participate.

John Locke, who is widely seen as the founding father of liberalism, set out in his *Two Treatises on Government* (1689) the case for widespread liberties based on 'natural rights'. Locke, like other thinkers in the Enlightenment then sweeping across Europe, developed a conception of human nature that was very different to the 'political man', which had characterized thinking in ancient Greece. He argued that people were self-interested and fulfilled when they were freely pursuing their own interests and the right to property. This required a private sphere that was beyond the reach of government, an argument echoed a century later by the great prophet of free-market economics Adam Smith. A similar belief in limited and representative government was also central to the American Founding Fathers' thinking about a new 'republic'.

The Declaration of Independence in 1776 stated that 'all men are created equal' and that governments derive their 'just powers from the consent of the governed'. But Thomas Jefferson, its principal author, held that there was a 'natural aristocracy' of publicly minded men who would be chosen for office by an electorate that was mainly comprised of white property-owning males. The Constitution that followed in 1789 provided for a House of Representatives, chosen from districts, a Senate, representing the states, and a president who, like the Senate, would be chosen by electoral colleges rather than by direct vote, which initially enhanced the power of 'notables'. Moreover, the fact that the president did not sit in Congress was part of an elaborate system of checks and balances that sought to limit the power of both leaders and the people. Federalism, which allocated major responsibilities to a lower level of government, further limited central power. Underpinning this new republic was the rule of law, including a Bill of Rights (1791), and a Supreme Court that could overrule laws passed by the president and Congress.

Although the Founding Fathers did not term America a 'democracy', the word spread rapidly across the West during the nineteenth century. This partly reflected the influence of *Democracy in America* (1835) by Alexis de Tocqueville. The pioneering French social scientist argued that America's Constitution had solved the problem of the 'tyranny of the majority' which had haunted Western thinking ever since Plato had voiced his fear about majoritarian rule. Moreover, de Tocqueville believed that what he saw as America's egalitarian society, encompassing different Churches and other independent bodies, served both as a forum for egalitarian participation and as a further check on the government. He largely neglected the racism that was suffered by non-whites (he stayed mainly in the North) and the inferior status of women, though he saw American women as influential compared to Europeans.

Although the British and American systems differed in major ways, they formed the basis of a model that became known as 'liberal democracy'. It involves four interlocking features. First, it accepts popular sovereignty, that only the people can legitimately authorize governments. Second is the provision for equal citizens to freely and regularly elect their representatives to govern, usually from a political party. The third is the idea of limited government, which is curtailed by checks and balances and backed by the rule of law to protect liberal freedoms such as free speech or worship: liberal democracy specifically rejects the idea that the majority is necessarily right. The fourth is the need for a vibrant 'pluralist' society of independent groups that would help different points of view to flourish. In the marketplace of ideas, the heart of liberal democracy, various people with competing demands air their views, compromise and reach consensus. Liberal democracy thus brokers the peaceful resolution of differences of opinion among the populace.

It was this form of government that Fukuyama celebrated during the final decade of the twentieth century. Yet his pervasive optimism failed to take into account two assumptions about the working of liberal democracy. The first was that it requires large numbers of people to believe that the system is fair and gives an equal voice to all. The second is that it assumes a relatively equal society, or at least one where most people accept considerable political and economic inequalities. But, as we will see, in recent decades these assumptions have been increasingly tested and will be for years to come.

Fear of the Masses

Direct democracy did not die in ancient Greece. It later became central to the political and social upheavals of eighteenth-century France.

Jean-Jacques Rousseau, the great Enlightenment prophet of direct democracy, was born in a Swiss Federation that had practised a limited form of people power since the Middle Ages. In works like *The Social Contract* (1762) Rousseau depicted the ideal state as egalitarian and small, which he believed would allow a form of 'general will' to emerge, involving a high level of agreement among the people (unlike liberalism, which celebrates difference). Rousseau famously held that 'man is born free' but 'everywhere is in chains', pointing to corrupting social influences like religion. Not surprisingly, Karl Popper listed Rousseau, as well as Plato, among his enemies of the 'open society', arguing that their views were central to the communist and fascist claim that man needed to be 'forced to be free'.

Although many liberals were active in the early stages of the French Revolution, the disciples of Rousseau came to play a prominent role. The most infamous was Maximilien Robespierre, who sought to overthrow the power of the aristocracy and Church, holding that 'the government of the Revolution is the despotism of freedom against tyranny'. Robespierre presided over a 'reign of Terror' during which the 'enemies of the people', including the King and Queen, were guillotined. Less well known, in 'revolutionary marriages' a naked priest and nun were bound together before being drowned, which was a common form of group killing for thousands of ordinary Catholics.

Robespierre was later sent to the guillotine, and following an interregnum a dashing young general, Napoleon Bonaparte, rose to power. The turbulent events of the Revolution, and Napoleon's elevation to Emperor by direct popular vote in a referendum, cast a long shadow. Aside from their impact on the course of European history, these developments were also important because they reignited broader fears about the appeal of charismatic demagogues to the mass public.

These fears returned with a vengeance after the First World War, when large numbers of people flocked to the Fascist Benito Mussolini and Adolf Hitler. But they also emerged elsewhere, including in the US, where as we have seen a tradition of populism has long been visible, continuing through figures like Father Coughlin, the Roman Catholic priest who became a national celebrity in the 1930s with his radio addresses to a weekly audience of 30–40 million listeners. He claimed to speak for the plain people, denouncing educated Easterners and the 'luxury of Park Avenue', defending fascist welfare policies and launching thinly disguised attacks on rich Jews and open ones against communists.

Around the same time another populist figure emerged in the US: Huey Long, a champion of the poor against big business who was first elected as Governor and then Senator for Louisiana, where he attracted a strong following. In 1934 Long founded the 'Share Our Wealth' campaign, promising a major redistribution of income and fortune. Echoing the populist People's Party attacks on plutocracy, Long asked ordinary Americans whether it was right that more of their nation's wealth was owned by twelve people than by the other 120 million, and promised a minimum family income of $5,000 (around $90,000 today). He was building a major movement until he met an assassin's bullet.

The rise of fascism in Europe and a concurrent revival of America's populist tradition deepened suspicions about people power. This was reflected in a school of elitist liberal-democratic scholars like the Harvard-based Joseph Schumpeter, who argued that the essence of stable democracy was not mass participation but rather rule by competing and enlightened party elites. Politicians should eschew campaigns that pander to popular passion and prejudice and start to view apathy as a positive asset, because it was likely to remove the least well-educated and more extreme voters from the marketplace of ideas. At the same time, scholars of the US presidency celebrated strongmen like Franklin Delano Roosevelt and Harry Truman for leading rather than following public opinion.[5]

Such elitism was reinforced by early work on American voters. During the 1950s, the scholars Philip Converse and Paul Lazarsfeld found that most people's political beliefs lacked coherence and stability and there were few informed 'good citizens'.[6] As the intellectual Democrat Adlai Stevenson, who ran unsuccessfully for the US presidency in the 1950s, replied to a supporter's claim that 'every thinking person' would surely vote for him: 'That's not enough. I need a majority.'

By this time, American liberals also had a new cause for concern. There was a powerful 'enemy within' in the form of hysterical anti-communist campaigns led by Republican Senator Joe McCarthy. Democrat Senator J. William Fulbright summed up these concerns, arguing that McCarthy 'has so preyed upon the fears and hatreds and prejudices of the American people that he has started a prairie fire which neither he nor anyone else may be able to control'. The vicious and often unsubstantiated witch hunts against suspected communists were an important backdrop to Richard

Hofstadter's influential formulation that populism was a 'paranoid style', a phrase that he felt captured the 'sense of heated exaggeration, suspiciousness and conspiratorial fantasy' that not only ran through McCarthy's campaign but could be traced back to a long line of movements in American history, including the nineteenth-century anti-Catholic Know Nothings and the People's Party. Hofstadter argued that, unlike leaders of those earlier movements who felt they were central to their nation and were fending off threats to an established way of life, the modern populist 'feels dispossessed: America has been largely taken away from them and their kind, though they are determined to try to repossess it and to prevent the final destructive act of subversion'.[7]

McCarthy and later figures such as the conservative Barry Goldwater, who ran for the US presidency in 1964, also influenced the thinking of sociologists like Daniel Bell and Seymour Lipset, who traced the roots of populism to people who had few qualifications, lived outside the big cities and who experienced 'status tensions' as a result of a rapidly modernizing society. While McCarthy's bullying and dishonest style were eventually confronted head on by brave liberals, his previous high approval ratings further boosted fears about the masses on both sides of the Atlantic.

In post-war Europe, meanwhile, concerns about mass support for a fascist revival remained strong. This was especially true in Western Europe, which unlike the East was not under communist control, where such fears were stoked by the finding in 1949 that nearly 60 per cent of West Germans believed that Nazism had been a good idea, but one that had been badly carried out.

Acute anxiety about the ability of democracies to revive was also reflected in research in the 1950s by the American sociologists Gabriel Almond and Sidney Verba, who found that in Italy and West Germany the roots of liberal democracy were shallow.[8] In West Germany, rising support for democracy was viewed largely as a result of rapid economic growth, while despite similar conditions in Italy very few trusted fellow citizens and their political system, which included a corrupt Christian Democratic Party, a major communist party and the neo-fascist Italian Social Movement, which remained active until the mid-1990s (to insiders the party's acronym 'MSI' stood for 'Mussolini Lives For Ever'). Another cause for concern was the sudden rise and fall of the Poujadists in 1950s France, further reigniting worries about the ability of charismatic leaders to appeal to alienated groups.

The Power of International 'Governance' Elites

After the Second World War, these fears contributed to the growth of what would become known by scholars as international 'governance' structures. The post-war era saw a gradual diffusion of power away from democratically elected national governments to transnational organizations, from politicians at the national level who had been elected by citizens to non-elected 'expert' policymakers and lobbyists who operated in the international sphere, beyond the realm of democratically accountable politics.

This shift was enacted in the establishment of the IMF in 1944, the United Nations in 1945 and the General Agreement on Trade and Tariffs in 1948, which in the 1990s morphed into the World Trade Organization. These bodies were designed to foster international order, encourage greater economic stability and spark growth across the West by lowering or removing barriers to trade between states. Supporters of governance argued that the transfer of power to more remote transnational bodies was necessary because some issues – like managing economic globalization, or dealing with large flows of refugees – required decisions to be made above the nation-state level.

However, right-wing critics saw these distant and amorphous structures as fostering liberal cosmopolitan agendas that had not been sanctioned by national governments or the people, and which also empowered groups like the UN at the expense of American power. They were joined by critics on the left, who saw them instead as vehicles for the extension of American economic power and the spread of capitalism, which we explore in Chapter 5.

One important example of this move towards multi-level international governance arrived in Europe in 1958, when six nations – Belgium, France, Italy, Luxembourg, the Netherlands and West Germany – came together to form the European Economic Community. This is worth exploring, as the process of European integration has since become central to the political turbulence of the late twentieth century, including not only Brexit but the rise of national populism.

At the heart of this process is what in 1957 the Treaty of Rome termed 'ever-closer union', the idea that the nations of Europe would gradually become increasingly integrated, not only economically but also in later years politically and socially – to many, the obvious response to two major wars that had torn Europe apart.

Crucially, during the early years the push for European integration avoided educating the people about what was happening or mobilizing their mass support, other than through broad statements about the need to unite Europe to prevent future fratricidal wars. Instead, integration was pushed forward by an elite consensus, with the construction of complex legislation devised in the interests of the people, but not *by* the people.

One problem was that as decisions over key issues moved up to the European level, longer and less transparent chains of delegation reduced the accountability of those who were making the decisions. This also made it difficult, if not impossible, for elected politicians at the national level to be accountable to their national citizens, while also having to deal with the growing number of treaties, demands, players and processes that now surrounded them.[9]

It had been less of a problem in earlier years. At least until the 1990s, there had been what scholars called a 'permissive consensus', whereby people seemed content to leave complex debates about integration to their politicians and bureaucrats. But when it was announced that Britain would hold a national referendum on whether or not to stay in the club in 1975, many liberal-minded elites felt uncomfortable, deploying arguments against giving the people a say that were similar to those used by nineteenth-century conservatives to oppose giving people the vote. This was reflected best in remarks on Britain's vote by Jean Rey, ex-President of the European Commission, in 1974: 'A referendum on this matter consists of consulting people who don't know the problems instead of consulting people who know them. I would deplore a situation in which the policy of this great country should be left to housewives. It should be decided instead by trained and informed people.' Many of Europe's leaders looked increasingly elitist, berating their fellow citizens for simply exercising their right to express an opinion – something that would reappear after the 2016 Brexit vote.[10]

The reality was that there had never been mass support in Britain for European integration. While at the 1975 referendum the Brits voted to stay in by a clear margin of two to one, the result hid a notable lack of enthusiasm. As two scholars noted at the time, while the Brits had voted to stay, hoping it would boost Britain's stagnating economy, there was 'no girding of the loins for the great European adventure'.[11] Support was wide but never deep.

As the years passed, European integration picked up pace. Another big step was the Maastricht Treaty in 1992. This introduced the symbolic term 'European Union', furthered political not just economic integration, established the idea of EU 'citizenship' and laid the foundation for a 'Euro' single currency. By now it was clear that people in Europe wanted more of a say and that quite a few were not happy with the direction of travel. But only three countries held referendums on the Maastricht Treaty. While it easily passed in Ireland, the French only narrowly approved it by a 51:49 per cent margin and the people of Denmark required two votes to get the 'right' decision, first rejecting it and then in a second vote approving it narrowly, prompting the most serious riots in the country's history. In Britain, despite a major parliamentary rebellion, it passed. But this time the people were not given a say.

Although some voters used referendums to vent their frustration with national politicians, by the 1990s it was clear that indifference and opposition to the European project were on the rise. Between 1979 and 2014, the average rate of turnout at elections which decided who would represent the people in the European Parliament slumped by twenty points to a record low of 43 per cent. In many countries only one in three people bothered to vote, while in some it was fewer than one in two.

This distinct lack of enthusiasm for a European Parliament that could not initiate legislation, combined with fears about an elite-driven agenda, was far from irrational. As President of the European Commission, Jean-Claude Juncker once explained in an interview at the close of the twentieth century: 'We decree something, then float it and wait some time to see what happens. If no clamour occurs and no big fuss follows, because most people do not grasp what had been decided, we continue – step by step, until the point of no return is reached.'[12]

One of these steps arrived in 1999 when the Euro single currency was launched. Once again, the people were not given a vote. When they were, in Denmark in 2000 and in Sweden in 2003, a majority rejected it. Even in Germany, where the Deutsche Mark was a symbol of the country's post-war economic miracle, there was significant opposition. Polls suggested that only a minority saw the Euro single currency as a good decision – a view that from 2013 onwards would be exploited by the national-populist Alternative for Germany.[13]

There was also evidence that a serious divide was open-ing up. As the single currency was launched, researchers found that whereas more than seven in ten politicians across Europe felt proud of their 'European' identity, among the public the figure was only one in two. This prompted the authors to observe: 'One might wonder whether the govern-ments and politicians responsible for the Maastricht Treaty were living in the same European world as the people they were supposed to represent.'[14]

Crucially, in the early years of the twenty-first century public anxiety over European integration also became com-bined with rising concerns about immigration and nation-al identity, issues that bled into one another in the minds of many.

One of the core pillars of the EU is the free movement of labour, which allows people from EU member states to work and settle in other member states. The result was major flows of workers across borders as people from low-wage economies in Europe went to work in stronger ones that of-fered higher wages and better conditions. Many people in Europe supported the move, but significant numbers also saw it as a threat to their national sovereignty, culture and ways of life. Britain, especially, saw hundreds of thousands of low-skilled workers arrive from poorer states like Poland, Bulgaria and Romania. Shortly before Brexit, around one in two British people felt that membership of the EU was now undermining their nation's cultural identity. Many now felt that the EU was turning into something quite different from the economic trading area that they had initially been prom-ised. These worries would become central to the Brexit vote.

Further evidence that the 'permissive consensus' was over came in 2005 when a proposed European Constitution that would have extended the EU's reach into areas like justice and immigration was rejected by 54 per cent of the French and 61 per cent of the Dutch. In the same year, an annual survey found that only around half of people in the EU saw their EU membership as 'a good thing'. Opposition was notably stronger among those without degrees and workers who not only struggled to relate to distant institutions but also shared a strong distrust of their political representatives and a belief that this integration was now threatening their national group.[15]

Nonetheless, the EU ploughed on. By 2008, many of the changes that had been proposed in the Constitutional Treaty had found their way into the Lisbon Treaty, although once again this was not put to the people. Only the Irish held a referendum, and when they said 'no' the government held another after obtaining limited concessions. This one passed, but in all other countries, even ones that had held referendums in the past, ratifying the Lisbon Treaty was left to the 'safe' hands of parliamentary elites and kept well away from ordinary people.

The disconnect was even sharper when the global financial crisis, Great Recession and sovereign debt crisis ripped through Europe (see Chapter 5). As the sheer scale of the turmoil became clear, the President of the European Commission, José Manuel Barroso, spoke of the need for 'exceptional measures for exceptional times'. In return for bailing out collapsing economies, the 'Troika' of the European Commission, European Central Bank and IMF demanded that several countries in Europe now implement harsh austerity measures that included massive cuts to public spending and tax rises. International financial markets put further pressure on governments to accept the terms of the bailouts and implement the austerity.

This had big political implications. In 2011 in Italy, the pressure, combined with fears that the Eurozone's third-largest economy was about to collapse and take the Euro single currency with it, led to the appointment of a technocratic, non-party government under a former EU Commissioner named Mario Monti. Only the national-populist League voted against it. Monti presided over sweeping austerity, raising taxes, the pension age and making it easier to sack workers. One of his ministers broke down in tears as she announced income cuts for pensioners. Monti was deeply unpopular and the events stoked considerable change. Though the next election in 2013 was won by the centre-left, a new populist party called the Five Star Movement broke through after tapping into people's disgust with the political establishment and endemic corruption. It was led by a former comedian, Beppe Grillo, who a few years earlier had launched a national 'Vaffanculo Day' against corrupt politicians (translated as 'Fuck Off Day').

Similar views were being voiced in Greece, where even before the crisis people had felt frustrated with endemic corruption and the malfunctioning of their institutions. While negotiating the bailouts, Germany's Finance Minister, Wolfgang Schäuble, even suggested that, given Greek hesitation about the proposed austerity, the country should postpone a national election and install a technocratic government similar to the one in Italy. In 2015, a new anti-austerity and left-populist government in Greece called a snap referendum on the imposition of further austerity, which the Greek people rejected by a margin of 61:39 per cent. Nonetheless, under immense external pressure, the government accepted a bailout package that included larger pension cuts and tax increases than the measures which the people had just rejected. Unsurprisingly, it was around this time that 79 per cent of Italians and 86 per cent of Greeks reached the same conclusion: their voice no longer counted in the EU.

It is tempting to trace this reaction simply to countries that were hit hard by the crisis, but this is misleading. The divide was much broader and flowed from the fact that people and established elites were thinking in profoundly different ways. The international think tank Chatham House asked a large sample of Europe's political, civic and business elites and also the general public whether or not they felt that 'people like them' were benefiting from being part of the EU, and whether or not politicians cared 'what people like you think'. While 71 per cent of Europe's elites felt they had benefited, the figure plummeted to 34 per cent among the public; and whereas even 50 per cent of elites felt that politicians did not care what people think, the figure soared to nearly 75 per cent among the public.

Even some EU leaders acknowledged that a glaring disconnect had emerged. Shortly before Britain became the first country to decide voluntarily to leave the EU in 2016, the President of the European Council, Donald Tusk, conceded that: 'Obsessed with the idea of instant and total integration, we failed to notice that ordinary people, the citizens of

Europe, do not share our Euro-enthusiasm.' Yet this would not stop Tusk from urging Brexit voters to change their mind, or Jean-Claude Juncker from describing them as 'deserters', or his chief of staff from dismissing the result as 'stupid'.

Nor did many politicians in Britain hide their desire for a second referendum, calling on the people to think again. Unsurprisingly, you did not need to look hard to find frustration among ordinary people that those in power were still not taking their views seriously: 'What they really want to do', said one voter in a northern industrial town, 'is kill democracy. They didn't like the answer they got before and so they'll just keep asking until people agree. As if we are all mindless morons.'[16]

Ordinarily, you might have expected the EU to enter a period of self-reflection, to think seriously about the root cause of this growing discontent and to come up with a response. But instead, one year after the Brexit vote, Jean-Claude Juncker proclaimed that the 'wind is back in Europe's sails' and outlined steps for *more* integration, including deepening the EU's budgetary powers, expanding the Euro single-currency area and further eroding the right of nation states to veto EU policies. By this point the public backlash was far more evident.

At a string of elections during 2017 and 2018, the anti-EU Geert Wilders finished second in the Netherlands, nearly half of the French supported Eurosceptic candidates in the first round of the presidential election, the anti-Euro Alternative for Germany broke through for the first time and, shortly afterwards, Italy swung sharply to the right: the openly populist Five Star Movement and the League – both of which had voiced criticism of EU-imposed austerity and the Euro single currency – were asked to form a coalition government.

The Insular Elite

The rise of political distrust across the West has been compounded by the way in which politicians increasingly look the same and have become less representative of many of the people who elect them.

There has certainly been improvement in some key areas. Legislatures in major democracies like America, Britain and France are today far more representative of historically marginalized groups. In all three countries the proportion of female and ethnic-minority lawmakers recently reached record highs. America's 115th Congress in 2017–19 was the most ethnically diverse in the country's history. These changes should be applauded. But when it comes to groups that provide the core support to national populism – the working class and less well educated – it is an entirely different story.

Today, when these groups look at their representatives they often see people who have had a completely different upbringing, lead fundamentally different lives and hold very different values. Education lies at the heart of this divide. While the general trend in the West is one of rising numbers of college-educated citizens, in many democracies people who have not pursued education after high school still form large shares of the population. According to the Organization for Economic Co-operation and Development (OECD), in the year of Brexit and Trump those aged between twenty-five and sixty-four without the highest tertiary level of education comprised an average of 66 per cent of the population in the EU (including over 80 per cent in Italy) and 55 per cent in the US.[17]

This is especially true in the key Rust Belt states that propelled Trump to the White House. Not every Trump voter lacked a college degree, but it is worth reflecting on the fact that whites without degrees easily outnumbered their graduate counterparts by a ratio of 62:31 per cent in Iowa, 54:28 in Michigan, 55:29 in Ohio, 51:31 in Pennsylvania and 58:32 in Wisconsin. These numbers, and the extent to which voters swung behind Trump, led some to argue that the Democrats 'must do the hard thing: find a way to reach hearts and minds among white non-college voters'.[18]

One way forward is to make our political systems more representative of groups that, despite their large size, are largely absent from legislatures and the corridors of power. This applies to working-class voters too. In Britain, for instance, by 2017 the percentage of MPs who had had blue-collar jobs hit a new all-time low of just 3 per cent, half the number of those who had previously been lawyers.[19] The picture was a far cry from the past, when workers and non-graduates were not only a larger proportion of the population but had been far more prominent in their political systems. Whereas half of the ruling Cabinet in the famous pioneering Labour government of 1945 had had blue-collar jobs, only one of Tony Blair's Cabinet ministers in the late 1990s had done so. Although legislatures have never been anything like socially representative, in the past left-wing parties in particular, like Labour in Britain or the communists in France and Italy, did have a far more working-class 'face'.

This has now become a much wider problem as public office is increasingly dominated by the highly educated, a growing number of whom have spent their entire adult lives in politics. In the US, for example, in 2014 it was revealed that while unemployment benefits had expired for more than a million Americans, for the first time in history over half of those who had been elected to Congress were millionaires, with equal numbers of Democrats and Republicans. All of them were in the top 1 per cent of America's income distribution, a group that has also moved further and further away from the average citizen, as we explore in Chapter 5. In 2018, the median net worth of a Senator was $3.2 million and a Representative $900,000.[20]

In recent years highly educated elites have also become far more dominant. In the era of President John F. Kennedy, 71 per cent of House Members and 76 per cent of Senators held bachelor degrees. By the time of Barack Obama's second term in office these figures had risen to 93 and 99 per cent respectively – compared to a national average of only 32 per cent.

It is a similar story in Western Europe. Of the fifteen ministers in Angela Merkel's third Cabinet fourteen held Master's degrees, nine had a PhD, seven had worked at universities and two had been professors. In France, many of the political and media elite are still drawn from the *Grandes Écoles* (prestige schools), including President Emmanuel Macron. As the scholars Mark Bovens and Anchrit Wille have shown, since the 1980s the number of degree-holding Cabinet ministers in Western Europe has increased dramatically, with many also having Masters and PhDs. Others point to the same divide, concluding that the people elected to represent citizens are 'almost always wealthier, more educated, and more likely to come from white-collar jobs than the citizens who elect them'.[21]

This is not only about politics. Many people are now scrutinizing the corridors of power and see fewer people who look and sound like them. It is not hard to grasp why most of Britain's media failed to diagnose the working-class anger that was simmering throughout non-London England when around half of the country's leading columnists were educated at private school, more than one in two had Oxford or Cambridge degrees, and only one in ten were working-class.[22]

This is why scholars like Bovens and Wille rightly argue that Plato's dream of a meritocratic polity, run by 'philosopher kings', has more or less been realized. Yet whereas Plato's idealized ruling class was an ascetic brotherhood working for the common good in small city states, today's elites are cosmopolitan, distant and at times self-serving. E. E. Schattschneider once observed that one of the key risks in democracies is that they become dominated by pressure groups, lobbyists and businesses that represent the privileged while ignoring the less well off: 'The flaw in the pluralist heaven is that the heavenly chorus sings with a strong upper-class accent.'[23] Those who criticize national populists for being anti-pluralist would do well to reflect on this.

The gap in representation would matter less if the rulers and ruled held broadly similar views about key issues, especially those that have risen up the agenda, like immigration, European integration, refugees and Islam. But they do not. In the US and Europe researchers have shown how the growing divide between politicians and people has skewed the policymaking process towards the 'haves' rather than the 'have nots'. This is known as the 'exclusion bias', which refers to how certain groups are effectively silenced and not prioritized when it comes to public policy.

One person who has been particularly influential in this regard is political scientist Larry Bartels, who has shown that while a basic principle of democracy is that everybody's view should count equally, in the US politicians have become far more responsive to the wealthy and business, though studies have since suggested that this has been especially true of Republican politicians. Conversely, on a range of key issues – such as increasing the minimum wage – the views of left-behind, low-income voters 'were utterly irrelevant', while other analysts have illustrated how lobbyists have often been listened to more than the general public.

This political inequality has also been charted by the scholar Nicholas Carnes, who in his book *White-Collar Government* concludes: 'The effects on the well-being of working-class Americans are staggering. Business regulations are more relaxed, tax policies are more generous to the rich, social safety-net programs are stingier, and protections for workers are weaker than they would be if our political decision makers came from the same mix of classes as the people they represent.'[24] It is unsurprising that so many turned to Trump, who promised to push the pendulum back in their direction.

This divide between elites and voters will also likely widen further as more divisive issues like immigration remain at the forefront of our political debates. It is on these identity issues that we find some of the biggest differences between elites and voters. In a survey by Chatham House, for example, while 57 per cent of elites thought immigration had been good for their country, only 25 per cent of the public felt the same; and while 58 per cent of elites thought immigration enhanced their nation's cultural life, only 32 per cent of the public shared this view.

Nor did the differences stop there. Elites were more than twice as likely as the public to reject the ideas that immigration makes crime worse and puts a strain on the welfare state. In contrast, the public were much more likely to want to see powers returned from the EU to their nation state, to think that other countries will leave the EU in the future, to want to ban the mainly Muslim state of Turkey from ever joining the EU, to feel that their country should not have to accept any refugees, and to want to stop all further immigration from Muslim states, which more than half of people supported. Shaped by their different education and values, those who are in power are often far more liberal than the people who have put them there.

Against this backdrop, some have pointed to what they see as positive developments, including the arrival of a new 'participatory politics' as a potentially powerful counter to the rise of international governance elites and the growing role of vested interests and 'dark money' in party politics.[25] Benjamin Barber and James Fishkin wrote enthusiastically about the emergence of a 'strong' and 'deliberative' democracy in the West, a possible revival of the Classical Athenian commitment to informed and rational discussion among equal citizens.[26] This is often linked to optimistic views about the internet and social media, which are seen to offer arenas for discussion, arranging meetings, petitions and raising funds. These resources are open to even the poorest and are capable of reaching large audiences.

However, while the 'digital divide' initially meant that groups like the poor were largely excluded from the internet, problems of equal access (let alone political usage) remain: for instance, in the US recently a quarter of households did not have broadband access, especially in rural areas where people are often the most alienated from urban, educated elites.[27] Moreover, the legal scholar Cass Sunstein has shown how social media plays a role in polarizing voters by targeting messages at like-minded people. Empirical evidence points to the fact that many people on both sides of the political divide are highly selective in what they read and tend to see opposing views as deceitful even when the information comes from expert sources.[28]

These issues are linked closely to political correctness, which is targeted by national populists who argue that the closing down of debate over difficult issues like immigration has been encouraged by distant and more culturally liberal academic, urban and political elites. 'I think the big problem this country has', said Trump in 2015, 'is being politically correct.' His opponents in the media responded by attacking his braggadocio, xenophobia and sexism – giving rise to his recurring complaints about 'fake news'. But national populists do have a point.

Even left-leaning scholars like Mark Lilla link the growing polarization of America to the rise of 'identity liberalism', an increasing fixation or near-total obsession among Democrats and the liberal left with race, gender and 'diversity' rather than traditional left-wing concerns like how to improve conditions for *all* workers and tackle inequality.[29] The scale of this polarization is reflected in a growing tendency to view these issues from a partisan perspective. In 2017, for example, the Pew Research Center found that while 95 per cent of African American Democrats and 73 per cent of white Democrats agreed that 'white people benefit from advantages in society that black people do not have', only 23 per cent of Republicans agreed.[30]

While these views are partly a reaction to ongoing racism and discrimination, Lilla rightly argues there has emerged a new generation of liberals who are 'narcissistically unaware of conditions outside their self-defined groups, and indifferent to the task of reaching out to Americans in every walk of life'. Hillary Clinton talked much about African Americans, Latinos, LGBT communities and women, but she spoke much less about working-class whites without degrees. When large numbers instead turned to Trump they were presented as 'angry white men', a misleading caricature that in Lilla's eyes absolves liberals of recognizing how their obsession with diversity encouraged these voters to think of themselves as a disadvantaged group who were being ignored and whose identity was under threat. They were reacting against the growing rhetoric of diversity, or what they saw as 'political correctness'.

Nor was this a fringe debate among scholars. A 2016

survey by Gallup found that 73 per cent of Americans felt that political correctness had become a serious problem in their country. It has clearly cemented support for national populism among people who feel not only that they have been pushed out of the conversation, but that when they do try to voice their worries they are stigmatized as racists.

Resentment is further caused when liberals adopt a 'militant democracy' approach of the type introduced in West Germany after the defeat of Nazism. This allowed for the banning of propaganda and movements that were seen as seriously threatening liberal democracy. The US First Amendment enshrines a commitment to free speech, but there has been a growing move towards banning controversial speakers on college campuses, which should be a haven of legal free speech. Although polls show that many Millennial students are open to being exposed to free speech, in recent years bans have extended to conservative thinkers like Charles Murray.

In the 1980s, Murray argued that welfare led to a 'dependency culture' from which it was difficult to break out. Critics saw this argument as targeted especially at African Americans, which was reinforced by Murray's highly controversial writings concerning racial differences in intelligence, which virtually all scholars reject. More recently, he has pointed to problems among a 'new lower' white class, which he argues is characterized not only by a lack of work ethic but also by weak family, communal and religious ties.[31] This too aroused criticism, though Murray was right to point to problems caused by the breakdown of community and traditional values, such as the 'producerist' work ethic.

Nonetheless, such bans and the publicity they attract have played a role in stoking not only polarization but also a broader suspicion of college education. Once again there are strong partisan differences. While 83 per cent of Trump voters thought that 'too many people are easily offended these days over language', only 39 per cent of Hillary Clinton's voters felt the same. But while 59 per cent of Clinton's voters were of the opinion that 'people need to be more careful with language to avoid offending people', the figure tumbled to just 16 per cent among Trump voters.

Since the 2016 presidential campaign there have also emerged sharper partisan differences in attitudes towards college education, which national populists argue is complicit in cultivating political correctness. In the US, they point to the fact that among tenure-track professors, registered Democrats outnumber Republicans by a ratio of at least 12:1, while in some institutions the figure is 60:1.[32] This imbalance has led some scholars to call for greater ideological diversity on campus, but it has no doubt played a role in increasing Republican pessimism about the effect of college education. By 2017, only 36 per cent felt that its effect was positive compared to 71 per cent among Democrats.[33]

This really matters because the political correctness agenda is *increasing* support for national populism. Cultural norms, such as the tendency to conflate legitimate concerns over immigration with racism, can backfire. During the 2016 US presidential election a team of psychologists examined the effect of exposing moderate Americans to what they called 'restrictive communication norms'. They found that priming people to think about political correctness – about the fact that there are norms in society that discourage them from saying anything that is offensive to particular groups – led them to become *more* supportive of Trump.[34] Expressions of racism are obviously unacceptable, but there is a clear sense among large numbers of voters that attempts to police debates around 'diversity agendas' have gone too far, and if anything are making things worse.

Distrustful Democrats

These broad trends helped to create room for national populists, who contend that liberal-democratic politics no longer represents ordinary people and that politicians, as well as other elites, cannot be trusted. This message resonates with large numbers of citizens in the West.

People are not giving up on democracy. In the shadow of Brexit and Trump many excitable writers argue that people in the West, but especially the young, are losing faith in democracy and drifting towards authoritarian rule. This is deeply misleading. Lots of people feel frustrated about how their democracies are working, but most remain firmly committed to the democratic system, as do the young. In 2017, the Pew Research Center found that across the US and Europe an average of only one in ten rejected democracy (from 5 per cent in Germany to 17 per cent in Spain). When you consider that many of these states had only a short history of democratic rule, were grappling with the lingering Great Recession, an ongoing major refugee crisis and the rise of populist movements these figures are actually remarkably small. Or consider the World Values Survey. Overwhelming majorities of people – typically at least eight in ten – not only give positive assessments of democracy but also think it is important to live in a country that is governed democratically.

Look too at the US. Despite alarmist reactions to the Trump presidency, in 2017 the Voter Study Group found that an overwhelming majority of Americans (86 per cent) felt positively about democracy, while more than eight in ten regarded it as important to live in a democracy. Around the same proportion saw democracy as preferable to any other kind of government. They also found no evidence that support for democracy has been in decline or is especially low among young Americans. Actually, young Americans were *less* likely than their older counterparts to voice support for non-democratic alternatives. Furthermore, among those few Americans who *did* voice negative views about democracy, most opposed rule by a 'strong leader' or 'army rule', underlining how dissatisfaction with democracy does not automatically translate into support for authoritarian rule.[35]

Some evidence suggests that significant numbers of people do seem receptive to being ruled by a 'strong leader' – according to the Pew Research Center, 29 per cent in Italy, 26 per cent in Britain, 24 per cent in Hungary and 22 per cent in the US. But while even these numbers are still fairly low, what exactly is this question tapping? Was Tony Blair not a strong leader? Ronald Reagan? Margaret Thatcher? The key point is that the fundamentals appear clear: overwhelming majorities of people agree that democracy is a good way of governing their societies (see Figure 3.1).[36]

And much of this holds true when you look at national populist voters. They are generally not anti-democrats

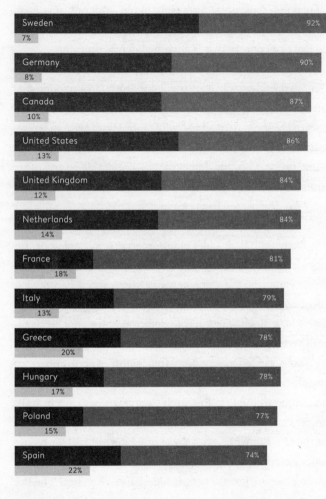

Figure 3.1 — Percentage of population who believe that representative democracy is:

- ■ Very good
- ■ Good
- ■ Bad

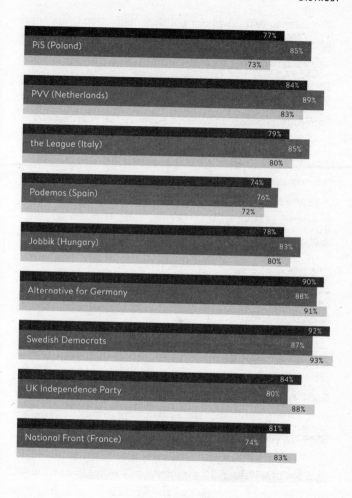

Figure 3.2 — Percentage of population who believe that representative democracy is a good way of governing the country

■ Overall population
■ Among those with a favourable view of _____
■ Among those with an unfavourable view of _____

who want to tear down our political institutions. Since the 1980s, national populists in general (unlike neo-fascists) have eschewed racism, anti-Semitism and anti-democratic appeals. Opposing democracy is no longer a vote winner. Nor do their voters want to overthrow the democratic system. Figure 3.2 compares levels of support for representative democracy among people who are favourable to national populism and those who are not. In several of these democracies national populist voters are actually *more* supportive of representative democracy than the general population. In Britain, Poland, Italy, the Netherlands, Hungary and Germany, eight or nearly nine in ten of these voters feel that representative democracy is a good way of governing their countries. Differences between these voters, the general public and those who oppose national populism are small or non-existent.

It is also worth pointing out that significant numbers of people have *always* felt unhappy with how their democracies are working, yet this has not spiralled into major upheavals. Even in 1944, as Winston Churchill led Britain towards victory, Gallup found that the British were evenly divided between those who felt their politicians were out to help the country and those who thought that politicians were merely in it for themselves. So we should be careful before falling into the trap of thinking that the world is going to hell in a handcart.

But at the same time there are challenges, the most pressing of which is a rising tide of political distrust across much of the West. In Britain, since Churchill's era the average level of public disapproval with the government of the day has increased by around twenty points to surpass 60 per cent, while general dissatisfaction with the prime minister of the day has also soared.[37] Meanwhile, the number of people who feel that politicians put the national interest ahead of that of their own party has slumped.

People elsewhere have also become less trusting. In established democracies like France, Germany and the US, even before the Great Recession fewer than four in ten people voiced confidence in their legislatures.[38] This was also true in new democracies in Eastern Europe, where in countries like Bulgaria and Hungary the 'honeymoon period' that followed the transition to democracy soon faded.

In the US, the arrival of a far more favourable climate for populists was visible long before Trump. In the 1960s, there occurred a striking collapse of public trust in politicians and government, which has been heightened in recent years by the decline of Democrat-Republican bi-partisanship and Congressional deadlock, brought on in part by widening ideological differences which has meant that both sides are less willing to back down. While there have been exceptions, such as the economic growth of the Reagan era in the early 1980s and after the terrorist atrocities on 11 September 2001, over the past half-century Americans have become much less trusting of Washington (see Figure 3.3).

Consider how the picture has changed since the 1960s. In 1964, 76 per cent of Americans trusted their government 'most of the time' or 'just about always'. Yet by the time of Barack Obama's re-election in 2012 this figure had plummeted to just 22 per cent. Along the way, Americans also became more convinced that their institutions no longer work for

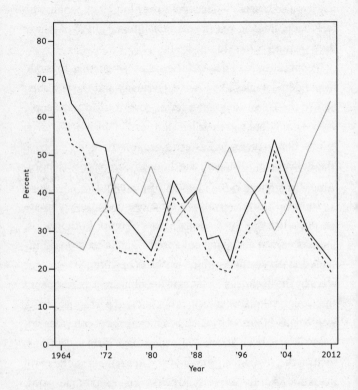

Figure 3.3
Percentage of US population who believe that:

——— Government can be trusted
- - - - Government is run for the benefit of all
——— Government officials are crooked

everybody. Between Lyndon Johnson in 1964 and Barack Obama in 2012, the percentage of people who felt the government was being run for the benefit of all slumped from 64 to 19 percent, while the percentage who suspected it was being run for a few big interests soared from 29 to 79 per cent. These longer-term trends make it all the more remarkable that so few saw Trump coming, who rightly perceived that a 'silent majority' of voters in America felt they had been completely cut adrift.

For many people, this distrust is wrapped up with a sense that they no longer have a voice. Back in 1964, 70 per cent of Americans rejected the idea that the people did not have a say in what the government did. But by 2012, nearly one in two felt they were no longer listened to. This sense of being shut out is especially pronounced among the left-behind. By 2012, while 41 per cent of college graduates felt voiceless, the figure spiralled to 64 per cent among those without a high-school diploma. While only one in three middle-class professionals felt voiceless, more than half of blue-collar workers did.

America is by no means exceptional. In 2017, Ipsos-MORI explored whether or not people felt that traditional politicians 'do not care about people like me'. The numbers who agreed were striking – 45 per cent in Sweden, 52 per cent in Germany, 58 per cent in Britain, 67 per cent in the US, 71 per cent in Poland, 72 per cent in Italy and 78 per cent in France.[39] The global average was 63 per cent.

In Britain, had you been looking at the long-term trends then you would have seen Brexit coming. Between the eras of Margaret Thatcher in 1986 and David Cameron in 2012, the working class and those with no educational qualifications were twice as likely as middle-class professionals and graduates to agree strongly that people like them have no say in government; only a few years before Brexit, the figure for the working class was nearly 40 per cent. The equivalent figure for the middle class was only 16 per cent.

Or look across the European Union. Over the past decade, on average between 37 and 50 per cent of people have felt their voice no longer counts, although in countries like Greece and Italy the figures have been much higher (see Figure 3.4). Again, these views were strongest among the left-behind. The voiceless are not only audible, but now comprise a large share of the population in virtually every Western state, a group that extends well beyond the left-behind.

These feelings of voicelessness help explain why lots of people are now instinctively receptive to the model of 'direct democracy' that we discussed at the outset of this chapter, including greater use of referendums. The Pew Research Center recently asked people whether voting 'directly on major national issues to decide what becomes law' would be good or bad. Germans answered 'good' by a majority of 74:23 per cent, the French by 74:25, Americans by 67:31 per cent and the British by 56:38.[40] The figure was even higher for supporters of national populism, underlining our point that while many do not want to replace democracy they do want more of a say in how their societies are governed.

Some are understandably nervous about this model. Critics of referendums list a variety of fields in which they should be eschewed, including: emotive ones like the death penalty; ones which make illegal what some see as human rights,

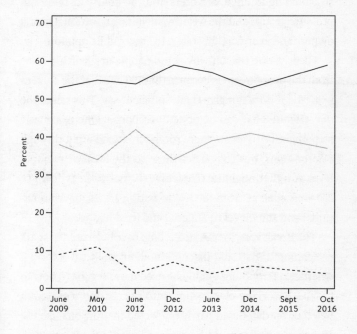

Figure 3.4
Responses to the statement 'My voice counts in the EU':

— Disagree
— Agree
----- Don't know

such as the choice of sexual lifestyle; or ones where there are complex arguments or potential dramatic changes in public policy, like the Brexit referendum. Critics also point to the so-called 'ignorance' of voters and the ability of powerful pressure groups and the wealthy, including traditional media owners and even foreign states, to sway public opinion.

Clearly, one reason why some people are drifting away from the mainstream is because they believe that the current settlement does not give them sufficient say. This raises the question of what can be done in response. One pragmatic step might be to create more room for citizen input through referendums, but to restrict these to the local or regional level. Another might be to devolve further powers down to citizens, such as from the EU to nation states, or from national and state level to regional and local bodies.

The Brexit vote, for example, could have been used to spark a meaningful national discussion about political reform – whether referendums should be used more regularly, how to get more working-class people into the corridors of power, whether outdated and partly unelected institutions like the House of Lords should be replaced with a more accountable and transparent second chamber, perhaps comprised of citizens, and which of Britain's economic and political institutions should be moved outside London and into areas that have been cut adrift. Another way forward might be to choose local or regional representatives by lottery or randomly select a large number of people to join 'citizens' assemblies' in which people discuss and debate policy. Similar points have been made about reforming American democracy, including by the scholar John P. McCormick, whose radical suggestions include a wealth ceiling on eligibility for election to Congress.[41] Such interventions might go some way to countering the populist charge that the people have no voice.

These initiatives might not halt national populism, as a country like Switzerland shows, with its long tradition of direct democracy and a highly successful populist party. But implementing a package of changes would go some way to addressing the underlying sense, shared by large numbers of people in the West, that they are not being listened to by an increasingly distant and insular elite.

However, the rise of national populism is only partly rooted in these concerns, so next we turn to explore the second 'D', namely people's fears about the possible *destruction* of their national group, values and ways of life.

CHAPTER 4

Destruction

Few debates about national populism fail to mention immigration; this is why it is crucial to explore exactly how this issue and the wider ethnic transformation of the West are creating room for revolts like Brexit, Trump and populists in Europe. Again, we need to step back and take in the broad view.

While many Western nations, not least the US, have experienced immigration in recent centuries, more recent flows have often been unprecedented in size, involved different types of migrants, and are more broadly ushering in an era of what we call 'hyper ethnic change'. This is causing significant fears and resentment among large numbers of voters, which will likely accelerate.

However, we reject the popular claim that national populism is simply a refuge for racists and people driven by an irrational fear of 'the other'. While racists are undoubtedly drawn to national populists, by no means everybody who votes for them is racist. Rather, national populists often raise legitimate questions such as what number of immigrants can be accommodated, what skill set they should have and whether new arrivals should have access to the same benefits as long-standing citizens.

Anxieties about the scale and pace of ethnic change are not simply rooted in economics and the availability of jobs. Despite what many on the liberal left claim, and as nearly twenty years of research have shown, what is just as important, if not more so, are people's fears about how immigration and ethnic change are seen to threaten their national identity. Our overarching argument is that national populism partly reflects deep-rooted public fears about how a new era of immigration and hyper ethnic change could lead to the *destruction* of their wider group and way of life.

We do not think that our societies are becoming more racist. When you look at the evidence, in many countries blatant racism is actually in decline. But many people do still feel intensely anxious about how their communities and nations are changing, perhaps irrevocably. National populists are appealing strongly to people who share distinct and legitimate beliefs about how this rapid change poses cultural and demographic risks. Before we explore these ideas, however, we first need to look at the ethnic transformation of the West and the arrival of hyper ethnic change.

Hyper Ethnic Change

We disagree strongly with the historian Noah Yuval Harari, who wrote in his bestselling book *Sapiens* that nationalism is losing ground: 'More and more people believe that all of humankind is the legitimate source of political authority . . . and that safeguarding human rights and protecting the interests of the entire human species should be the guiding light of politics.'[1] Such arguments often focus on generational change and exaggerate the scale and the pace at which tolerant youth are replacing their less tolerant elders.

There are good reasons to expect that people's feelings of attachment to the nation state will remain strong in the coming years. One is simply because of how many nations are now changing in rapid and profound ways. Both citizens and governments are grappling, often unsuccessfully, to come to terms with this new era of high immigration and ethnic churn; it is unsettling traditional norms, values and ways of life and is stoking a backlash from citizens who see it as a demographic and cultural risk. Exploring this broad process enables us to see that throughout human history immigration has often met with a backlash in the receiving country. It also allows us to compare recent ethnic change with an earlier era, which in turn helps us to understand better the seismic events of today.

Historic immigration has certainly strengthened nations; today, many major ones include people who can trace their immigrant ancestors back well over a century. What became known as Britain, for example, flourished following a wave of immigration from Ireland that helped drive the Industrial Revolution in the eighteenth century. The US grew out of colonies founded by Protestants who were often fleeing persecution, while great waves of immigration in the nineteenth century included Catholics, Slavs, Jews, Chinese and Japanese, whose hard work and skills helped make America the richest country in the world. Etched on the pedestal of the iconic Statue of Liberty are the words: 'Give me your tired, your poor, your huddled masses yearning to breathe free, the wretched refuse of your teeming shore.'

But it is important not to underestimate the tensions to which this immigration gave rise, especially when the numbers of incoming migrants were high and the pace of change rapid. Even in the US, the land of the 'melting pot', the epicentre of multicultural immigration, successive waves of immigrants, even European Christians, have long faced a hostile and even dangerous reception.

Alarmed by the continuing large-scale immigration from non-Protestant Europe, in the early twentieth century Congress appointed a commission to prepare a report on 'desirable' races. Its author was a Representative whose eugenicist adviser, Madison Grant, had written the 1916 bestseller *The Passing of the Great Race*, which separated the world into the tripartite Caucasian, Mongoloid and Negroid division (Hitler described the book as his Bible).[2] Influenced by this report, Congress passed an immigration law in 1924 based on national quotas linked to past immigration, which prioritized north (white) Europeans.

The rise of the 'second' Ku Klux Klan in the 1920s reflected how widespread this racialized world view had become. The first KKK had been formed after the Civil War, terrorizing newly liberated African Americans and whites who cheered the end of slavery. The Klan's revival was sparked by the film *The Birth of the Nation* (1915), which portrayed it as heroic defenders of downtrodden Southern whites (who in practice went on to impose segregation on 'liberated' slaves and removed their voting rights). At its peak, the KKK claimed 5 million members, mainly Protestants worried by the rise of 'uppity blacks' and immigration. The Klan faded from view but white racism remained pervasive, especially in the South. During the 1930s, continuing hostility to potential immigrants was reflected in the way in which refugees from Nazi Germany were kept out, ostensibly on the grounds that they might become 'public charges', though 200,000 Jewish refugees eventually gained entry.

It was only after 1945 that immigrants like the Irish and Italians began to lose their second-class-citizen status. Nonetheless, public hostility to migrants and minorities remained widespread. In the late 1950s only 38 per cent of Americans told Gallup they would be willing to vote for a well-qualified person for president who happened to be black. There were even open doubts in 1960 about whether John F. Kennedy, a wealthy war hero who came from a Catholic family, could successfully run for the presidency.

America's immigration story was then transformed. The 1965 Immigration and Naturalization Act, which Lyndon Johnson signed at the foot of the Statue of Liberty, profoundly changed the flow of people coming into America. The old quota system favouring people from Europe was replaced by a new system that allowed entry for family members of US citizens, skilled workers and political refugees. Over the next fifty years America experienced considerable change both in the numbers and origins of immigrants. This included sharply rising numbers of immigrants from Asia, the Middle East and Africa. The percentage of the 'foreign-born' population in America had peaked between 1880 and 1920 at almost 15 per cent, but had then fallen below 5 per cent by 1970. However, by 1990 it had jumped to 8 per cent and by 2015 was over 13 per cent, the Pew Research Center estimating that it will be 18 per cent by 2065 on current trends. As before the 1920s, most of the new arrivals and illegal immigrants (who make up about a quarter, according to Pew) have been unskilled.[3]

This changing immigration story was reflected in the numbers. Back in 1900, the two largest foreign populations in the US had been the Germans (2.7 million) and Irish (1.6 million). Fifty years later it was the Italians (1.5 million) and Russians (1.1 million). But from the 1980s onwards Mexico emerged as a much bigger source of inward migration. By 2013, three years before Trump's presidency, Mexicans were by far the largest group (nearly 12 million), followed by Chinese (2.4 million) and Indians (2.0 million). Whereas in 1960 around 84 per cent of all immigrants to America had come from Europe or Canada, by 2014 this figure had dipped below 14 per cent.[4]

Furthermore, many long-time Asian, Latin American and other non-European US citizens used the new rules to bring in their extended families, who in turn brought theirs, beginning what Trump would later call 'chain migration' (about 65 per cent of immigrant visas have been based on family ties, and only 15 per cent on the basis of employment).[5] By the time of Trump's victory in 2016, America was far more ethnically and culturally diverse: according to the US Census Bureau, the main groups were 61 per cent white (non-Hispanic), 18 per cent Hispanic and 13 per cent African American, while Pew estimated that just over 1 per cent of Americans were Muslim (the Census Bureau does not ask questions about religion).[6]

These changes have been matched by ones in the religious profile of the population. In the 1970s, 81 per cent of Americans had identified as white Christian, but by 2017 that number had nearly halved to 43 per cent. Today this decline is also underpinned by a sharp generational divide: while nearly half of Democrat pensioners identify as white Christian, the figure tumbles to only 14 per cent of Democrats aged between eighteen and twenty-nine.

Some welcome this increasing secularity as part of a wider process of liberalization that extends to issues like abortion and women's rights. But others have pushed back. White Christians still vote in relatively large numbers, partly in an attempt to uphold traditional values about the patriarchal family and the 'right to life'. And they increasingly line up behind the Republicans: Christian voters comprise 73 per cent of Republicans but only 29 per cent of Democrats. In spite of Trump's divorces, derogatory and offensive statements about women and past support for abortion, more evangelical Christians voted for him in 2016 than for Mitt Romney in 2012, seeing him as likely to deliver on key policies such as appointing conservative justices who might reverse secular liberalism.

America has not undergone this process alone. Parts of Western Europe have also experienced radical and fast-paced ethnic change. When Britain emerged victorious from the Second World War it was almost entirely white, but full employment attracted immigrants from the West Indies, India and Pakistan, Commonwealth countries that were not subject to controls until new legislation in the 1960s. This generated unease among voters. A watershed moment came in 1968, when the Conservative politician Enoch Powell broke an elite consensus of silence and addressed people's concerns directly, using incendiary language. The former university Classics professor infamously warned that 'Like the Roman, I seem to see the River Tiber foaming with much blood.' What became known as the 'rivers of blood' speech advocated the repatriation of non-white immigrants to stop what Powell argued would spiral into violence. Powell was ostracized and his career never really recovered, yet polls at the time found that his views had widespread support, not least among 74 per cent of the working class who, according to Gallup, agreed. Majorities of British people have backed reductions of immigration ever since.

The post-war economic boom in France similarly attracted a great wave of immigrants, including Muslim Algerians who were part of metropolitan France until 1962 (though there had been significant Muslim immigration after the First World War, partly to compensate for the vast number of French dead and injured). Poor relations between the host nation and its colonial immigrants reached a nadir in 1961, when French police massacred Algerians demonstrating in favour of independence.

A key problem Muslim migrants faced was France's assimilationist approach to the integration of immigrants, which required them to adopt French culture and identity. While this had worked well in the past for those such as white Belgian and Italian Catholics, it left Muslims increasingly isolated in urban areas, a ghettoization that was further reinforced by fears of racism and housing policies that encouraged their segregation. The historic separation between Church and state caused further problems over issues like girls wearing the hijab to schools, which the rising national-populist Jean-Marie Le Pen was happy to exploit (though he had no objection to the wearing of crucifixes and using as the party's symbol the Catholic nationalist hero Joan of Arc, who was burnt at the stake by the English).

Changes were also under way in West Germany, where the post-war economic boom had likewise been driven partly by large numbers of refugees who had fled communism. Later immigrants who came from the former Yugoslavia and Turkey were called 'guest workers' (*Gastarbeiter*), as it was assumed they would return home once they had made some money. Although few did, public displays of anti-immigration politics remained on the fringes, suppressed not only by the strong economy but also by the legacy of Nazism, which rendered these views unacceptable.

However, it all changed during the 1990s with the arrival of a new wave of immigrants from former communist states and the Middle East, many of whom were attracted by the unqualified right of asylum that had been included in West Germany's 'Basic Law' (Constitution) as a means of atonement for Nazism. In 1992, nearly half a million applied for asylum. This led to a spike in attacks on immigrants, in some cases murderous ones, and the rise of the neo-Nazi National Democratic Party, which was notably stronger in Eastern Germany. The German government responded to the twin problems of integrating newcomers and countering rising extremism by bringing asylum rules more in line with international norms in order to cut the numbers coming in, accompanied by local policies to further integration.

By the end of the twentieth century, therefore, the US and much of Western Europe had witnessed large and often unprecedented waves of immigration which were also often more visibly and culturally distinct than earlier ones, and which then accelerated during the first two decades of the twenty-first century as the ethnic transformation of the West reached new heights.

This has been especially apparent in the US where, by 2011, more than half of all cities were majority non-white. Cities like Austin, Tucson, Charlotte, Phoenix and Las Vegas have now tipped into 'majority-minority': people from minorities comprise a majority share of the population. By 2016, whites were also a minority in the states of Nevada, Texas, New Mexico, California and the District of Columbia, while for the first time in history white non-Hispanic children under ten years old had become a minority across America.

In Western Europe, meanwhile, by 2015 some countries had a higher percentage of foreign-born populations than the US. This ranged from 11 to 17 per cent in Austria, Sweden, Britain, Germany, France and the Netherlands.[7] In the decade before the Brexit vote, Britain also witnessed historic ethnic shifts as net migration (more people coming in than leaving) surged. As often low-skilled workers from other EU member states like Poland, Bulgaria and Romania moved to Britain, net migration soared from 50,000 per year in the late 1990s to reach record highs of more than 300,000 per year by the time of the Brexit vote.

In parts of the West, these dramatic shifts have been especially visible in the cities where, as sociologists point out, a population comprising more than 170 nationalities is now the rule rather than the exception.[8] While cities in North America like New York, Los Angeles and Toronto have long lacked a dominant majority group, European cities are now also witnessing profound change. Brussels, Geneva, Frankfurt and Amsterdam are already majority-minority. For the first time in history, by 2011 white Britons in London had become a minority, as they also are in Birmingham, Leicester, Luton and Slough. Head to the popular Pret a Manger fast-food chain in London and you will be served by somebody from the more than 105 different nationalities that work there.

This trend of rapid ethnic change looks set to accelerate. For example, only one in three schoolchildren in cities like Amsterdam have Dutch parents, while in countries such as Britain minority ethnic pupils recently accounted for over 70 per cent of the increase in student numbers at primary schools.

The picture is very different in Central and Eastern Europe, where in countries like Hungary and Poland the foreign-born population remains below 5 per cent. But this has not stopped national populists from being highly successful, partly because public worry over immigration is not only shaped by the actual number of immigrants or refugees entering a country or by the proportion of minorities, but is subjective in nature.

People living in ultra-conservative countries that have strong national populists but low immigration often look at what is happening in the West with horror and alarm. Indeed, the markedly different immigration story across much of Eastern Europe partly explains why the refugee crisis that erupted in Europe was opposed so fiercely by them. Countries like Bulgaria, Poland and Romania had experienced net *emigration* after joining the EU, as many young people left for higher-wage economies in the West; but they also had strong nationalist currents, which meant that they saw the arrival of culturally and ethnically distinct refugees, as well as domestic minorities like the Roma, as a threat to their identity and community. Many leaders and people in Central and Eastern Europe loathe what they see as a cosmopolitan and liberal Europe in the West.

While there is no Protestant equivalent in Europe of the powerful American evangelicals, the issue of religious demographic change should also not be ignored. Most national-populist voters are not religious, but there are nuances. While the religiously active in Europe are *less* likely to support national populism (because they vote for Christian parties where these exist), orthodox believers in some states like Belgium, Norway and Switzerland have felt more threatened by these ethnic shifts and been shown to be *more* likely to support national populists.[9]

Catholicism has also been a powerful influence on Fidesz in Hungary and Law and Justice in Poland. Both seek to preserve religious and traditional beliefs in what they view as an increasingly liberal and secular world. They also see Catholic Churches in other parts of Europe, such as Germany and Italy, losing the influence they once had in politics, while the number of Muslims is on the rise. In 1963, for example, 400 new priests were ordained in West Germany, but by 2015 the number for the whole of Germany had fallen to just fifty-eight. In the decade prior to 2016, 525 Catholic Churches and 340 Evangelical ones closed their doors for the last time.[10] The remaining Christians in Germany talk of the rise of a 'society without God', a fear populists tap into.

Outside the US and Eastern Europe, the connection between national populism and religion is weaker. Although national populists like Marine Le Pen and Geert Wilders talk about defending a 'Judeo-Christian tradition', there is no evangelical attempt to convert, reconnect with God or fill church pews. Instead, they target the growing number of Muslims in Europe, claiming that they want to defend liberal traditions, the Christian roots of Europe or connect with Jews to defuse the charge that they are 'fascist'.

These arguments became far more strident amid the refugee crisis that began in late 2014, and which eventually saw more than 2 million refugees and migrants seek asylum in Europe. With the exception of the earlier conflict in the Balkans, this marked a notable change from refugee flows in the past, not least because many refugees from countries like Syria, Afghanistan or Somalia were Muslim.[11] The crisis quickly revived fears in Europe about Muslim immigration, which many national populists have long presented as a specific cultural and demographic threat to the West. In countries like France, where the proportion of Muslims is projected to rise from 9 per cent to 17 per cent by 2050, Marine Le Pen compared Muslims praying in the streets to the Nazi occupation: 'It's an occupation of swathes of territory, of areas in which religious laws apply . . . for sure, there are no tanks, no soldiers, but it's an occupation all the same and it weighs on people.'[12]

Such claims are linked closely to the idea of 'Eurabia', which was developed by the writer Bat Ye'or and whose broad outlines have been supported by journalists including Oriana Fallaci in Italy, Douglas Murray in Britain and Daniel

Pipes in the US. Scholars like Bernard Lewis also adhere to aspects of it, having talked about a 'clash of civilizations' long before the phrase was popularized in the 1990s by Samuel Huntington, partly as a riposte to Francis Fukuyama's 'end of history' thesis.[13] Bat Ye'or argued that the move towards Eurabia first emerged in relation to the growing rapprochement during the 1970s between what was then called the European Economic Community and the Arab oil powers, against the background of the third Arab-Israel war. Linked to this was a rethink of how Europe was seeking to construct a European identity, which had previously stressed shared Christian culture and the threat from Islam as far back as the Crusades.

The Eurabia thesis holds that, just as European defences against Islamic states were being lowered, Muslim immigration into Europe was on the rise, a population characterized by higher-than-average birth rates. Some conspiratorial accounts posit this as a deliberate plot, citing statements like that of the Turkish President Recep Tayyip Erdoğan in 2017, who called on Turkish families in Europe to have five, not three, children each in revenge against what he argued was the West's 'injustices'. The Eurabia thesis circulates widely among national populists.

The nightmare vision of thinkers like Bruce Bawer is the introduction of sharia law: 'thieves would have their arms amputated . . . adulterous women would be stoned to death; so would gay people'.[14] In the short term, Muslims are charged with creating 'no-go zones', areas dominated by highly conservative interpretations of Islam which exclude non-Muslims and clamp down on dissent and deviancy, an argument popular among the Alt-Right in the US, who point to Europe's burgeoning Muslim populations. The thesis, however, involves population projections that most serious analysts regard as exaggerated (see below). Moreover, there is no serious evidence of any Islamic plot to 'colonize' Europe, even if groups like ISIS think it useful to have Muslim refugees on the continent. That said, the idea also plays on the anti-Muslim sentiment that has developed widely in the West and is likely to find a receptive audience for many years to come.

Clearly, not everybody will feel alarmed by these demographic shifts. But for many, as we will see, this considerable immigration and ethnic change raises the real possibility that their once-dominant group will soon be a minority as their nations continue to become far more ethnically and culturally diverse. Liberal and left-wing commentators correctly note that such a development would not necessarily mean that whites would lose their political and economic power, a fear stressed by white supremacists and the Alt-Right during Trump's campaign.[15] But these trends are fuelling considerable public anxiety, which in turn will continue to feed national populism.

Fears about Destruction

We take a very different view from those who argue that the West is drifting into an era that will be characterized by the decline of the nation state, the spread of transnational identities and a shift towards a liberal cosmopolitan world order in which borders will increasingly become redundant.

The truth is that many people still feel very committed to their nation state. According to the esteemed World Values Survey, overwhelming majorities of people across the US and Europe say they feel strongly attached to their nation (an average of 82 per cent), see themselves as part of their nation (93 per cent) and would be willing to fight for their nation (90 per cent).[16] While some pundits talk about withering national attachments, the reality is that they remain strong.

At the same time, large numbers of people feel instinctively negative about how their nations are changing, not just economically but also culturally and demographically. Before exploring these changes, it is important to resist the claim that we are all becoming more racist. Over the past fifty years, many nations have seen a steady decline in support for blatant racism, of the sort that we discussed in Chapter 2. This is not to say that racism has evaporated, because clearly it has not, but rather that general attitudes have shifted in important ways in most Western countries.

Consider the following question: would you feel comfortable if one of your relatives married somebody from a different ethnic group? This is a classic marker of traditional racism, and yet across much of the West the number of people who would feel uncomfortable has plummeted. Look at the US, where today around one in six newlyweds marry somebody from a different group. In 1958 more than 90 per cent of Americans disapproved of inter-group marriage. Today, 90 per cent approve. In Britain, more than half of the population opposed inter-group relations as recently as the 1980s. But today fewer than one in four do.[17]

These trends help to explain why movements that are

blatantly racist have been much less successful than those that replaced arguments about race with appeals that focus on culture and values.[18] Trump panders to xenophobic stereotypes of Mexicans and others, but he still sounds very different from the racist George Wallace, who proclaimed in his 1963 inaugural speech as Governor of Alabama: 'Segregation now, segregation tomorrow, segregation for ever.'

Cultural fears arise from concerns, shared by many, about immigrants who cannot speak the language, minorities who do not respect women's rights, the practice of female genital mutilation and other cultural traditions that appear to undermine or challenge the established community, or ethnic and religious groups which do not seem to integrate into wider society. Demographic fears flow from a belief that the scale and pace of immigration put the longer-term survival of the national group at risk, amounting to intense concern about its possible *destruction*; they are not necessarily grounded in objective reality but they are still potent. Many people feel that ethnic shifts are now completely out of control and that their much-cherished ways of life are under imminent threat.

Immigration has certainly become a far more pressing concern. It has crept up the agenda across much of the West. Furthermore, it is also an issue that often bleeds into others, like border security or strains on public services. In the US, for example, whereas in 2001 only 2 per cent of the population saw immigration as a top problem, by 2006 the figure had surged to 19 per cent, amid Congressional disputes and mass protests in major US cities; and while it subsequently fell, by 2014 it was back to 17 per cent, reflecting new debates over refugees from Central America. In early 2018 it was still at 15 per cent, making it the second concern (behind dissatisfaction with government).

The picture has been similar in Europe: whereas in 2005 only 14 per cent saw immigration as a key issue, by 2016 this figure had doubled to 28 per cent, making it the second-top priority (behind unemployment). The growth of public anxiety about immigration was also underlined in the spring of 2018, when surveys by YouGov found that immigration and terrorism were seen as the top two concerns across a large range of European democracies, reflecting widespread worries over Islamist terrorism and the refugee crisis. In Britain, between 2000 and the Brexit vote in 2016 the percentage who saw immigration as a major problem soared from 7 per cent to 48, making it the top concern in the country.

Many people in the West also feel instinctively pessimistic about the effect of this change. In 2017, for example, Ipsos-MORI ran a global survey and found that large majorities not only felt that there were too many immigrants in their nation, but that immigration is 'causing my country to change in ways that I don't like' (see Figure 4.1).

These broad trends hide differences, of course. Not everybody feels this way. In countries like the US, there is considerable polarization. In the mid-1990s there was not much difference between Democrats and Republicans in the extent to which they felt that 'immigrants strengthen America because of their hard work and talents': 32 per cent of Democrats thought so and 30 per cent of Republicans concurred. The two groups were separated by only two points. But by 2017, after years of toxic debates, the Obama presidency

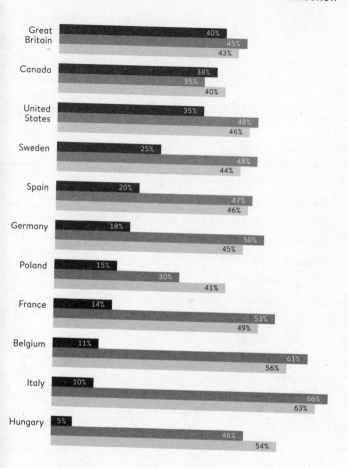

Figure 4.1

Percentage of population who agree that:

- Immigration has had a positive impact
- There are too many immigrants in our country
- Immigration is causing my country to change in ways that I don't like

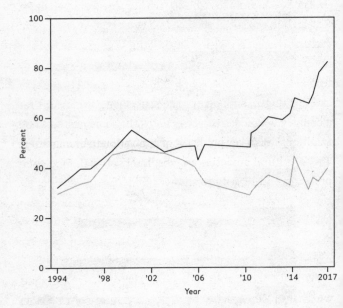

Figure 4.2
Percentage of US population who say immigrants
strengthen the country because of their hard work
and talents.

——— Democrat / leaning Democrat:
——— Republican / leaning Republican

and Trump's divisive campaign, this had spiralled to a forty-two-point difference, as Democrats swung far more strongly behind a pro-immigration position and Republicans were far more pessimistic.

The key question is: why do some people feel so anxious? Research in the social sciences suggests that worries about cultural change are just as important as economic ones, if not more so. Already in 2008, when scholars looked at nineteen nations in Europe, they found that, aside from the educational divide, support for the statement, 'It is better for a country if almost everyone shares the same customs and traditions' was a key predictor of opposition to immigration. These cultural anxieties are absolutely crucial. One comprehensive review of 100 studies that looked at how people across the West think about immigration concluded that while arguments which focused on economic self-interest 'fared poorly', people were far more anxious about how immigration impacts on their nation and its culture.[19]

Worries about cultural incompatibility – for example, whether Muslims share the West's commitment to gender equality, or immigrants will respect and uphold domestic cultural traditions – influence the type of immigration that people support. Americans are most approving of immigrants who have college degrees, good language skills, good job experience and who have legally visited America in the past. But they are much more hostile towards immigrants who have no plans to work and who come from more culturally distinct Muslim states like Iraq, Somalia or Sudan. In Britain, people are likewise more opposed to immigrants from Africa and South Asia.[20] Such cultural conflicts are key because they challenge the well-worn belief that in order to overcome anxiety and national populism, all you need to do is create jobs and growth. Rather, tensions over perceived differences in culture and values will likely remain.

This backlash has been especially acute in Central and East European states like Poland and Hungary. In the latter, the national-populist Prime Minister Viktor Orbán built a fence to close down the so-called 'Balkan route' and portrayed the mainly Muslim refugees as 'invaders'. Together with the national-populist governing Law and Justice party in Poland, and also politicians in the Czech government, Hungary refused to participate in an EU-backed quota scheme that allocated a proportionate number of refugees to individual member states. Orbán even ordered a referendum on the issue, which was easily won, though it was boycotted by opponents of the government as part of a wider protest against his move to what he openly called illiberal democracy.

During the 2018 national election campaign Orbán returned to the attack, claiming that opposition parties 'in the pay of foreigners' wanted to come to power 'so that they can demolish the fence and accept from the hand of Brussels the compulsory [immigrant] settlement quota'. Although East European countries are loath to provoke a rupture with the EU as they are major net beneficiaries of EU funds, this ongoing crisis underlined big differences in opinion about the powers of nation states and the desire to limit immigration.

The refugee crisis has also had a major impact on Germany. The Chancellor, Angela Merkel, took an executive decision to open Germany to refugees on humanitarian grounds, though Germany's ageing population may have been another consideration. More than a million arrived, including a large number of unaccompanied minors. The national-populist Alternative for Germany had already been on the rise following its criticism of taxpayer-funded bailouts for troubled states in the Eurozone, but amid the refugee crisis it shifted its focus to security and identity threats. In 2017 the party entered into parliament, winning almost 13 per cent of the vote and ninety-four seats.

Crucially, today worries about immigration and refugees have also become entwined with wider fears over security. After the 9/11 attacks in the US, Europe witnessed a number of major terrorist atrocities, from London to Madrid. The refugee crisis coincided with the occurrence of over sixty acts of 'Jihadist terrorism' in Europe and North America between 2014 and 2017, which left 424 dead and 2,000 injured. Unsurprisingly, therefore, the refugee crisis started to stoke fears that not all those entering Europe were genuine refugees and that some of them might be incompatible with Western culture. The latter claim included footage of so-called 'mass sexual assaults' in Germany during New Year celebrations in 2016, as well as the fact that some refugees were involved in terrorist attacks in Paris, Stockholm and Berlin.

Terrorism has certainly also come from the extreme right, as we have seen in the case of Anders Breivik in Norway. The US has also suffered attacks, including a mass shooting in 2015 in a Charleston African American church by Dylann Roof, who killed nine and injured one in his attempt to initiate 'race war' (a tactic that has widely circulated among white supremacists for decades, ever since the publication of *The Turner Diaries* in 1978 by a leading US neo-Nazi, William

Pierce). Yet among the public, the refugee crisis has mainly ignited fears over Islamist terrorism.

Especially in Europe, where Muslim populations are much larger than in the US, the potential for home-grown terrorism seems strong, while small but not insignificant numbers of European Islamists have fought with ISIS in the Middle East. Muslims make up over 60 per cent of France's prison population, a recruiting ground for extremism, while counter-terrorism officers have estimated that 11,400 Muslims in France are radicalized extremists. Such numbers are difficult to verify, though in Britain scrutiny of the failure of the security services to prevent terrorist atrocities in London and Manchester forced officials to acknowledge that there were 23,000 jihadist extremists in Britain, 3,000 of whom were under investigation or active monitoring.

What is clear is that large numbers of people have bought into the idea that refugees will increase the risk of terrorism – according to the Pew Research Center, more than 70 per cent of Poles and Hungarians, 60 per cent or more of Italians, Dutch and Germans and over half of the British, Greeks and Swedes. On average, almost 60 per cent of Europeans felt this way.[21]

There is also fairly widespread support for a far more restrictive policy response. Though Trump was widely condemned for introducing a travel ban on predominantly Muslim states in 2017, a survey by Chatham House revealed that 55 per cent of people across ten European countries *agreed* that all further immigration from Muslim states should be stopped, a figure that was significantly higher in Austria, Hungary and Poland, where people are especially

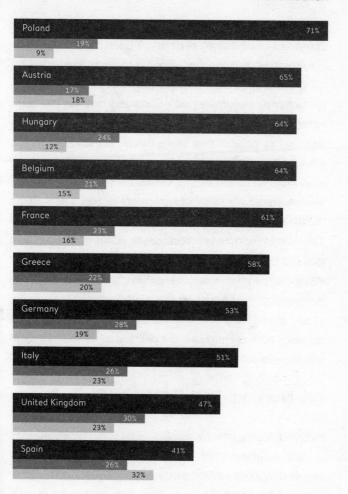

Figure 4.3
All further migration from mainly Muslim countries should
be stopped:

- Agree
- Neither agree nor disagree
- Disagree

anxious about refugees (see Figure 4.3). In 2018, another survey revealed that 63 per cent of Germans wanted their country to adopt a tougher response to the refugee crisis.[22]

These broad ethnic changes and security threats are already having major political effects and may yet continue to reduce trust among ethnic groups, hinder welfare reform and lead to polarization along ethnic lines. The Harvard scholars Steven Levitsky and Daniel Ziblatt argued that there is no example in history of a successful multi-racial democracy where the once-majority group has become a minority.[23]

The mainstream has by and large failed to respond effectively to this angst, largely because the values of many in politics and the media mean that they accept or celebrate these ethnic shifts. Although there are growing signs that some in the mainstream right are turning to national-populist-lite policies to halt the tide, the general failure to address people's fears has given national populists the political space to make their promises distinctive.

Are National-Populist Voters Racist?

National populism has tapped directly into these concerns about immigration, but, as we have seen, this is not to say that most of their supporters are necessarily racist. This is an important point because misdiagnosing the nature of such concerns could easily make things worse.

Let's consider how national populists think about their wider national community. Around the time of Brexit and Trump, the Pew Research Center asked people what they thought was important to being considered part of the nation – whether or not someone can speak the language, whether they share customs and traditions and, at the most restrictive end, whether they were born in that country. Large majorities of people across the West, irrespective of their political beliefs, feel that speaking the language is *very* or *somewhat* important. At least 95 per cent of the Dutch, Brits, Hungarians, Germans, French, Greeks and Poles think so, as do more than 90 per cent of Americans, Swedes, Spanish and Italians with, on average, those on the right twenty points more likely to.

What about sharing customs and traditions? The picture begins to change. There is still widespread support, but it is less intense. More than 90 per cent of Hungarians, Greeks and Poles, over 80 per cent of Americans, Brits, Dutch, Italians and French, over 70 per cent of Germans and Spanish and over 60 per cent of Swedes feel that sharing the nation's cultural heritage is important to being part of the national community. Those on the right, however, including national populists, are especially likely to think so: while 66 per cent of Le Pen's voters in France feel it is *very* important, only 39 per cent of French socialists think the same way; while 81 per cent of Nigel Farage's supporters hold this view, only 44 per cent of Labour supporters agree. So, while large numbers of people across the West feel that sharing customs and traditions is important, national populists are especially likely to do so. Such views are also more pronounced among older generations and those with less education, pointing to the underlying key divides: while 54 per cent of Americans with only a high-school education see cultural compatibility as key, just 33 per cent of graduates think the same; while 28 per cent of those aged between eighteen and thirty-four hold this view, the figure is 55 per cent among the over-fifties.

What about whether or not being born in the country is an important marker of belonging to the nation? Support for this ethnic attachment is much lower among the public at large: while 73 per cent of people across the US and Europe think that being able to speak the language is very important and 47 per cent felt the same way about sharing customs, only 31 per cent regarded birth in the country as very important. This does, however, mask variations. While 52 per cent of Hungarians value an ethnic attachment, only 32 per cent of Americans and 13 per cent of Germans agree.

National populists, again, are more likely to subscribe to this view. For example, 57 per cent of Farage's supporters and 41 per cent of Le Pen's felt that being born in the country was an important prerequisite to being part of the nation. Rather than stressing 'civic' ties, such as respecting institutions or the rule of law, some national-populist voters put stronger emphasis on 'ethnic' ties like ancestry, as well as whether or not other groups are seen to be compatible with their nation's culture. Nevertheless, it is also true that many of those who are drawn into national-populist movements do *not* view the world in this way and are not obsessed with ethnicity or ancestry. This is important, as it suggests that to dismiss national-populist supporters en masse as ignorant bigots is actually wide of the mark.[24]

This broader outlook helps us to make sense of why national populists are more likely to regard immigrants, refugees, minorities and culturally distinct Muslims as a threat to their national identity and way of life. It also throws light

Being able to speak the national language is important

97%

92%

88%

Sharing national customs and traditions is important

86%

84%

90%

Being born in the country is important

58%

55%

43%

Figure 4.4

Percentage of population who believe that language, customs and ancestry are important.

■ Europe
■ United States
■ Canada

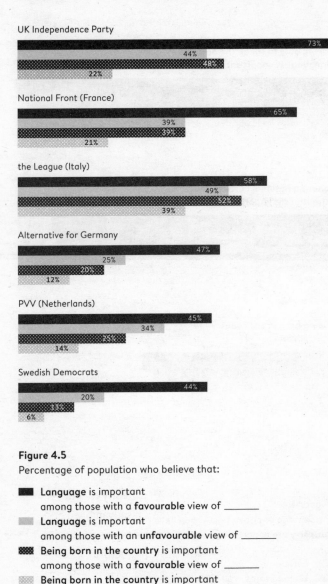

Figure 4.5
Percentage of population who believe that:

- **Language** is important
  among those with a **favourable** view of _____

- **Language** is important
  among those with an **unfavourable** view of _____

- **Being born in the country** is important
  among those with a **favourable** view of _____

- **Being born in the country** is important
  among those with an **unfavourable** view of _____

on why they distrust politicians and transnational institutions like the EU, which they see as failing to halt the threats to their cherished nation or, even worse, encouraging its destruction.

That national populism is not simply a refuge for die-hard racists has been shown by others. For instance, of the people who were drawn to Nigel Farage in Britain, only one in five thought that blacks were less intelligent than whites (a classic measure of racism), but nearly two-thirds saw Islam as a danger to the West.[25] After looking at what motivated national-populist support across six democracies in Europe, the scholar Jens Rydgren has similarly demonstrated how these voters' main concern was not to express an irrational hatred or fear of 'the other' but rather to voice their scepticism of immigration, their desire to reduce the levels of immigration and slow the pace of change. Questions that tapped blatant racism, such as whether or not people opposed having an immigrant as their boss or one of their relatives marrying an immigrant, were *less* revealing than those that asked whether people simply wanted fewer immigrants in the nation, but not necessarily because they were racist.[26]

Such findings underline the problems and risks that come with branding all national-populist supporters as 'racist', let alone 'fascist'. Consider one example of how this can backfire. Ahead of European Parliament elections in 2014, British politicians and journalists charged UKIP with racism after the party released billboards suggesting that low-skilled immigrants were undermining employment opportunities for domestic British workers. The attack went down well among graduates, middle-class liberals and ethnic minorities, few of whom supported UKIP. But it further alienated workers and social conservatives who shared legitimate worries about the effects of historically unprecedented rates of immigration. It also ran the risk of alienating the much larger 70 per cent of *all* people in Britain who shared the belief that low-skilled workers looking for low-paid work should not be allowed in Britain. Playing the racism card reinforced a sense that an established elite had little time for people who thought differently about these issues. When all the votes had been counted, UKIP became the first party other than the mainstream Conservatives and Labour to top the poll in a nationwide election since 1906, albeit with under 27 per cent of the vote.

Wanting a tighter immigration policy or fewer immigrants is not in itself racist. Rather than being driven by racial hatred, most national populists see the quest for lower immigration and slower ethnic change as an attempt to stem the dwindling size of their group, to advance its interests and (in their eyes) avoid the destruction of their culture and identity.

Threatened White Enclaves?

Another myth is that public worries over immigration are divorced from the real world, that national populism only appeals to people who have no experience with immigrants or minorities and who hunker down in threatened white enclaves. This is linked closely to the notion that in the long term the inevitable contact that will occur between different ethnic, racial and religious groups will curb prejudice – an idea that in the social sciences is called 'contact theory'. This was inspired by early work during the Second World War which found that the more voyages whites in the US Merchant Marine took with African Americans, the less prejudiced they became.[27]

But there are good reasons to challenge this line of thinking. First, it does not fit easily with evidence that the people who vote for national populists often live in close proximity to ethnically diverse neighbourhoods, or in communities that are actually undergoing rapid ethnic change. Some scholars like Robert Putnam have argued that in the latter, citizens will, at least in the short term, become less trusting of others, less willing to co-operate, build fewer bridges with other people and withdraw from the wider world (the idea that immigration can produce a decline in mutual regard and trust has also been voiced by thinkers like Paul Collier).[28]

Others argue that what really matters is the *quality* of contact between different groups and that most people only experience brief or 'fleeting' contact which can reinforce negative stereotypes and entrench hostility. But we can also explore real-world examples like the US. Despite a long and rich history of immigration and a national story that is built around the 'melting pot', nevertheless in 2016 more than 62 million Americans decided to elect a president who had promised to clamp down on various forms of immigration.

This had largely been predicted by the scholar Samuel Huntington, who more than a decade before Trump had argued that the profound changes taking place were likely to generate 'a move by native white Americans to revive the discarded and discredited racial and ethnic concepts of

American identity and to create an America that would exclude, expel, or suppress people of other racial, ethnic, and
cultural groups'. He pointed to historical experience to argue
that this was a highly probable reaction 'from a once dominant ethnic-racial group that feels threatened by the rise of
other groups'.[29] In fact, long before Trump scholars had already shown that whites living in communities that were experiencing rapid ethnic change were more likely to feel at
risk and become supportive of a more restrictive immigration policy. For example, a rapid increase in the relative proportion of Latinos or Hispanics in US counties was positively
associated with a hostile reaction to these groups among
white Americans.[30]

There is no doubt that some Americans living in counties that later switched to Trump had witnessed remarkable
ethnic shifts. Many areas where Trump's message resonated
had been historically white, but then during the early years
of the twenty-first century had witnessed a rapid influx of
non-white and mainly Latino newcomers. During the US primaries, Trump won the vast majority of counties where the
rate of ethnic change had at least doubled between 2000 and
2015, driven in large part by the arrival of Latino workers –
places like Carroll County in Iowa or Hendricks County in
Indiana, where Latinos went to work in meat-packing plants
or airports.[31]

One example of a rapidly diversifying area that swung
behind Trump is Arcadia and the surrounding communities in Trempealeau County, Wisconsin, once a railroad
town that had been built mainly by European immigrants.
Between 2000 and 2014 it went from being nearly all-white

to more than one-third Latino, as Mexican, Honduran and Salvadoran workers flocked to dairy farms, furniture makers and chicken plants. The local church added a Spanish Mass, a Latino bakery popped up on the high street, a school went from being all-white to 73 per cent Hispanic and road signs were translated into Spanish. While the county had voted for the Democrats in every presidential election since 1988, in 2016 Trump defeated Clinton by thirteen points.

Crucially, in these areas unemployment often remained lower than average, yet Trump's call to build a wall on the Mexican border and prioritize American workers struck a chord among those who felt uneasy about how rapidly their communities, and nation, were changing. Studies of the Trump vote have since found that living in areas where the proportion of Latinos had increased sharply over the past decade was a key predictor of this support, even after taking into account economic conditions like the number of manufacturing jobs. Trump's support was thus partly an 'adversarial reaction' among Americans who felt under threat from the rapid expansion of Latino populations in their own communities.[32]

Rapid ethnic change was also central to the Brexit victory, where Leavers feared what these sudden ethnic shifts meant for their national group, values and ways of life. One idea that gained currency was that Brexit had been driven by white people in all-white areas where there were no immigrants. This was popular among writers who argued that because immigrants were not present, 'they were held partly to blame for the all-too-real, but much deeper-seated, economic difficulties experienced by locals'.[33] But it was wrong. This argument might have seemed true had you looked only at the *static level* of immigration. For example, of the twenty areas with the lowest proportion of non-white residents, fifteen voted for Brexit, while of the twenty areas with the largest proportion, eighteen voted Remain. But if you look instead at the *rate of ethnic change* the picture changes.

Even after researchers took account of the overall amount of immigration as well as the age and educational profile of an area, support for Brexit was stronger in areas that during the preceding decade had experienced rapid inward migration, such as the coastal town of Boston in Lincolnshire. Between 2001 and 2011, the percentage of people in Boston who had been born outside Britain increased fivefold, to over 15 per cent. While in 2001 the foreign-born community consisted of around 250 Germans, by 2011 there were nearly 65,000 workers from EU countries like Poland, Lithuania and Romania. In only a very short period of time some local schools reported that 62 per cent of children were from immigrant backgrounds. Three-quarters of people in Boston voted for Brexit.

We can also look at evidence elsewhere in Europe. Over the past two decades, numerous studies have shown how the supporters of national populism often inhabit areas that are very close to more ethnically mixed communities (the so-called 'doughnut effect'), or that have experienced rapid ethnic change over a short period of time.

In France, the larger the proportion of immigrants or ethnic minorities in a region, the greater the likelihood that people voted for Le Pen. In the Netherlands, national populists have polled strongest in areas with high numbers of immigrants and where people felt anxious about the effects of immigration and crime, associating these ethnic changes with the deterioration of their neighbourhood and threats to their way of life (this support then flattened as areas became far more ethnically dense).

In other parts of Europe, like Belgium, support for national populism has been stronger in areas with larger numbers of Muslims, while the proportion of non-Muslim immigrants made no difference. In Germany, support was higher in regions that experienced a sudden increase in the number of minorities over a short period of time. In Switzerland support was driven by a feeling among people that immigration posed a threat to their community, which in turn was stronger in areas that had larger-than-average numbers of immigrants from the former Yugoslavia and Albania. And in Sweden support has been greater in areas that have not only economic problems but also higher numbers of immigrants, or which border diverse communities.

Importantly, these findings are backed up by larger studies. Though scholars continue to debate and disagree about exactly how these immigration flows interact with the prevailing economic conditions, almost all of them find that support for national populists is usually higher in areas that are experiencing ethnic change or which border more diverse communities.[34]

Irrational Nationalism?

Some readers will inevitably see such attitudes as a reflection of irrational nationalist fears which are promoting xenophobia and racism. But the way we think about these issues is shaped by our own politics. As the British thinker

David Goodhart has argued: 'Modern liberals tend to believe that preference for your own ethnic group or even your own nation is a form of racism. Conservatives regard it as common sense and resent being labelled as racist.'[35]

In debates about the philosophical legitimacy of nationalism, liberal and left-wing critics point out that nationalists cannot identify a single key feature that holds people together. Although nations commonly have one language, Switzerland has several. Similarly, having a state religion is not necessary: the Netherlands has been divided historically between Catholics and Protestants, while Geert Wilders is agnostic. Reflecting this lacuna, the Marxist historian Eric Hobsbawm argued: 'no serious historian of nations and nationalism can be a committed political nationalist . . . Nationalism requires too much belief in what is patently not so.'[36] Certainly, holistic nationalism has at times proved a highly dangerous force, as Nazism shows.

Yet rejecting outright the legitimacy of the nation renders any serious understanding of national populism impossible. In fact, at precisely the same time that national populists were starting to win significant support in Western Europe, new thinking began to emerge about the nation as a cultural group, though one which was not necessarily ethnic, characterized by a shared identity and civic values. A good example comes from David Miller, who has sought to show that nationalism is a form of 'meta-ideology', relevant to a wide range of liberal and left-wing policies, and involving far more than love of specific features of a country's landscape and particular way of life which are commonly associated with 'patriotism', or nativists' concern with boundary creation.[37]

His argument can be broken down into three parts. First, that people can legitimately claim a national identity based on a shared sense of history and values, including a sense of national mission, though this does not mean that they cannot have other identities, such as their social class or gender. In other words, the desire to belong to a nation should not be seen as some sort of pathological perversion and/or automatic proof that one is intellectually foolish.

Second, while nationalists defend the interests of the nation, Miller holds that these are 'ethical communities', namely their members have a greater sense of duty and obligation towards those within their national community than to others. They also have a greater right to rewards: consider people who fought for their nation in wars, or who paid taxes all of their lives, compared to someone who has just arrived in the country as an economic immigrant. Miller sees this ethical side as important for a series of socially desirable policies like redistributing income, which needs not only an efficient state but also one that inspires widespread trust. The significant redistribution of resources around society requires us to identify closely with our fellow citizens. Without this trust and a wider sense of common belonging, such a system of redistributing the nation's resources would break down.

Third, the people who form a national community have a right to self-determination. In other words, people can choose what form of government and state they want to live under.

Such views predictably provoke a lively response. For example, a strong sense of nationalism does not always guarantee support for redistributionist policies: witness the US, where even among whites there has been opposition to extensive redistribution and welfare programmes. The prevailing doctrine of self-determination can also be a recipe for fragmentation, which in practice could make even rich, small states less sovereign. Indeed, a key argument for the EU is that it pools sovereignty to gain greater protection from bodies such as multinational companies, which seek to drive down production costs and pay tax where rates are lowest. However, theorists like Miller are not arguing whether, say, Britain would be better off in or outside the EU. The point is that people have a right to choose to preserve what they see as their national independence and identity.

A prominent advocate of similar views is David Goodhart, who has argued within the context of Britain that the sharp rise in immigration threatens the nation's welfare state, as many people do not feel that new arrivals should immediately qualify for the same social rights as long-standing tax-paying citizens. Large-scale immigration can also threaten the unwritten contract between different generations, whereby people are willing to pay higher taxes for the benefit of those who follow. This is linked to the way in which, as we have seen, many people across the West still feel a strong sense of attachment to their settled communities, common norms and the nation state. The liberal left is far more individualistic in its thinking and has generally failed to comprehend these attachments.

Relatively similar points have been made by the social psychologist Jonathan Haidt, who describes himself as a US 'centrist'. Haidt argues that the anthem of 'globalists' is John

Lennon's: 'Imagine there's no countries. It isn't hard to do. Nothing to kill or die for . . .'. Haidt counters that love of one's nation does not necessarily imply any sense of dangerous superiority, rather as the love of one's partner does not demean others. Having a shared sense of identity, norms and history promotes trust – and societies with high trust 'produce many beneficial outcomes for their citizens: lower crime rates, lower transaction costs for business, higher levels of prosperity, and a propensity towards generosity, among others'. What is often seen as racism can be deeply bound up with people's moral concerns, especially in trying to protect their group or society from what they see as a major 'normative' threat to their identity and values (though Haidt makes it clear that he does not use the term 'moral' to endorse racism).[38]

For Haidt, there is a crucial moral difference between liberals, who stress autonomy, and conservatives, who stress community and in some cases divinity, between those who are more concerned with fairness and avoiding harm and those whose focus is on care, reciprocity and defending a community that they believe is being destroyed. While Haidt underplays the moral and communal concerns of some liberals who are far from rational egotists, he rightly points to the way in which national populists see their own arguments as moral.

Critics of national populists whose automatic response is to damn them as irrational, as largely uneducated nationalists and racists, would do well to ponder these approaches.

Peering into the Future

Public worries over immigration and ethnic change, and the concomitant intellectual debates, look set to intensify rather than fade. This is because hyper ethnic change will not only continue but accelerate.

One reason for this is that while the countries that tend to send immigrants are growing quickly, as are settled ethnic minority and immigrant communities, much of Europe and North America as a whole is experiencing birth rates that are below what is called the 'replacement level', namely the level at which a population exactly replaces itself from one generation to the next. Consider a few trends. Deaths have exceeded births in Germany since 1972, in Italy since 1993 and in much of Eastern Europe since the mid-1990s. This means that, without large-scale immigration, many nations in the West, particularly in Europe, are now staring at population decline.

According to EU data, more than a dozen states are projected to experience natural population decrease in the coming decades, including Greece, Italy, Hungary and Portugal; ironically, some of the countries that are the most fiercely opposed to immigration and refugees are simultaneously forecast to have the fastest-shrinking populations in the world. By 2050 the populations of Central and East European states like Bulgaria, Hungary, Latvia, Lithuania, Poland and Romania are estimated to shrink by at least 15 per cent, due to low birth rates, high mortality and the fact that young people are moving to higher-wage economies.

Contrast this, for example, with the picture in Africa, from where many of the refugees entering Europe originate. Over the coming decades the population of Nigeria, which has already increased more than threefold since 1960 to nearly 190 million people, is forecast to expand to more than 300 million by 2050. This will leave that country, which has slightly more Muslims than Christians, as the third-most populous in the world and well on its way to eclipsing the population of the European Union. While the world's population is expected to hit nearly 10 billion people by 2050, more than half of this expected growth will occur in Africa, where today 60 per cent of people are under twenty-five years of age.[39] In fact, some estimate that whereas the entire population of Africa will reach about 4.5 billion people by 2100, by this time the population of the EU will have fallen to only 465 million.[40]

Even without famine, government collapse or war it is hard to believe that such demographic shifts will not affect the number of people trying, legally and illegally, to enter the wealthier West. Perhaps policymakers will find a way of encouraging these populations to remain, but if they cannot – which seems likely – then the questions that are being asked by national populists about immigration and its associated problems will become even more important.

Western nations, therefore, look set to witness considerable ongoing ethnic change and demographic pressures. Increasingly, native-born citizens will become aware of the shrinking size of their own group relative to immigrants and minority communities. In the US, for example, the share of the immigrant population more than doubled between

1960 and 2016 to reach nearly 14 per cent, while at the same time the nation's fertility rate halved. This is partly what lies behind the fact that whereas whites made up 87 per cent of the population in 1950, by 2050 this figure is forecast to fall to 47 per cent. In Britain, by the 2050s the percentage of the population comprised of ethnic minorities and non-native whites is forecast to increase to 44 per cent, by which time these groups will also account for half of all children up to the age of four.[41] In Western Europe, by 2050 the foreign-born population is predicted to reach between 15 and 32 per cent in several states, while countries like Sweden and the Netherlands will probably have majority foreign-origin populations by the end of the century. The Pew Research Center forecasts that by 2050, and even if there is no further inward migration, the proportion of the population that is Muslim will more than double in Britain, Denmark, Finland, France, Italy, Norway, Portugal, Spain and Sweden. With continued inward migration, this could reach 14 per cent across Europe – a significant increase, though nothing like the exaggerated 'takeover' prophecies of Eurabia doomsayers – yet it is nonetheless likely to generate political effects.[42]

Some might argue that the impact of these trends will be minimal as religion fades from view and minorities are integrated into the liberal mainstream. Certainly, it is important not to overlook the rising numbers of Muslims who are changing aspects of their values. Pew found that in the US in 2017, 52 per cent of Muslims accepted homosexuality, up from 27 per cent in 2007 (and more than evangelical Christians at 34 per cent).[43] But it is also true that younger immigrants from outside Europe tend to be more religious than the host community and are often just as religious as their elders.[44] In countries like Britain and the Netherlands, this factor is compounded by a tendency to live in relatively closed communities which reinforce lifestyles. While religious decline is mainly occurring in Catholic European states, differences in fertility rates, migration flows and age structures mean that Western Europe may be *more* religious at the end of the twenty-first century than it was at its beginning. Europe may reach a 'de-secularization' phase, when declining rates of religious affiliation are offset by the growth of religious (and younger) immigrant-origin populations.[45]

Muslims and Islam are already targeted by national populists, who present them as a cultural and demographic threat to the West, while many in the mainstream play on the threat from a small number of violent Islamists, including home-grown terrorists. There is certainly a ready audience for these campaigns. In 2018, the Pew Research Center found widespread public support for the idea that 'Islam is fundamentally incompatible with our country's culture and values', ranging from 53 per cent in Italy to over 40 per cent in Denmark, Germany, Netherlands and Switzerland. Exclusionary campaigns against Islam may encourage Muslims to turn to religion for shelter, or make them more willing to engage in political action to defend Islam, increasing the likelihood of a cycle of mobilization.[46]

Clearly, these ongoing cultural changes and the fears they engender are powerful drivers of the national-populist revolt. However, this does not mean that we should completely ignore economic perspectives, as we will see in the next chapter.

CHAPTER 5

Deprivation

The economic system that characterizes the West is known as capitalism, models of which have differed over time since the beginnings of its rapid rise over 400 years ago. The most significant change in terms of its impact has arguably taken place in the last fifty years, and is a further factor in the rise of national populism.

After the devastation of the Great Depression in the inter-war years, governments across the West began to take more responsibility for ensuring the economic well-being of their citizens. This involved a commitment to achieve high employment and expand welfare, though provisions varied considerably, from thin ones in the US to extensive 'cradle-to-grave' systems in Europe, where the state played a major role.

This culminated following the Second World War in the so-called 'Golden Age' – a new era of growth, rising wages and increasing equality of income and wealth. Yet it was short-lived and by the 1970s had come to an end as 'stagflation' (inflation accompanied by lower growth) reared its head. Against this backdrop, free-market fundamentalism returned with a vengeance. During the 1980s this neoliberalism, as it became known, went global.

In the twenty-first century, however, neoliberalism's

record has come under increasing attack. Growth rates in the West have been disappointing, while the global financial meltdown that ensued in 2008 and sparked the Great Recession led to a crippling wave of fiscal austerity policies in many countries, including dramatic cuts in government expenditure and services and misery for millions of citizens. Moreover, neoliberalism has significantly altered the distribution of income and wealth. The economist Thomas Piketty has shown that across the West inequalities have returned to levels that were last seen over 100 years ago[1] – in contrast with the elite 1 per cent, who have become far richer, lead separate lives and have no serious awareness of the concerns that unite 'left-behind' voters.

To make sense of the way in which these historic economic developments have helped to fire national populism, we need to step back and consider the rise of capitalism over a long period. This allows us to make several key arguments. The first is that Western capitalism is an ethic that celebrates the pursuit of self-interest as a means of maximizing economic growth for the benefit of all (Asian capitalism has a more collectivist ethos). As the fictitious, but all too real, financier Gordon Gekko infamously opined in the film *Wall Street* (1987), 'Greed, for lack of a better term, is good.' Lack of effective controls over greed in the banking sector helped trigger the Great Recession, yet not a single Wall Street chief executive was prosecuted.[2] This is no doubt what induced Gordon Gekko in the 2010 sequel to *Wall Street* to gloat that greed was not only good, but 'now it's legal'.

Another point is that this state of affairs marks a radical departure from the past. Historically, capitalism was legitimized by much more than its ability to deliver widespread material benefits. Initially it was underpinned by religious values that celebrated work and a shared community. Capitalism's ethos was also reinforced by nationalism, which countered socialist calls for greater equality. In addition, especially in post-war Europe, economies were characterized by redistributive taxation, full employment and generous welfare nets. Today, the impact of religion on social values is much weaker, while the revival of nationalism challenges the rise of globalized capitalism.

These points lead to our overarching argument that today's national-populist revolt is partly linked to the rise of neoliberalism, in particular through a growing sense of relative *deprivation* that unites large numbers of citizens. This does not refer merely to objective deprivation, such as the experience of living on a low income, losing a job or enduring slow economic growth. Rather, it encompasses strong fears among people that both they and their group are losing out relative to others in society, that a world of rising prosperity and upward social mobility has come to an end for them, and with it not just hope but also respect.

Many scholars argue that cultural concerns, especially immigration, are paramount when explaining the appeal of movements like Trump or Brexit, noting the weak correlation between voting and people on low wages. However, what matters more in the economic context is people's state of mind – their *subjective* perceptions about how their own position and that of their wider group is changing *compared to others in society*. This sense of relative deprivation affects far more than just the poorest at the bottom of society: it extends to full-time workers, parts of the middle class and also young voters.

The Legitimation of Early Capitalism

Although private property has existed in most societies since time immemorial, capitalism only developed rapidly after the seventeenth century, following a confluence of several factors in Europe, including new thinking that accompanied the Reformation and the Enlightenment.[3] But to make sense of the way in which the evolution of capitalism made room for national populism, we should focus on the way in which it was initially legitimized in the eyes of the people.

The term 'capitalism' did not enter common usage until the late nineteenth century, but its seminal manifesto was Adam Smith's *An Inquiry into the Nature and Causes of the Wealth of Nations* (1776), which argued that people are best occupied pursuing their private interests. Far from seeing this as a threat to the social order, Smith proclaimed the virtue of hard work for individuals and held that an 'invisible hand' would lead to the efficient allocation of resources within the free market. As a result, he advocated what became known as the 'laissez-faire' view of government, arguing that its role should be kept to a minimum so as not to interfere with individual rights and the dynamism that the new economic order would create.

Smith was writing at a time when the Industrial Revolution was gathering pace and dramatically changing societies in the West. It created what Karl Marx termed a new 'bourgeoisie', a ruling economic elite who controlled both 'the means of production', especially factories and raw materials, and 'the means of coercion', such as the army, police and legal systems. The elite stood over the 'proletariat' or workers who, having previously been tied to the local community and land through the medieval bonds of feudalism, now toiled for low wages in the factories and cities.

Marx argued that this new, unequal settlement was unsustainable because class divisions alienated people from their common humanity, while the relentless quest for profit would lead the capitalist elite to replace their workers with machines. This in turn would induce the impoverished masses to rise in revolution, ushering in the age of communism – at least that was the theory. Yet in the West the violent worker-led revolution that was predicted in his *Communist Manifesto* (1848) failed to appear. Despite periodic slumps like the Long Depression of the 1870s, the capitalist system had been initially legitimized by unprecedented growth, which delivered benefits for increasing numbers of people. Although these gains were distributed very unequally, in richer countries 'an aristocracy of labour' emerged – better-off workers who focused less on fomenting revolution than on achieving better wages and working conditions through trade unions, like the ones who founded the British Trades Union Congress in 1868.

Historically, capitalism was further legitimized in two other important ways – through religion and nationalism, which often overlapped. The first clearly capitalist countries to emerge after the sixteenth century were England and the Netherlands, both seafaring countries, where Protestantism proclaimed not only the virtues of hard work and saving but also each nation's special mission to spread commerce and prosper. For many Americans in the nineteenth century this took the form of 'manifest destiny', the belief that the country was characterized by a unique people and institutions who had a God-given destiny to move west (which included the ethnic cleansing of Native Americans). By the turn of the twentieth century the Christian celebration of charity – reinforced by populist and progressive attacks on the greed of an emerging plutocratic business and financial elite – contributed to the setting up of well-endowed and much-publicized bodies, such as the Rockefeller Foundation, to promote good causes like education and public health (in 1913 John D. Rockefeller was worth around $400 billion in today's money, compared to 2018's richest man, the Amazon CEO Jeff Bezos, who is worth a mere $150 billion).

The nineteenth century was also a time when nationalism was spreading widely. In Europe this was encouraged by political and economic elites who saw it as a way of countering the rise of socialism, though another concern was the need to raise disciplined mass armies which were used to instil nationalist values. In major powers and emerging mass democracies like Britain and Germany this took the form of 'social imperialism', which involved the state providing basic welfare such as health care and old-age pensions, while also promoting pride in Empire and burgeoning national wealth. In the US, a Protestant producerist ethos celebrated the nation as the home of hard-working individuals who wanted to get on in life. This culture was also adopted by successive waves of immigrants, who from the

1840s onwards came from Catholic and other religious backgrounds, mainly as economic migrants seeking new lives in the 'land of opportunity'.

The legitimacy of capitalism, however, then came under major strain after the Wall Street Crash in 1929, which plunged large parts of the West into the most serious depression of the twentieth century. Between 1929 and 1932, US output fell by 30 per cent, 13 million workers lost their jobs, unemployment rocketed to 25 per cent, and there was a 40 per cent reduction in annual family income. Although the term 'American dream' was popularized at this time to remind people that they lived in a land of great opportunities, many dwelt in poverty and despaired for the future.

In Europe, meanwhile, by the time Adolf Hitler came to power in 1933 Germany's rate of unemployment had surged to 30 per cent. Although most unemployed voters supported the communists, Hitler polled strongly among the 'working poor' – people who were in work, often self-employed, but who struggled from one month to the next and feared communists.[4] In Fascist Italy depression hit hard too, though the government successfully responded by increasing the role of the state. The Nazis did the same, copying Fascist welfare programmes that included subsidized holidays. By 1939 the Nazis were building the largest hotel in the world for workers on the island of Rügen (in the new millennium its shell was converted into luxury flats and a hotel).

Welfare Capitalism and the Golden Age

The Great Depression helped to create a body of opinion that was favourable to increasing government intervention in the economy. In democracies like Britain it was the Conservatives who extended welfare provision, while in Sweden social democrats during the 1930s pioneered an extensive welfare state, a model that attracted many admirers in the US.[5] America's response to the Great Depression is especially revealing about the growing belief that unbridled capitalism needed to be curbed, not least to weaken the potential appeal of fascism and a revived populism in the US in the shape of Huey Long.

In 1932, America elected as President the Democrat Franklin Delano Roosevelt, who promised a 'New Deal'. Although the US had relatively low levels of state intervention in the economy, other than in fields like 'anti-trust' controls to curb the monopolies and oligopolies so hated by the populists, the New Deal pointed to an important change of direction. It included controls over banking, which had been a central cause of the crash, massive infrastructure programmes to provide immediate work and long-term growth, and new benefits for the retired, unemployed and dependent mothers. Further reforms recognized the right of most workers to join trade unions, which gave them stronger bargaining power to improve wages and conditions.

There were still problems. People in work relied on companies for benefits like health insurance and many did not offer such rewards, while those in dire need often had to rely on charities and churches. Many blacks were effectively excluded, as social security did not cover farm workers and domestics. Nevertheless, the New Deal's achievements are significant, especially as they were achieved against fierce opposition from free marketeers who were far from silenced by the Great Depression.

By the late 1930s, the belief that government had a major role to play in managing the economy and ensuring people's well-being was boosted by the impact of the liberal British economist John Maynard Keynes.[6] In 1936 his book *The General Theory of Employment, Interest and Money* had an immediate global influence. Whereas the New Deal had focused on microeconomics, Keynes was more concerned with the macro-management of the whole economy. He argued that it was possible to smooth capitalism's recurring cycle of booms and slumps through government policy. As an economy moved into recession, spending should increase, not be cut to balance the budget as the prevailing wisdom dictated. Key to this was the 'multiplier effect', the idea that government expenditure not only helps those whom it directly affects but has a broader ripple effect across society, creating a virtuous circle (workers employed on new infrastructure projects spend their wages in local businesses, who in turn hire more workers, who buy more, and so on).

Keynes led the British delegation at the 1944 Bretton Woods conference, which established the key economic institutions and policies that would guide the West through the post-war era. These included fixed exchange rates managed by the IMF in order to prevent the competitive devaluations that had broken out in the 1930s in an attempt to make a country's goods cheaper in the export market. A General Agreement on Trade and Tariffs sought to promote free trade to counter the growth of protectionism – for example, the 1930 US Smoot-Hawley Tariff Act had imposed duties on around 20,000 products, leading to 'beggar my neighbour' retaliation by countries like Canada and France and a damaging major decline in trade. Moreover, the need to rebuild a war-ravaged Europe, alongside fears of expansionary communism, resulted in the 1948 Marshall Plan whereby the US sent around $100 billion in today's dollars to help restore Europe's confidence in the future.

American interests, including the belief that free markets would benefit its major corporations, drove much of this. However, the US accepted that differences would exist in the West's economic and welfare regimes. Britain was included in the Marshall Plan despite the way in which its post-1945 social-democratic Labour government was enacting radical reforms that included high rates of marginal income taxes (around 90 per cent), the nationalization of key industries like coal and steel and utilities like electricity and gas, and the introduction of an initially totally free National Health Service at the point of use. This was done against bitter opposition from Winston Churchill and the Conservatives, though after returning to office in the 1950s they accepted most of the reforms and increased health spending. The Labour government also had to cope with a legacy of wartime debts, plus borrowing to cover its worldwide colonial and anti-communist roles (Britain was not to repay its final instalment to the US until 2006).

As the West moved into the post-war era the American economy continued the boom that had begun in the late 1930s. Following difficult starts, so too did much of Western Europe, though no country had a GDP even half the size of that of the US. While there was a left-wing and intellectual strand of anti-Americanism in countries like France, many people in the West came to buy into the hedonistic and optimistic American dream symbolized by increased ownership of consumer goods like cars, refrigerators and televisions.

This was a time of rapid growth and is now seen as the Golden Age of capitalism, a period between the late 1940s and the early 1970s when prosperity was widely enjoyed. It was an era that witnessed the West German 'economic miracle', as the country rose from the ashes of defeat to enjoy the largest GDP in Europe, and France's *les trente glorieuses*', thirty years of strong performance that transformed the country into Western Europe's second-largest economy, while joblessness virtually disappeared (a factor which attracted immigrants, as it did in West Germany).

Occasionally, public support for political outsiders rose briefly on the back of miscellaneous grievances. As we have noted, in 1950s France the French Poujadist movement enjoyed some short-lived success, while in the 1960s the neo-Nazi National Democratic Party of Germany won a few seats in several state parliaments. But in general, politics seemed to have been 'pacified' by growth, prosperity and lingering memories of war. It was also a time when the bonds between the people and the mainstream parties were strong, as we will see in Chapter 6.

The Golden Age, however, did not stem simply from

Keynesian policies and new international economic institutions. Even before the Second World War, military expenditure had created a boom while new technologies developed for war inspired product innovation, such as civil jet aeroplanes. The Cold War continued these trends, with free-market America spending vast sums of government money on defence and prestige projects like the space programme (in the same way, major subsidies to private railroads had encouraged America's rapid drive westwards in the nineteenth century). These furthered the development of major new technology sectors and products like the internet, personal computers and smart phones, including an infant Apple that was the beneficiary of the federal government's Small Business Investment Company.[7] It was different in Britain, where the state pumped money into declining 'lame-duck' nationalized industries that suffered from a lack of investment, poor managers and disputes with assertive labour unions.

High US defence expenditure, however, soon became a source of major economic problems. In the 1960s the escalation of the Vietnam War coincided with President Lyndon B. Johnson's 'Great Society' and 'War on Poverty' programmes which, coming after the Civil Rights movements, had a strong focus on the economic plight of African Americans. Together with the vast cost of war, these added to rising US government debt and inflation, which contributed to a loss of faith in the Bretton Woods fixed exchange rate mechanism. While at the end of the Second World War the US had held over half of the world's gold reserves, by the turn of the 1970s its holdings were insufficient to meet potential demand for 'dollar convertibility' into gold, as required by Bretton Woods, and in 1971 convertibility was suspended by the US.

The world quickly moved on to a floating exchange rate system whereby the value of currencies was determined by supply and demand. The result was that some countries saw their currency depreciate, making imports dearer without exports necessarily improving significantly. Growing inflationary pressures were heightened when oil-producing states in the Middle East responded to the 1973 Arab-Israeli war by hiking the price of crude oil fourfold. Although Western GDPs did continue to grow, rates slackened and in some countries the new spectre of stagflation loomed.

Among richer countries, Britain was particularly affected: inflation peaked in 1975 at a staggering 26 per cent. Compared to the relatively stable era of the 1950s, by 1982 unemployment had soared more than sixfold to 12 per cent (the true figure being higher, as politically motivated ways of measuring unemployment changed). Faced with a falling pound, Britain requested a record loan of $3.9 billion from the IMF (about $18 billion in 2018 money), which in turn required drastic cuts in spending and government control of the money supply. These changes sparked a wave of strikes by public-sector workers during the freezing 'Winter of Discontent' in 1978–9, which gave rise to shock news stories such as the dead lying unburied by local authority workers.

The scene was set for the rise of a very different economic wisdom on both sides of the Atlantic, which would change the face of the West and help pave the way for national populists.

The 'New Right' and Neoliberalism

The term 'New Right' became commonplace after Margaret Thatcher was elected Prime Minister in 1979 and Ronald Reagan President in 1980.[8] Both politicians shared a strong opposition to communism while domestically they trumpeted the need for major tax cuts, rolling back the 'big' state and fighting inflation. Another string to Thatcher's bow was her hostility to the idea of a highly integrated federal Europe, warning in her 'Bruges speech' that Britain had not just spent much of the 1980s reversing state socialism only to see 'a European super-state exercising a new dominance from Brussels'. In some ways, the term New Right is a misnomer as many of its arguments were not new. But it is useful shorthand to highlight the new-found confidence of free marketeers and their proposed solutions, a point encapsulated in Thatcher's 'TINA' riposte to her left-wing critics – There Is No Alternative.

The New Right also attracted vast new funds from business and the rich, especially in the US, which financed influential think tanks like the Heritage Foundation (1973), the Cato Institute (1977) and the Centre for Policy Studies in Britain (1974).[9] It also bankrolled campaigns aimed at the public, including the new technique of targeted mailing, opinion-forming elites and policymakers, while also financially supporting sympathetic politicians.

We do not need to examine New Right thinking in detail but we can identify some of its key aspects, as they help explain why New Right ideas were so powerful after the 1970s and why they contributed to the rise of national populism. While some of these ideas, such as the importance of entre-preneurial dynamism, are shared by many national populists, others, like unrestricted free trade, are anathema.

Broadly speaking, there were two main wings of the New Right – a radical one and a traditionalist one. Among the former, extreme 'libertarians' championed 'negative' freedom as the ultimate goal, the most radical of them believing that government should provide little more than defence and the maintenance of the rule of law so as not to interfere with in-dividual liberty. Within the traditionalist wing were Christian fundamentalists who opposed liberal policies like the legali-zation of abortion and women's rights, as well as neoconserv-atives who were more concerned with the alleged harmful cultural consequences of 'big' government, especially welfare systems, which they believed created dysfunctional people and groups that became dependent on benefits, a charge often targeted at ethnic minorities in the US after the 1960s.[10]

The main economic guru of the New Right was the Aus-trian Friedrich von Hayek, who published his voice-in-the-wilderness attack on the rise of the big state, *The Road to Serfdom*, in 1944. Three years later he set up the Mont Pel-erin Society, which increasingly attracted disciples from aca-demia, business and journalism. Hayek did not accept Adam Smith's belief in an 'invisible hand' leading to 'perfect' mar-kets, as he acknowledged that there could be 'market fail-ures', such as domination by monopolies. But he responded by setting out an 'epistemological' defence of free markets in which he argued that state intervention meant not only a loss of liberty but bureaucratic inefficiency, as planners lacked the entrepreneurial ability to act effectively on the myriad pieces of information which markets pass on about demand and supply.

Against an economic slowdown, by the 1980s New Right ideas had become a new orthodoxy, especially in the US and Britain. Though these economic theories were often completely divorced from an understanding of a nation's culture, society and values, they were also becoming important in developing countries, being pushed by a 'Washington Consensus' led by the US Treasury Department and the US-dominated IMF and World Bank.

This was a very different model from those that had helped the rise of major new economic players in the post-1945 era, and which had correctly taken into account local practices and values. The emergence of Japan as a trading superpower involved extensive liaison between government, banks, business and labour unions, backed by tariff and non-tariff barriers to protect industries (such as standards that were unique to Japan). By the 1970s, dynamic new capitalist powers were coming to the fore in the shape of so-called 'Asian tigers' like South Korea, where the state played a major role in guiding the economy and caring for the people.

In sharp contrast, the main tenets of neoliberalism or 'neoliberal globalization' have been: cutting taxes and shrinking government; privatizing state assets and deregulating business and finance; identifying low inflation rather than full employment as the key goal; and globalizing the economy further by opening up domestic markets to international capital and trade, as well as to much larger numbers of immigrant workers.[11] Neoliberalism was held to be beneficial both to developing countries *and* wealthy ones.

The powerful appeal exerted by some of these neoliberal panaceas is illustrated by the way in which even many social democrats on the centre-left were influenced by them. During the 1990s, Bill Clinton and Tony Blair claimed they were charting a new third way between capitalism and traditional social democracy. The latter had combined socialism with pluralism, including an acceptance of a mixture of state and private markets (exemplified by Britain's reforming 1945–51 Labour governments). By the late 1990s Blair's 'New Labour' governments had ditched their old signature policies – the nationalization of key industries such as household utilities and rail transport, for example, and high rates of taxation on richer people – though classic redistributive policies aimed at the poor remained important, including the introduction of a minimum wage which slowed the rising inequalities of the Thatcher era.

Meanwhile, when Bill Clinton signed the North American Free Trade Area (NAFTA) Bill in 1993, linking the US, Canada and Mexico, he argued that it meant 'American jobs, and good-paying American jobs'. Most economists have held that NAFTA has generally been beneficial, promoting worldwide growth. But some rightly see it as encouraging an economic model that has increased the appeal of the national-populist promise.

Let's take one example: Mexico has gained American car plants, while US companies benefited from lower costs and consumers from cheaper cars. Yet moving production meant that high-paid and steady US jobs in manufacturing were lost. Moreover, Mexico began to import corn from US agribusinesses, which drove people off the land. Together with the removal by Mexico of state price controls on some food as part of trade liberalization, this encouraged further immigration into the US, both legal and illegal. Although most economists hold that automation and globalized trade are the most important factors in job losses in rich countries, immigration seems to have made it harder for less skilled workers in the US to get pay rises.[12]

Public Backlash

These problems were not lost on ordinary Americans. Long before the financial crisis and Great Recession large numbers of people were already instinctively sceptical about free trade and receptive to the argument that America needed to put American workers first.

Gallup has regularly asked Americans whether they see foreign trade as an opportunity for growth through exports or as a threat to their economy because of imports. Even in 1994, the year NAFTA was launched, already 40 per cent of Americans saw it as a threat, while since then considerable public anxiety has remained. Between 2000 and 2018, on average 38–40 per cent of Republicans, Independents and Democrats saw foreign trade as a threat to the US economy, illustrating how there has long been a receptive audience for the likes of Trump and Bernie Sanders, both of whom voiced criticism of free trade.

But worries about free trade have been especially intense

among the key groups for national populists, including non-graduates and older social conservatives. Over the past two decades, Gallup found on average a nearly twenty-point gap between the percentage of college graduates who saw foreign trade as an opportunity (66 per cent) and the percentage of non-graduates (48 per cent) who felt the same way (see Figure 5.1).[13] This picture has also been confirmed by others.

As Trump celebrated the end of his first year in the White House, the Pew Research Center found that whereas one in three of all Americans felt that NAFTA had been 'bad for the United States', this statistic concealed major variations. Older, less well-educated and self-described conservatives were far more negative about how free trade had affected the nation: while nearly 70 per cent of young Millennials felt it had been good for the US, only 48 per cent of those aged over sixty-five agreed; while 70 per cent of postgraduates thought it had been good, only around half of Americans with some high-school education or less agreed; and whereas three-quarters of liberals thought free trade had strengthened America, fewer than one in three conservatives felt the same way.[14]

Trump pitched direct to these concerns by targeting what he argued were unfair practices that harmed American workers. As he told the Davos World Economic Forum in 2018, he supported trade as long as it is 'fair and reciprocal' – a reference not only to the balance of trade, but also to how producers in developing countries often violate Western norms.[15]

This angst has also clearly been on display in Europe, where national populists like Marine Le Pen appeal to citizens who feel worried about what she calls 'savage globalization'.

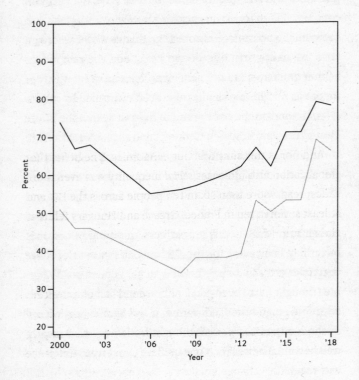

Figure 5.1
Percentage of adults saying foreign trade is an opportunity
for economic growth, amongst:
— College graduates
— College nongraduates

Question: 'What do you think foreign trade means for America? Do you
see foreign trade more as an opportunity for economic growth through
increased US exports or a threat to the economy from foreign imports?'

Even in 2017, as the financial crisis began to drift into the rear-view mirror, more than one in three people across the continent felt that globalization threatened national jobs and companies, though in countries like France and Greece the ratio was more than one in two. Once again, this concern has been visibly sharper among specific groups. People from the lower-middle class and working class were twenty points more likely than the upper-middle class to feel under threat from globalization.

And nor is this simply about economics. The belief that globalization also increases *social* inequality was even more widespread. More than six in ten people across the EU and at least seven in ten in France, Greece and Hungary felt that globalization fuels social inequalities, underlining how it is incredibly misleading to associate anxieties over globalization only with economic effects.[16]

Turning to the deregulation side of neoliberalism, an excellent case study of its problems is the banking meltdown that led to the Great Recession, which had a political impact well beyond its direct economic effects. An important cause was regulatory change, including the repeal in 1999 by Bill Clinton of the New Deal legislation which separated the commercial and investment arms of banks, and in Britain a failure by three successive Labour governments to regulate carefully enough the financial services industry. These developments underline how social democrats accepted aspects of neoliberal policies without fully thinking through the potential consequences, not least for ordinary workers.

Greater freedom for the banks was reinforced by the rise among professional economists of the 'efficient market hypothesis', which made policymakers think that banks could correctly assess the risks in different markets. Many hailed the 'Great Moderation', arguing that independence for central and other banks meant that economies were becoming far less volatile than in the troubled 1970s.[17] But this was wrong. Instead, low interest rates helped increase demand for loans, including from people with poor credit ratings in the booming US property market. These assets were then bundled up and traded extensively as self-interested credit-ratings agencies seeking new business classified them as safe – as was brought home in the film *The Big Short* (2015), based on the book by Michael Lewis, when a stripper explains how she was allowed to take out multiple loans on five different properties. This came unstuck in a major way when the housing price bubble burst.

In countries like the US and Britain, governments bailed out banks as they were 'too big to fail', threatening to bring down the entire system (a moral hazard which may have encouraged risky lending more generally). While some of the most senior bankers were guilty at the very least of corporate and personal greed, none in the US were prosecuted, though in Britain Sir Fred ('the Shred') Goodwin, the CEO of the Royal Bank of Scotland which suffered vast losses, was pilloried in the media and stripped of his knighthood. US financiers paid around $150 billion in fines, but only some smaller fry were ever convicted.

The result, unsurprisingly, was a strong public backlash. In the US, the Tea Party rose to prominence in 2009 and peaked the next year, when it commanded support from one in three Americans. Although its immediate cause of concern was a proposal by President Obama to bail out bankrupt homeowners, behind this was an attack on big government and Washington elites, reinforced by growing hostility to Obama personally and other issues such as immigration. President George W. Bush's 2008 Emergency Economic Stabilization Act authorized the US Treasury to spend $700 billion to buy high-risk assets and create new funds which were supplied directly to the financial system as part of a policy of 'quantitative easing' to stimulate the economy. While this was supported by a majority of Democrats in Congress, together with a smaller proportion of Republicans, almost eight in ten of those who flocked to the Tea Party opposed the bailouts, compared to only one in ten Democrat voters. For many Tea Partiers, the objection was about morality as well as the over-reach of big government – a belief that the good guys in Joe Public were being punished while the bad guys suffered no real consequences.[18]

Lavish bailouts also sparked a strong revolt against Wall Street from the left-wing Occupy movement. Beginning in Zuccotti Park in New York City's financial district, it soon broadened into global street protests and sit-ins concerned about issues like corporate greed, social inequality and the dominant power of banking and business elites. Although well-publicized clashes with police led to a fall-off in support, a 2011 poll found that nearly 60 per cent of Americans agreed with the concerns of the protesters.[19]

Amid the meltdown, there was also a wider collapse of trust. Whereas in the late 1970s around 60 per cent of Americans had trusted banks either a great deal or quite a lot, over the next thirty years the number consistently declined and

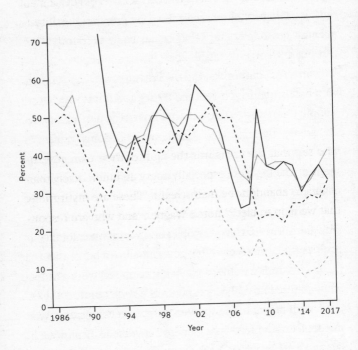

Figure 5.2

Public confidence in:

—— The Presidency

—— The Supreme Court

----- Banks

----- Congress

The average is based on fourteen institutions Gallup has asked about annually since 1993 (newspapers, public schools, banks, organized labour, Supreme Court, criminal justice system, Congress, television news, big business, police, Church or organized religion, military, medical system, presidency).

by 2012 had reached a record low of 21 per cent. As shown in Figure 5.2, this went hand in hand with a broader loss of faith in Congress, the presidency, big business and the Supreme Court. Trust in these key institutions reached its nadir in 2010.

The belief that one's own representatives – individuals who had been elected to look out for the people and their welfare – were instead complicit in the meltdown intensified this anger. Markus Wagner has shown that in Britain, people who felt that the crisis was the fault of their own government or the EU were especially angry and more likely than others to abandon the mainstream. 'These are institutions that we help to elect,' noted Wagner, 'and who are responsible for our welfare, so anger is perhaps an understandable response.'[20]

But this anger was especially visible in southern Europe where, after the crisis, support from the EU and IMF was often conditional on governments implementing harsh cuts in public expenditure and structural reforms like liberalizing labour markets, which in turn were encouraged by financial markets that raised interest rates on loans to countries that were felt to have excessive public debt. This provoked sharp criticism from the Keynes-influenced Nobel Prize-winning economists Paul Krugman and Joseph Stiglitz in the US, who argued that stimulating growth and countering inequality should play a greater role.[21]

However, the European Central Bank (in line with German policy, which has a fear of inflation that dates back to the rise of the Nazis, together with a desire for budgetary rectitude) rode roughshod over national politics, imposing austerity on the southern democracies of Greece, Italy and Spain. This resulted in higher unemployment, especially among the young, lower or static living standards for many, and a decline of faith in mainstream politics.

Italy saw especially remarkable changes after the crisis and its slow recovery from recession. Easily the largest party in the 2018 elections was the Five Star Movement, formed, as we have seen, by a comedian only nine years earlier. Its programme is an eclectic populist mix of hostility to mainstream politicians, support for direct democracy and criticism of EU-imposed austerity. Another movement, the national-populist League, emerged as the largest party on the right and only narrowly failed to replace the centre-left Democratic Party in second place after taking a tough anti-EU, anti-immigrant and anti-refugee line. Together, the two populist movements attracted more than half of all Italian voters and did well among the young.

Rising Inequality

While the Great Recession was the most spectacular development to hit neoliberalism in the West, wider economic factors have also played a role in driving the national-populist revolt. In particular, we need to probe more carefully the corrosive consequences of rising inequality and worries about relative deprivation, linked to fears about the future.

So-called 'New Optimists' like the Swedish neoliberal Johan Norberg argue that, broadly speaking, humans today live in an age of great optimism and progress.[22] Certainly, global indexes that track people's quality of life are generally rising, 2016 being the first year when fewer than 10 per cent of the world's population lived in 'extreme poverty', compared to 72 per cent in 1950. During the same period, global average real incomes per head rose by nearly 500 per cent. But these frameworks are not ones that most ordinary people would recognize as they relate little to day-to-day life.

Instead, many people in the West now feel deeply concerned about an economic settlement that feels increasingly unequal and unfair. As Thomas Piketty showed in his bestselling book *Capital in the 21st Century* (2015), the trend towards greater equality of income and wealth in the West, which began around the First World War and gathered pace after 1945, has now been reversed.

We will mainly focus here on earnings, but issues about growing discrepancies in wealth should not be forgotten, especially as they have longer-term implications for inequalities which are likely to deepen political discontent. In America, for example, whereas in 1973 the share of national income going to the top 1 per cent had fallen from nearly 20 per cent in 1928 to below 8 per cent, by 2012 it was back up to almost 19 per cent. Although the greatest changes in the West took place in the Anglo-Saxon countries, most others have witnessed growing inequality.

A major cause of the return of this inequality is rising salaries for the most highly paid. In the US, back in 1965 the CEOs of major companies were paid around twenty times as much as their average employee, but by 2012 they were being paid more than 350 times as much. In Britain, the ratio between the salaries of CEOs in major companies and the earnings of the average worker rose from 45:1 in the mid-1990s to 129:1 in 2016. In continental Europe the picture is more mixed, but an OECD report in 2017 highlighted similar trends.[23] In the 1980s, the average income of the top 10 per cent of earners in Europe was about eight times that of the bottom 10 per cent. By 2016 it had risen to nine and a half times, and it is still rising.

We also need to consider changes in taxation on incomes. In the US the highest federal band of personal taxation fell from over 70 per cent in the 1970s to 28 per cent during the Reagan era. In 2017 Trump claimed that his major tax cuts would benefit ordinary Americans, but the main gains will come for the rich and businesses, further increasing inequality. Although in countries like Denmark and Sweden the top rates of income tax remain above 50 per cent, these too have fallen since the 1970s.

Moreover, in many Western countries there is a growing tendency to marry people of similar socio-economic status, including education, income and wealth.[24] At the top end of the social scale this is creating a new aristocracy of wealth, whereby children are likely to retain their high socio-economic status. As well as benefiting from higher education and family networks, the vast majority will inherit considerable assets, including housing, which is today well beyond the grasp of many Millennials.

In contrast, there is a very real risk that less skilled and less well-educated young people will permanently be left out of the labour market, a marked difference from the full employment of the Golden Age. For example, even as the Eurozone area was leaving recession behind in 2017 the average rate of youth unemployment was still at 19 per cent, while in countries where national populists have made serious inroads it is even higher, including 31 per cent in Italy and 23 per cent in France. Clearly, it is not all about objective unemployment. Youth unemployment has been considerably lower in states where national populists have also done very well among the young, as in Austria. But such figures feed into a broader sense of angst among some people, including the young, that they are being left behind relative to others.

This is further reflected in trends of inequality, which are often examined by looking at what are called 'Gini coefficients'. On this measure, 0 equals complete equality whereas 1 is complete inequality. They confirm that over recent decades inequality has risen across the West and is higher in the US and Britain (see Figure 5.3). Perhaps more surprisingly, they show how inequality has sharpened over the last generation in classic social-democratic Sweden, which has been more influenced by neoliberalism than fellow Scandinavians in Denmark or Norway, and where there has been a dramatic rise of the national-populist Sweden Democrats. A similar trend can be seen in Germany, where the influence of neoliberalism is reflected in the spread of a new 'Denglish' language containing words such as 'Jobcenters', and in the Hartz reforms of the labour market, launched by a social-democratic Chancellor in 2002, which restricted welfare and included sanctions on the unemployed who refused reasonable offers of work.

These trends are intimately connected to the rise of economic insecurity, which is reflected in falling numbers of full-time, secure and well-paid jobs that give workers a sense of respect, dignity and social status, and which in the

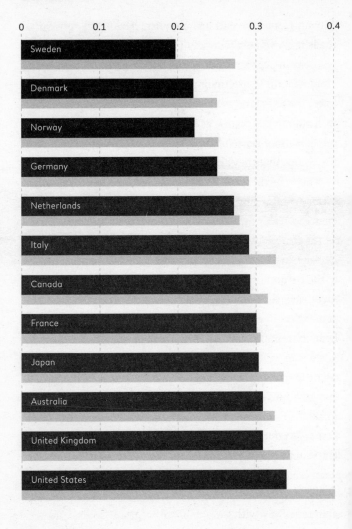

Figure 5.3
Gini coefficient (0 = perfect equality, 1 = perfect inequality)[25]

■ 1985
■ 2013 (or latest)

US were often linked to benefits such as company-provided health care.[26] There, almost 60 per cent of the labour force is paid hourly wages rather than annual salaries. In France, employment in car production, once a major manufacturing sector, almost halved between 2000 and 2015. In Sweden, car production fell from a record 366,000 in 2007 to 163,000 by 2012, losing Saab along the way. Even when a country's official data on employment appear strong, as in Britain and the US, they often conceal the rise of temporary, part-time, self-employed and insecure jobs.

Some link rising inequality and insecurity to the declining power of trade unions, which in earlier decades helped give workers stronger bargaining power to improve their wages and conditions. Certainly, across much of the West the proportion of unionized workers has declined significantly. Between 1990 and 2016, the number slumped from 38 to 23 per cent in Britain (and to just 8 per cent among those aged between sixteen and twenty-four), while in the US between 1983 and 2015 it almost halved, from 20 to 11 per cent. In the US retail industry, now the largest employer, the decline of unions has undoubtedly been a major factor enabling owners to cut labour costs. In countries like Germany, where labour laws and unions are stronger, workers have better conditions and wages.

Workers have good reasons to feel angry. By 2017, the share of GDP going to them in advanced economies was 4 per cent *lower* than it had been in 1970. However, while the decline of unions has reinforced a feeling among workers that they no longer have a voice, IMF figures show that over half of this decline in their share of GDP can be explained by automation, which has reduced the demand for labour.[27] In the US, for example, since 1980 but especially during the 2000s, a combination of automation, offshoring and globalization liquidated nearly 7 million manufacturing jobs – more than one-third of all manufacturing positions. Such issues will be exacerbated in the future, as automation increasingly takes over low- and medium-skilled administrative jobs. Indeed, a British 2017 study indicates that in this sector, automation could slash 30 per cent of jobs by 2030. Although some economists argue that automation will create jobs through demand for devices like robots and through increased consumer spending resulting from lower prices, it is widely agreed that the process has been an important check on wage increases for the less skilled.[28]

These currents are unlikely to weaken in the short term. In 2017 even the IMF, once a bastion of neoliberalism, argued that 'excessive levels of inequality can erode social cohesion, lead to political polarization, and ultimately to lower economic growth'. It proposed 'inclusive growth', arguing that serious consideration be given to higher taxes for the rich, a universal basic income and the positive role of public expenditure in education and health.[29]

This was followed in 2018 by Kristalina Georgieva, World Bank CEO, stating that growing income gaps in the EU were providing 'fertile ground for populism'. World Bank research pointed to gaps within as well as between countries. For example, Poland's per capita GDP had risen from half the EU average in 2000 to 69 per cent by 2015, but internal divisions had grown. More generally, technological advances have boosted the number of creative and analytical jobs by

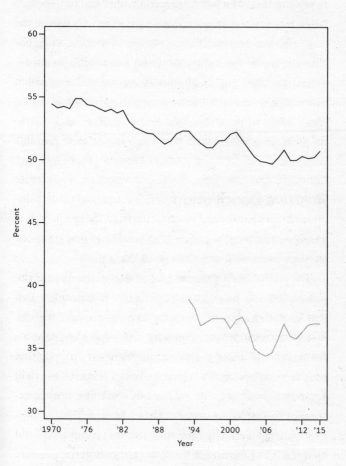

Figure 5.4
The share of national income paid to workers in:

—— Advanced economies

—— Emerging markets and developing economies

15 per cent over the last fifteen years, but manual jobs have fallen by the same amount, with particularly high losses in countries like Austria, Greece, Hungary and Italy. Together with the report from the IMF, these facts highlight the legitimacy of concerns about growing inequalities even within professional circles. National populists might disagree about what to prescribe, but many of them would have no problem agreeing with this diagnosis of their nation's ailments.

Relative Deprivation

The rise of national populism is clearly about more than objective economic scarcity: some of these movements have arisen in the most affluent and stable countries on the planet. This can be explained by the fact that people's economic worries are not only rooted in narrow concerns about money but encompass community, self-respect and people's strong anxiety about their own and their group's position relative to others. As the Harvard scholars Noam Gidron and Peter Hall point out, one reason why the wider transformation of the capitalist system matters in explaining national populism – and why economic factors cannot simply be disregarded – is because it has impacted strongly on people's perceived levels of respect, recognition and status relative to others in society.

Over recent years, white male workers who have few qualifications and are therefore ill equipped to navigate the economic storms have become especially likely to feel as though their status in society has declined relative to others and they are no longer fully recognized and valued members of wider society.[30] These are people who have borne the full force of the economic winds – the decline of secure, permanent and well-paid jobs, and a knowledge economy that puts a premium on the college degrees they do not have. In the US, some have succumbed to opioid drug addiction, which some commentators describe as an epidemic. Many more of them have rebelled against the political mainstream, which often only promises more of the same.

This sense of relative deprivation is critically important. It can relate not only to people's self-worth, but also how they think about the political system and society as a whole. It may be reflected in the feeling that the economic settlement is no longer working for ordinary people, that politicians and government are giving priority to the rich and powerful, or that immigrants and other newcomers are being given special treatment at the expense of the national group. If politics is seen as unresponsive to the concerns of ordinary people and failing to deliver equal and fair outcomes, this will fuel a feeling of being relatively deprived, making it increasingly likely that people will seek out more radical political solutions. Established politicians are blamed for either causing this inequality or for failing to stop it.

Indeed, researchers have already shown how these macroeconomic trends are having powerful political effects. In the early years of the twenty-first century, one study of twenty democracies in Europe found that in those with higher inequality, citizens were not only less likely to believe that their political system was working well but were also less trusting of key institutions. Others have likewise found that inequality can curb support for liberal democracy, especially among left-behind citizens who lack the skills and qualifications that are needed to keep pace.[31]

There is also evidence to suggest that inequality is fuelling other challenges to the mainstream, including increasing public opposition towards the integration of European democracies. Even before Brexit, between 1975 and 2009 people across Europe often responded to rising inequality by blaming the EU for the widening gap between the rich and poor and subsequently withdrawing their support for the further cohesion of European economies and societies. Again, this was especially true of the left-behind. The effect of inequality in driving opposition to the EU was almost twice as great on those with few or no qualifications than on the most highly educated.[32]

Crucially, however, feelings of relative deprivation are not simply to do with objective indicators like low incomes, poverty metrics or unemployment, which are actually poor predictors of support for national populism, as discussed in Chapter 1. It is worth restating that people at the very bottom tend to withdraw from politics altogether, while the unemployed support left-wing movements or populist parties that do not link economics to immigration, such as Italy's Five Star Movement, which did well among unemployed Italians. Rather, it is when the wider economic environment triggers a broader feeling of relative deprivation that spreads further up the social and economic system and a politician emerges to give voice to these grievances that they translate into political action.

The critical role of relative deprivation shines through in

research on both sides of the Atlantic. As Justin Gest vividly documents in his book *The New Minority*, based on hundreds of interviews with workers in the US and Britain, this profound sense of injustice is not rooted simply in concerns about tangible economic resources such as lost jobs or absent welfare. Rather, it flows from a more diffuse sense of cultural, political and social loss.

Many of the people who were drawn to national populists like Donald Trump or Nigel Farage had long been used to difficult financial conditions and even took pride in their ability to 'get by' in tight circumstances, contrasting themselves with a work-shy, immoral and welfare-dependent white underclass. What motivated them was a sense that, relative to others, they and their group had lost out, whether to more affluent middle-class citizens or to immigrants. Not only had they been demoted from the centre of their nation's consciousness to its fringes, but affirmative action had given further advantages to minorities while anti-racism campaigns had silenced any criticism about these rapid and deeply unsettling social changes.[33]

In a similar way, the social geographer Christophe Guilluy has written about the growth of a 'peripheral France', comprised of people who have been driven from the urban centres by deindustrialization and gentrification, who live apart from decision-making centres, and who have come to feel strongly excluded from the national conversation. He argues that approximately 40 billion Euros were spent between 2004 and 2013 on extensive refurbishing of mainly ethnic-minority housing estates in cities (*banlieus*), but nothing like this was invested in similarly depressed areas inhabited by native French people, fuelling resentment against what was seen as favouritism towards immigrants. These are people who often state that immigration is a major concern, but who are also influenced by their broader worries over social loss and fears about the future; Guilluy sees many of them turning to Marine Le Pen and the National Front.

In former East Germany the process of change has been different, but concerns are similar. While there was significant inward government investment, in the decade after re-unification over 10 per cent of its population moved to the West (though some *Wessis* hoping to make their fortunes moved the other way, a further source of resentment). Those remaining tended to be less educated and older, and now endure unemployment rates about 50 per cent higher than in the West. Rural and small-town areas have often suffered most, as in the US. Although many who remain take a pride in their locality and traditions (*Heimat*), they are bitter about their economic position and feel that they lack any ability to reverse their inferior economic and social status. It is hardly a surprise that this was the source of Alternative for Germany's greatest gains in the 2017 national elections.

These potent worries over relative deprivation are not fringe concerns. The feeling that Western economies are rigged in favour of the rich and powerful, together with the belief that the main parties no longer care about ordinary people, is widely shared. Today, many people are clearly at least open to considering more radical alternatives. This is reflected in the finding, in 2017, that at least two-thirds of people in Britain, France, Hungary, Italy, Spain and Belgium agreed that 'a strong leader is needed to take the country back from the rich and powerful'. While these voters are not looking for a fascist-style dictatorship, there appears to be clear support for a new and more radical path.

There is much further evidence of major discontent with the current economic settlement. For instance, 55 per cent of Americans, 64 per cent of Brits and 77 per cent of Germans agreed with the statement, 'The poor get poorer and the rich get richer in capitalist economies.'[34] And when asked whether 'strong community and family life is as important to well-being as a strong economy', 78 per cent of Americans, 79 per cent of Brits and 83 per cent of Germans concurred, suggesting that large numbers of people do not want a society that is only organized around the pursuit of profit and growth. This might go a long way to explaining why many voters in Britain rejected the case for remaining in the EU, which was based exclusively and narrowly on economic forecasts and appeals to self-interest.

Such surveys and polls show that there are large numbers of people who not only believe that their societies are broken and in decline, but who also appear convinced that in the future their children will find life even harder than they did, as we show in Figures 5.5 and 5.6. In 2016, the year of Trump's election, only 24 per cent of Americans thought that life for their children's generation would be better than theirs today, a figure that fell to 11 per cent among Trump supporters. Trump's voters were not only around twice as likely as Clinton's to feel that their personal finances were worsening, and four times as likely to feel that the economy was getting worse, but they were also united by a profound sense of pessimism about the future: 62 per cent of Trump's

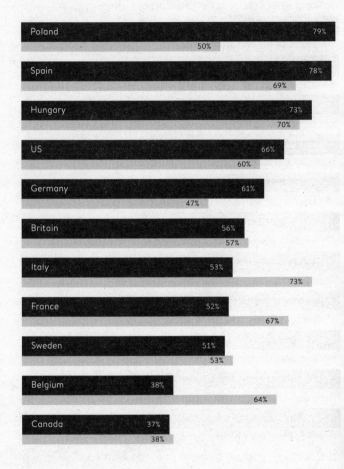

Figure 5.5
Percentage of population who believe that:

Society is broken
Society is in decline

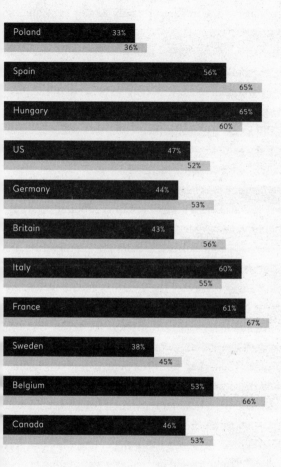

Figure 5.6

Percentage of population who believe that:

■ Their generation will have a worse life than their parents
▧ Today's youth will have a worse life than their parents

voters felt that life for people like them was worse than it was fifty years ago, compared to only 28 per cent among Clinton's voters.[35]

Nor are they wrong to feel this way. While 90 per cent of American children born in 1940 went on to earn more than their parents in real terms, only 40 per cent of the 1980 cohort have. Is it really surprising, then, that many American families think that paying for their children's college education is a risky gamble given the wider changes in the labour market and their own static income?

These feelings of relative deprivation are also important because they can act as a bridge between economics and culture. Though some argue that national populism is driven only by worries about cultural factors like immigration, its rise cannot be divorced from the way in which the broader economic transformation of the West has encouraged many people to feel a profound sense of loss.

We have already noted how support for Brexit was significantly stronger among people who felt that things were a lot worse for them than for other people. In the US, similarly, while there was little correlation between support for Trump and income, it became apparent if you looked instead at how people 'think broader social groups are doing – in short, whether the rich are getting richer and the poor getting poorer'.[36] Trump polled particularly well among people who felt that they were being left behind.

This creates room for national populists who promise to remove or at least reduce the influence of competing groups in society, punish the traditional parties and deliver a new economic settlement that prioritizes domestic workers.

More than twenty years ago, one scholar argued that national populists in Europe had struck upon a 'winning formula' that was a combination of tough right-wing positions on immigration and crime and a laissez-faire stance on the economy.[37] But this overstated the extent to which national populists were content with the free market, which was often linked to their objections to the way in which the traditional parties had used the state sector in countries like Austria, Italy and the Netherlands to distribute benefits to their friends and allies.

Today it is an even more misleading formula. National populists now differ in big ways on economic policy, and many subordinate their economic policies to their intense opposition to cultural issues like immigration. Some national populists, like the Freedom Party in Austria, appear broadly comfortable with free markets, though they seek to retain extensive welfare benefits for existing citizens. Others, like Nigel Farage, argue that lower growth is a price worth paying if it means fewer immigrants, more jobs for British people and more united communities, as this 'matters more than pure market economics'.[38] But some, like Marine Le Pen in France and similar figures in Eastern Europe, go further, advocating economically left-wing policies such as more state aid for troubled industries and restrictions on the free flow of capital and goods.

It might be thought that this points to major potential for left-wing populists, and certainly the rise of Podemos in Spain and Bernie Sanders' campaign in 2016 fit this argument. However, in general leftist populists have done far less well than national populists. There are two reasons for this.

The first is that national populists tap more widely into the 'Three Ds' of distrust, destruction and relative deprivation. Left-wing populists are critical of established politicians and the economic settlement, but they neglect the equally intense concerns over ethnic change and the possible destruction of the wider group, identity and ways of life. Too often, the left views this immigration angst solely as a by-product of objective economic grievances when it is in fact a legitimate concern in its own right and, as we have seen, is rooted in broader subjective worries about loss and relative deprivation. This means that the left is often outflanked by national populists who speak to people on all three levels.

The second reason is that whereas national populists often differ on economics, they have increasingly sought to set out an alternative to the status quo, including the adoption of policies that in the past were advocated on the left, like calling for more infrastructure projects and improving pay. These economic positions are not as important in explaining their support as opposition to immigration, but they do play an important role by diluting the distinctiveness of their left-wing competitors and entrenching the appeal of national populism to workers who conclude they are 'on the same side'.

Like the other trends that we explored in the context of democracy and the nation, it seems unlikely that these economic winds will calm in the short term. If anything, there are good reasons to expect them to gain even more strength, which will serve to sustain potential support for populists who rail against the status quo.

De-alignment

The political, demographic and economic roots of national populism have been visible for decades, and have been strengthening notably in recent years. As we have seen, several deep and long-term currents combined to create room for the likes of Donald Trump, Marine Le Pen and Matteo Salvini.

But these currents have also swirled alongside a fourth key trend in the West, which has further opened the door to national populists. This concerns the way in which the traditional bonds between people and the traditional parties have become much weaker over time, and also how the underlying dividing lines in politics have changed. This is what we call 'de-alignment'.

We are now living in a very different situation to that which existed during the 'classic era' of mass politics in the mid- to late twentieth century. Unlike then, when people's loyalty to the traditional parties was much stronger and political battles were mainly fought over questions about economic redistribution and the state, today our political systems are grappling with major changes.

These include higher rates of volatility at elections, a growing willingness among some citizens to back new parties, the rise of new value-led conflicts, stronger feelings of alienation and apathy, especially among the working-class, and a striking decline of bedrock support for movements that were once dominant, such as social-democratic parties in Europe. Amid this change, national populists have recruited impressive support from workers, while others point to new opportunities for the old guard. In the US and Europe, some argue that while centre-left parties may be struggling to retain their working-class voters, a new era of hegemony might nonetheless be opening up, supported by expanding immigrant and minority populations, the spread of liberal values and the rise of culturally liberal youth.

We will explore these broad changes in this chapter. Back in the 1960s two scholars – Philip Converse and Georges Dupeux – argued that people would be less likely to defect to populists if they felt loyal to the established parties.[1] Yet while this was the case during part of the second half of the twentieth century, in many countries these bonds are breaking down, sometimes dramatically. Many of us are now living in a political world that is more volatile, fragmented and unpredictable than at any time since the birth of mass democracy. And these changes are unlikely to be reversed any time soon.

The 'Classic Era' of Alignment

Political parties are central to modern democracy, but this was not always the case. As we saw in Chapter 3, the model of direct democracy that flourished in ancient Greece was one that made more room for ordinary citizens. This could work in small city states, but great thinkers like Aristotle never imagined that democracy could be practised across much larger countries – for example the US, with a population of more than 325 million citizens, or the EU, which brings together twenty-eight states with a combined population of more than 500 million.

Nor were parties central to the growing body of thought that, after the seventeenth century, sought to adapt democracy to larger states and led to the creation of what we now call liberal democracy. Instead, parties were viewed with suspicion, as vehicles that were likely to divide societies and be captured by special interests. Thomas Jefferson stated that 'If I could not go to heaven but with a party, I would not go at all.'

But during the nineteenth century political parties did spring up, largely to fulfil important functions as societies grew in size and, amid the Industrial Revolution, became more complex. On the one hand, they helped simplify choices, 'educate' citizens and mobilize their votes. On the other, they were a training ground for new leaders who would govern the country and help to broker compromise among the different elites and interest groups in society.

People in Europe and the US soon developed a strong sense of allegiance to these parties and these long-term and stable attachments became a way in which many thought about politics, the world and themselves: their chosen party was linked to their job, family and social class. These allegiances were often 'inherited' during childhood, and people would see, throughout their lives, the big debates of the day from this partisan perspective.

Competition between the parties, meanwhile, was shaped by things like the type of electoral system that was being used and the ways in which societies were divided. In major democracies like Britain and the US, a simple majority electoral system favoured the emergence of two big, dominant parties, while in many European states proportional systems produced more parties and also made it easier for new ones to break through.

The first parties to develop in the nineteenth century had a strong middle-class base, reflecting how the (male) working class was excluded from voting in most democracies. This meant that parties mainly supported economically liberal and socially conservative values. However, as the West moved into the twentieth century, and as workers and a growing number of women gained the vote, a significant number of workers did turn to conservative parties. This was not simply because they held socially conservative values. In countries like Britain and Germany they were also attracted by what historians call 'social imperialism', namely a combination of welfare measures to help poorer people, such as the introduction of old-age pensions, and the celebration of national greatness and expanding Empire. For example, the pre-First World War naval rivalry between Britain and Germany revealed extensive jingoism in the working and middle classes: 'We want eight and we won't wait' was the popular British call to build more dreadnought battleships to counter the German challenge.

In parts of Europe, during the late nineteenth and early twentieth centuries religious parties also emerged, especially Catholic ones. The latter's 'social Catholic' doctrine was inspired by the Papal encyclical *Rerum Novarum* (1891) about the changing relations of capital and labour. This was critical of what it saw as divisive aspects in the industrial revolution, including socialist thought among workers, and argued that the state should promote social justice and curb the excesses of the free market. This helped Christian Democrats in Germany and Italy broaden their support across class boundaries, even attracting non-Catholic conservatives. As the West moved into the post-1945 era some scholars came to describe these parties as 'mass' or 'catch-all' parties due to their ability to attract large and fairly stable coalitions of supporters.

Ranged against these centre-right parties were a variety of left-wing challengers. In some countries, like France and Italy (and Germany before Nazism), major communist parties arose. But more commonly, social-democratic parties became the main representatives of the working class. In Britain, this was linked to the rise of unions that were intimately bound to the Labour Party. It was also driven by a strong sense of class consciousness, a belief that Labour was creating a new and more equitable Britain, which was reinforced by strong working-class group identities in solidaristic mining villages or shipbuilding towns. When Labour formed its first majority government in 1945, many of its voters dreamed of creating a 'New Jerusalem', united by an almost religious sense of identity and hope.

In the US things were different. The development of the 'left-right' division that characterized European countries was hindered by several factors. The country's strongly individualist, producerist ethos and ethnic divisions among waves of immigrants during the nineteenth century acted as barriers to the rise of class consciousness and the spread of socialist thought. Moreover, after the Civil War the Republican Party had proceeded to 'reconstruct' the South to give newly liberated African American slaves a share in power. The result was that, during the late nineteenth century, the South became dominated by a white Democrat Party which removed voting rights for African Americans, imposed racial segregation and ruthlessly played the 'race card'. They accused their opponents – including the 1890s People's Party as well as Republicans – of promoting the interests of African Americans. However, especially in Northern cities, the Democrats increasingly made links with progressives, labour groups and African Americans, which against the backdrop of the Great Depression produced the coalition with Southern Democrats that led to four presidential victories in a row for Franklin Delano Roosevelt and, from 1933, the New Deal.

Meanwhile, the Republicans emerged as ardent protectionists of US industry, a major factor in the rise of the US as an economic superpower. Many of the plutocrats of the time, like Andrew Carnegie and John D. Rockefeller, were Republicans, but the party also attracted support among the working class and in some rural areas. Although there was a realignment towards the Democrats during the inter-war years, the Republican coalition was still strong enough to win the presidency for Dwight Eisenhower in 1952 and 1956.

For these reasons, while parties differed between countries, by the 1960s scholars were arguing that many of the West's party systems had effectively 'frozen'.[2] By this they meant that the underlying dividing lines in politics ensured that the major parties remained broadly the same, and that while parties sometimes changed their names, the basic 'party families' stayed intact. For example, while in the post-war period there have been more than ten names for the centre-right in France, its underlying base remained broadly stable and tended to come from the same groups in society. Although the vote for the major parties would ebb and flow and governments would come and go, most supporters tended to stay loyal to their party of choice, not changing their allegiance between major elections.

However, as the West passed through the second half of the twentieth century the status quo of relative stability and loyal electorates began to alter, and in major ways. Among the most dramatic manifestations of this was the breakdown of the Democratic American South against a background of Civil Rights legislation, followed by the rise of the 'Reagan coalition' which after the 1970s welcomed many white workers into the Republican fold. Europe, meanwhile, began to see the decline of traditional social-democratic parties, sometimes losing voters to the New Left and Greens, though larger numbers defected to conservative and national populists, a trend which would gather pace in the new millennium.

The Culture Conflict

These changes reflected how the underlying dividing lines in politics had begun to change. The industrial era in which mass democracy emerged gave way to the post-industrial and globalization eras. Rural areas began to shrink as people moved into cities. The number of blue-collar workers and people who belonged to unions declined, partly because industrial production was moving to regions like Asia and work was becoming more casual and less tied to regimented factories. The number of people going to church also fell, though church-going remained an important part of life in America and Eastern

Europe, as well as for immigrants. Meanwhile, the number of college graduates and economically secure middle-class professionals was on the rise, encouraged by the Golden Age of capitalism that we explored in the last chapter and widening access to college education. In later years, these voters would be joined by new generations such as the Millennials, who had been socialized in a world where the old dividing lines were even less relevant to their lives. They thought very differently to their elders about key issues like immigration, and generally felt less tribally loyal to a particular party.[3]

Over time, the issues that people debated also changed. During much of the classic era, which stretched into the post-war years, debates had been dominated by topics such as economic redistribution, jobs, taxation and the extent to which the state should intervene in the economy. But as the West entered the final decades of the twentieth century and the early twenty-first century, new concerns began to move up the agenda. The demographic and political changes that we have explored ushered in new and far more divisive debates about immigration, ethnic change, European integration, refugees and issues that bridged security and identity, like Islam and terrorism, which might not have been so disruptive had everybody held broadly similar views. But instead they exposed a much deeper 'culture conflict' in the West that was more a battle over competing sets of values.

The emergence of a new dividing line had first been noticed by scholars like Ronald Inglehart during the 1970s. The rise of the new, prosperous and college-educated middle class pushed new values and priorities to the forefront of politics. Many of these 'Baby Boomers' had been born after the Second World War and raised amid the post-war boom. In Europe they had also enjoyed generous welfare nets. All of this meant that their upbringing was fundamentally different from that of the earlier 'Greatest' and 'Silent' generations, who had come of age while trying to stay alive during the Great Depression and global wars. For these older generations, survival had never been secure: they had witnessed 18 million die during the First World War and some had experienced harsh poverty. In contrast, for the Baby Boomers full employment, individual rights, widening opportunities for upward social mobility and time to invest in (cheap) higher education seemed guaranteed, as did a new affluent lifestyle.

Because they were less worried about their basic economic and physical security and had passed through the liberalizing effects of higher education, these new generations were far more likely to adopt a different set of 'post-material' values. Unlike earlier generations that had been preoccupied by their material concerns about physical and economic security, post-materialists were far more interested in equality and lifestyle goals such as freedom of speech, self-expression and rights for all. They generally embraced a far more culturally liberal and internationalist outlook.

During the 1960s and after, many of these voters threw themselves into radical causes that were led by the New Left and sought to translate these values into political outcomes. They included the sexual and student revolutions, campaigns for civil and women's rights, opposition to nuclear weapons and the Vietnam War, support for immigration and rising ethnic diversity, environmental campaigns and the promotion of identities and organizations that transcended the nation state, like the EU and the idea of 'global citizenship'. Some voters decided to abandon the traditional parties to pursue these goals through green or more radical left-wing parties. Others stayed with the mainstream social-democratic parties, which became more liberal in order to win over these new voters.

In later years, post-materialists threw themselves into other causes: the expansion of rights for LGBT communities and minorities, anti-racism campaigns, climate change, multiculturalism and jumping on social media to express solidarity with #TimesUp, #MeToo or #RefugeesWelcome. They cheered on the liberal centrist Emmanuel Macron, but felt shocked and repulsed by Trump and Brexit. This value change across the West is what Ronald Inglehart called the 'Silent Revolution'.[4]

But not everybody joined the revolutionaries. Even in the 1970s, it was clear that many in the West did not support the change of direction. Amid the rapid cultural and societal developments being advocated by the New Left, people who had not been to college, as well as traditional social conservatives and those from rural and small-town communities which had not been subject to the winds of change, were apprehensive, if not alarmed, by the perceived rapid breakdown of order, values and ways of life. And they were about to stage a counter-attack.

Witness the growing use among conservatives of the term 'silent majority', first coined by President Richard Nixon at the turn of the 1970s. Although attitudes to issues like women's rights, race and sexual freedoms were changing rapidly, the term undoubtedly captured a widespread feeling that these changes were being driven by an active minority rather than by the American heartland, which respected tradition, paid taxes and willingly died in wars for their country.

The Silent Revolution soon spawned a backlash among voters, who flocked to an array of movements which argued that they too had a right to defend their communities and ways of life against cultural liberalism and its perceived corrosive effects. In the US this was reflected in the rise of groups like the 'Moral Majority', which held highly conservative views on family and religion. Its divorce from mainstream Republicanism was reflected in Pat Buchanan's socially conservative campaign against the Republican George H. W. Bush in the Republican primaries of 1992, which many of his followers saw as an attempt to fight back against a liberal assault on traditional values and a growing acceptance or even celebration of non-white immigration and ethnic change. Buchanan garnered 23 per cent of the vote, mainly from young and less well-educated men who felt disenfranchised and threatened by these changes, including the growing dominance of liberal graduates in politics and media.

In Europe, meanwhile, similar shifts were fuelling the sudden rise of national populists like Jean-Marie Le Pen in France and Jörg Haider in Austria, who were likewise symptoms of this emerging divide in values between liberals and traditionalists, as well as a growing gap between people and the older political parties. One of the first to notice the backlash was the Italian scholar Piero Ignazi, who termed it the 'Silent Counter-Revolution'. Ignazi argued that the sudden rise after the 1970s of neoconservatism had helped pave the way for national populism by legitimizing the right-wing focus on defending communal identities and traditions that had previously largely been ignored, even effectively banned from debate. 'A mounting sense of doom,' wrote Ignazi, 'in contrast to postmaterialist optimism, has been transformed into new demands, mainly unforeseen by the established conservative parties.' Calls for tough law and order, control of immigration and the reassertion of traditional values were becoming ever louder.[5]

As part of its defence of tradition, the Silent Counter-Revolution defended a patriarchal view of sexual relations in reaction to the rise of rights for women and their growing role in the workplace. This was a time of de-industrialization, when the development of new technologies was pushing men into what many saw as 'knicker jobs' like distribution and retail, rather than dangerous but 'macho' occupations like manual work in heavy industry. Given the gendered nature of its promises, it is unsurprising that a core feature of national populism has been its strong support among men, even if some politicians like Marine Le Pen and Donald Trump have recently polled well among some groups of women.

These value conflicts then accelerated further, and for two reasons. The first was that from the 1980s and 1990s onwards the polarizing issues of immigration, European integration, Islam and the refugee crisis moved up the agenda, as we saw in Chapter 4.[6] The second was that the rise of national populism itself drew even more attention to these debates and gave its followers a greater feeling of agency, a sense that they could now mobilize against the new liberal zeitgeist.

These changes widened the divides between college-educated middle-class liberals, the inheritors of the New

Left tradition, and a broad alliance of traditional conservatives and whites without degrees who flocked to the silent counter-revolution. The emergence of new issues also had big implications for the traditional parties, though few were quick to spot them. As classic anchors like class and religion began to wield less influence on voters, the new value conflicts often cut across traditional dividing lines. This further eroded the bonds that once kept people closely aligned to the traditional parties, for example causing blue-collar workers who felt instinctively anxious about immigration increasingly to question their allegiance to pro-immigration social-democratic parties.

Breaking Bonds

As the West moved through the final decades of the twentieth century, the new era of de-alignment came increasingly to the fore. From the 1970s onwards countless studies showed how growing numbers of people across the West were becoming ever more open to new movements.[7]

In the US, in the 1950s and early 1960s a solid 70–75 per cent of people had identified with either the Democrats or Republicans. But things then changed radically. By the time of George Bush's controversial victory in 2000 the figure had fallen to 59 per cent and by 2014, as Trump mulled over whether or not to run for the presidency, it had sunk to a record low of 56 per cent.

There were also other signs that America was ripe for an outsider like Trump, and which make it all the more remarkable that so few pundits saw him coming. Between 2003 and

2017, the proportion of Americans who felt that the traditional parties were doing an 'adequate job' tumbled from 56 to 34 per cent, while those who thought that a new third party was needed surged from 40 to 61 per cent.[8] According to the 2016 American Values Survey, more than 60 per cent of respondents said that neither major party reflected their opinions, compared to less than half in 1990. Meanwhile, the proportion who refused to identify with the main parties and said they were 'independent' jumped from 23 per cent in the early 1950s to a record 43 per cent in 2014. In fact, for five consecutive years before Trump beat Clinton at least four in ten Americans had identified as an independent, while the number of those who were loyal to the two big parties had reached its lowest point since the advent of modern polling.[9]

These trends did not hand Trump the presidency, of course, and some independents do 'lean' towards a party. But, broadly speaking, the growing number of people who feel less strongly attached to the mainstream has created a climate that is far more fluid and unpredictable. As scholars like Russell Dalton have pointed out, fewer Americans today express an allegiance to the main parties than at any time in the country's history.[10] Some Americans used to argue that this disconnect resulted from factors that were unique to America – for example the Vietnam War, Richard Nixon and the Watergate scandal, or Bill Clinton's divisive presidency and his threatened impeachment. But such debates ignore the fact that similar trends have actually been taking place across the West.

In Europe, by 2009 the percentage of people who did not feel close to any political party had increased to 45 per cent. It is certainly true that there have been variations. In

Eastern Europe, most new parties were not firmly implanted after the collapse of communism unless they had built on pre-existing social divides and networks, like the Catholic Church in Poland which played an important role in the downfall of communism. But increasingly fewer voters have felt loyal to the established parties.

Look at Britain, where the writing was on the wall long before the Brexit referendum. Whereas in the 1960s around half the population felt strongly aligned to one of the traditional parties, by 2015 only one in eight were. The Brexit issue, which was bound up with immigration, then cut directly across the traditional party electorates, though most visibly the Labour Party's, which has increasingly found itself dependent on two irreconcilable groups: pro-EU and pro-immigration middle-class liberals, and anti-EU and anti-immigration blue-collar workers.

On the morning after the Brexit referendum, Labour, which had officially campaigned for Britain to Remain in the EU, awoke to find that it controlled *both* the most passionately pro-Remain districts that were filled with affluent middle-class professionals and Millennial graduates, and the most strongly pro-Brexit districts where there were lots of pessimistic working-class voters who worried intensely about immigration, felt left behind relative to others and loathed the established political class.

When the dust had settled, two-thirds of Labour politicians found they represented pro-Brexit districts, though only a handful had campaigned for Brexit. The vote had cut through Labour's electorate like a hot knife through butter. This tension was reflected in the working-class northern

Labour district of Doncaster, where more than seven in ten had voted for Brexit, versus the more ethnically diverse, younger and hipster Labour district of Hackney and Stoke Newington in London, where eight in ten had voted to remain. The divide in values had found its full expression in the Brexit vote.

Though other states in Europe have not witnessed a similar referendum, the same underlying trends are clearly visible. In Sweden, the proportion of people who felt loyal to a particular party had slumped from two-thirds in the late 1960s to just 28 per cent in 2010, the same year that national populists entered parliament for the first time. In Germany, the world was stunned by the breakthrough of Alternative for Germany in 2017 – but had you been looking at the longer-term trends you would not have been surprised. Whereas in the early 1970s more than half of West Germans felt a strong allegiance to a party, by 2009 this figure had dropped to below one in three. Meanwhile, the proportion that felt only weakly committed to one or not committed at all surged by more than twenty points to 64 per cent. These ties were weaker in East Germany, which has a shorter history of democratic rule, and where 'West' Germans are seen almost as colonialists. Here the national populists won their strongest support, becoming the most popular choice of all for men.[11]

The established parties have also been weakened on other fronts. Since the 1970s, most major parties in the West have recorded a significant decline in their memberships, which in turn has curbed their ability to mount counter-campaigns against the populists. By the early twenty-first century, one major study found that party membership had

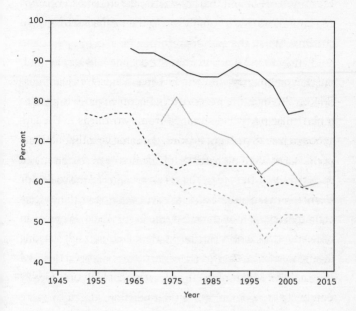

Figure 6.1
Percentage of party identifiers:

—— GB
—— Federal Republic of Germany
------ USA
------ France

consistently declined in all of Europe's long-established democracies. This downward spiral was especially marked in post-communist states that lacked vibrant civil societies and a tradition of competitive politics. Political parties, concluded the authors, were 'rapidly losing their capacity to engage citizens'. When the authors returned in 2012 to update the study they found not only that the decline had accelerated, but that membership had reached such a low ebb 'that it may no longer constitute a relevant indicator of party organizational capacity'.[12]

Scholars also developed new terms to signal the decline of the mass, catch-all party that had once been rooted firmly in civil society. In Europe, 'cartel party' entered the political-science vernacular, referring to parties that are run by elites and funded largely by the public purse (typically on the basis of past voting, which further hinders new parties).[13] Traditional parties turned to the state, often using tactics like state control of part of the broadcast media and patronage in the public sector to reinforce their position. More generally, parties became increasingly professional in the way they ran campaigns, often involving extensive teams including people like image consultants and pollsters and which, in the context of increasingly powerful media, stressed the personalities of individual leaders or candidates, developments which can be traced back in the US to Jack Kennedy and beyond.

This requires large sums of money, which especially in the US often comes from business and rich donors, raising fears about 'dark money'. However, the growing use of primary elections to choose candidates for a broad range of offices has led to debates about whether this practice has strengthened party members compared to party elites. Certainly, Trump's choice as Republican nominee, against the wishes of the Republican party leadership and with far less money to spend than rivals like Jeb Bush, is evidence that the power of party elites has weakened. However, even though in some states voters have to register an allegiance to vote in primaries, this does not have the same implications as party membership in Europe, which typically involves paying a small annual fee and receiving the right to participate regularly in local meetings (though few now do so). The social democrat Bernie Sanders, who mounted a powerful challenge for the Democratic presidential nomination in 2016, was not even a registered Democrat, though he caucused with the Democrats in the Senate. Nevertheless, while direct comparisons are impossible, the broad pattern of declining party membership is the same as in Europe.

There have certainly been exceptions. The large numbers of French people who flocked to Emmanuel Macron's new movement in 2017, or the surge of new members of Britain's Labour Party under Jeremy Corbyn since 2015, are two examples. But they have run counter to the norm, and even today Labour's membership is only half the size that it was in the 1950s. Furthermore, three-quarters of these new members are middle-class and usually university-educated professionals, while half live in London, well away from Labour's historic working-class bastions where large majorities had backed Brexit.[14]

Crucially, these shifts have also occurred among the young: in America, the refusal to align with the main parties is twenty-five points higher among today's under-thirties than it was for the equivalent generation in the 1960s, illustrating how this phenomenon is specific to the modern era. Similarly, before the Brexit referendum only 66 per cent of British twenty- or thirty-somethings identified with the main parties, compared to 85 per cent of the same age group back in 1983. In Germany, whereas in the mid-1970s around 20 per cent of under-thirties felt no real political attachment, by 2009 this figure had rocketed to 50 per cent. Clearly, young people are not giving up entirely on politics, but they are less loyal to the traditional parties.

With Brexit and Trump in mind, it is also true that when it comes to voting these typically more liberal youngsters have generally not packed a hard punch. In the US, at every presidential election since 1964 those aged between eighteen and twenty-four have consistently voted at lower rates than other generations (see Figure 6.2). And this appears to be getting worse. Between 1964 and 2012 the rate of turnout among young people fell from 51 to 38 per cent, meaning that when President Obama was re-elected in 2012 the turnout gap between those aged between eighteen and twenty-four and those over sixty-five was a striking thirty-one percentage points. This is why Hillary Clinton should never have expected a strong Millennial vote.

There are clear parallels with Britain's Brexit referendum, when Millennials turned out at much lower rates than older voters and were also more likely to over-claim they had voted. The estimated rate of turnout among people aged between eighteen and twenty-four was 64 per cent, compared to 80 per cent among those aged between sixty-five and

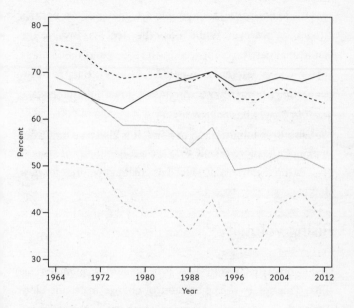

Figure 6.2
Voting rates in the US amongst people aged:

—— 65 years and over

----- 45 to 64 years

—— 25 to 44 years

----- 18 to 24 years

seventy-four.[15] It was thus rather ironic that a petition to overturn the Brexit vote received a large number of signatures in the young hipster London districts where Millennials had failed to mobilize when it really mattered.

This is not to say that people are giving up on politics altogether, however. While today they feel less loyal to the traditional parties, compared to the 1960s and 1980s many appear just as interested in politics, as likely to try to influence others how to vote, to contact governments, engage in protests and to use new media as a means of political as well as social interaction.[16] Rather, the point is that today there are lots more people who are not habitually or tribally loyal to the mainstream, which has created openings for new challengers.

Rising Volatility

One immediate effect of these broader shifts is greater volatility. This refers to the amount of change from one election to the next and the extent to which voters are willing to shift their loyalty from one party to another. The more volatility, the more people are switching between parties.

In Europe, after politics settled down following the Second World War the situation was fairly stable. But since the 1970s political systems have gradually become more volatile. This then accelerated during the 1990s and continued into the 2000s.[17] While it did not happen everywhere, politics in many democracies has generally become more unstable, chaotic and less predictable.

New movements have thus arisen more easily, whether

radical-left populists, Greens, parties that campaign on separatist issues, or national populists. Between 2004 and 2015 the mean share of the vote for the traditional parties in Europe declined by fourteen points to 72 per cent, while the share of the vote going to new challengers more than doubled to 23 per cent.[18] These general trends also conceal some fascinating examples of truly historic changes.

In Germany, Angela Merkel's centre-right Christian Democrats saw their vote drop in 2017 to its lowest level since 1949. In France, in the same year's presidential election neither candidate from the mainstream centre-right or centre-left even made it into the final round. Whereas in 2007 the centre-right party had then gone on to win 39 per cent of the vote on the first ballot at legislative elections, ten years later it took only 16 per cent. In Austria, the 2016 presidential election became a fight between a national populist and an independent after mainstream candidates failed to win sufficient support.

How you think about this will be shaped by your own politics. Optimists might reason that all of this change will help to keep the old parties on their toes and make them more responsive to people's demands. Pessimists might reply that this will only make politics more fluid and chaotic, opening the door to more change, more parties, more big swings at elections, more shaky coalitions and more unpredictable political decision-making. Such trends will make it hard if not impossible to achieve the stability that the financial markets, investors, policymakers and many citizens crave.

The US has been different in this respect, while also exhibiting some parallels. The first-past-the-post election system favours the two major parties, though there have been notable third-party candidates in presidential elections, including George Wallace who won over 13 per cent of the vote in 1968 and Ross Perot who won nearly 19 per cent in 1992. The racist Wallace's success reflected how the Democrats' hold over whites in the South was rapidly declining, while Perot's performance reflected the rising number of independents.

Behind these third-party votes were wider trends. Particularly since the 1970s, blue-collar workers, once the mainstay of the New Deal coalition, have realigned behind the Republicans. During Bill Clinton's shift towards the centre ground during the 1990s, while the Democrats became more appealing to the college-educated and women, blue-collar workers and Americans without a college education began to turn away.[19] Their number could have been greater had there not been an economic slowdown, which allowed Clinton to campaign on the slogan 'It's the economy, stupid', while attacking Republicans for their support of tax cuts which would mainly help the rich.

Yet by the 2016 presidential election the shifting landscape was clearly visible. According to the American National Election Study, Hillary Clinton only won around 4 per cent of her support from people who had previously voted for the Republican candidate Mitt Romney in 2012, despite the widely reported dislike of Donald Trump among mainstream Republicans. Trump retained the overwhelming majority of Republican voters but also made a wider incursion into the Democrat electorate, winning 13 per cent of Obama's 2012 voters. This suggests that while 2.5 million

Romney supporters switched to Clinton, more than 8 million of Obama's voters went to Trump, allowing him to win four states that Obama had carried in both 2008 and 2012.[20] The key switchers were whites without degrees.

While their anxiety over immigration and ethnic change were important 'push' factors for these voters, so too was their feeling that liberal urban elites did not understand people like them. It was also in key swing states like Michigan where the already declining influence of labour unions was clearly visible, furthering the likelihood of a move away from the Democrats.

But these shifts should not be traced simply to Trump. They too were a long time coming. The defection of white Americans away from the Democrats and their realignment around the Republicans began many years ago. As the scholar John Sides has shown (see Figure 6.3), it was actually during the era of President Obama, between 2009 and 2015, that the Democrats became visibly weaker among white Americans who had few qualifications.[21] Whereas the Democrats' lead over Republicans among Hispanics, Asians and African Americans has increased sharply in recent years, it is the Republicans who have established a growing advantage among whites – a lead that jumped to twelve points in 2010 and fifteen points in 2016, and which occurred almost entirely among whites without degrees. Furthermore, this lead was in place before Trump even started to campaign.

Turning to Europe, the trend towards greater volatility also began long ago, but then accelerated during the Great Recession. According to a major study of thirty democracies, not only did the financial crisis and its aftermath accelerate

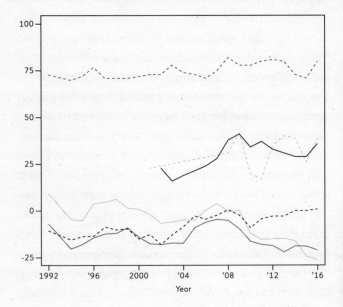

Figure 6.3
Democratic advantage in partisanship, amongst:

- - - - Black people
- - - - Asian
——— Hispanic
- - - White people, college degree
——— White people, some college
——— White people, high school

the divide between the 'haves and the have-nots' but it also drained support for the mainstream and fuelled greater support for populists on both the left and right. While national populism was well on its way before the crisis, the turmoil encouraged even more people to reconsider their allegiances, but especially where unelected bodies like the European Central Bank had intervened to impose austerity that most people opposed. In fact, in the shadow of the Great Recession the overall rates of volatility reached levels that had not been seen at any other point since the birth of mass democracy, including the turbulent inter-war years that had witnessed the rise of new communist and fascist parties.[22]

This is true even of rich and stable countries like Sweden, where since the 1950s the number of people switching their vote from one election to the next surged more than three-fold to reach 37 per cent by the early 2000s.[23] The once-dominant Social Democrats, who averaged 45 per cent of the vote between the mid-1930s and 1980s, were down to 31 per cent by 2014 – though they still provided the Prime Minister, showing that what happens at the government level is often not representative of what is going on at the grass-roots. As we will see, one important factor in this decline was the way in which many blue-collar workers disengaged from politics.

In Italy, this volatility is reflected in even greater changes. At the turn of the 1990s, the old party system collapsed amid a sea of corruption charges against both the two major governing parties, the Christian Democrats and Socialists, leading to the rise of the populist-conservative business tycoon Silvio Berlusconi. In 2001, his Go Italy (Forza Italia) won over 29 per cent of the vote, but by 2018 a reformed version was down to just 14 per cent. Berlusconi had become embroiled in scandals, political, financial and sexual, and the main centre-left party became bogged down in issues relating to how to respond to the Great Recession and ones of constitutional reform, including seeking to strengthen the government (a proposal defeated by a referendum in 2016). This presaged the remarkable rise of the populist Five Star Movement, which together with the national-populist League emerged to dominate Italian politics.

Or consider France. In 2016, the thirty-eight-year-old former banker and Finance Minister in the socialist government Emmanuel Macron started his own movement, En Marche! (Forward!). He had never run for elected office before, yet only one year later in the presidential elections the old order crumbled. Although since 1945 the French party system has experienced the rise of the National Front in the 1980s and the demise of the once-strong communist party, there has been a broad balance of left- and right-wing parties. In 2017 Macron pitched for the centre ground, in the first ballot squeezing out the mainstream centre-left and centre-right parties, which attracted a combined total of only 23 per cent of the vote, the lowest in modern French history. Macron faced off against the national-populist Marine Le Pen, who lost but walked away with support from more than one in three voters, a record for the party. In the legislative elections which followed, En Marche! won a commanding parliamentary majority, though at only 43 per cent the rate of turnout was a record low, revealing a dangerous trend of apathy as well as volatility.

Some commentators have since argued that the evidence points to a turning-back of the tide towards stability. In the shadow of the Brexit vote, for example, the prophets of political armageddon appeared to be dealt a sharp rebuke. In the general election of 2017, the two big parties, Labour and the Conservatives, completely dominated, taking over 80 per cent of the vote. Although Britain uses the simple majority system, which of course favours large parties, this was their highest combined share since 1970 (though not quite the 97 per cent achieved in 1951).

But claims about a new-found stability are wide of the mark. In reality, British politics was still in a state of major flux. The two elections that took place either side of the Brexit vote were the most volatile in the modern era: compared to the 1950s the rate of volatility had increased four-fold. This was largely because a once-stable two-party system had given way to the rise of an assortment of parties, from nationalists in Scotland and Wales to the national-populist UKIP. By the time of the Brexit referendum nearly one in three Brits had voted for parties other than the big two. The fact that they were now far more willing to diversify was reflected in the fact that in 2015 and 2017, a striking 43 and 32 per cent respectively changed their votes from the last election. So, while after Brexit the headline story was the return of the two big parties, underneath the surface the currents were swirling around like never before, leaving Britain open to new challengers.[24]

Apathetic Workers and Non-Voters

Had you been observing Britain's working class closely, you would have seen Brexit coming. More than a decade before the vote, deeper changes had paved the way for the shock result.

Though few tourists do, if you had ventured into the more industrial and struggling north of England then you would have sensed the coming rebellion. During the classic era, the old saying in many working-class communities was that even if you put a red Labour Party rosette on a donkey the people would still vote for it. Fast-forward thirty years and the situation had changed radically. Because of the wider transformations that we have explored, by the late 1990s the main parties were pitching far more to middle-class liberals, there seemingly being few incentives to speak directly to the working class, which also comprised a dwindling share of the electorate.

Social democrats had to find new ways of broadening their appeal. This is what led the likes of Bill Clinton in the US, Tony Blair in Britain and Gerhard Schröder in Germany to reach out more actively to the ascendant and more culturally liberal middle class which had arisen amidst the New Left crusades. Social Democrats embraced, or at least did not seek to overturn, key aspects of the neoliberal economic settlement. They drifted to the centre, which Blair and Clinton called the Third Way and Germans called the 'New Centre', while also pitching more directly to identity politics.

In Europe, social democrats often accepted cuts in generous welfare systems and diluted labour protections for workers. They became more supportive of post-material issues such as feminism, immigration and multiculturalism, expanding rights for minorities and tackling climate change. In Britain, Blair famously overturned his party's commitment to the public ownership of key industries and higher taxes, while talking much less about defending workers and weakening party links with unions. He soon had more support from the middle class than from the working class and assumed that workers had nowhere else to go.

But the assumption turned out to be wrong. In the short term Blair seemed to have won his gamble, as from 1997 he enjoyed three consecutive election victories, following four Labour defeats in a row to Margaret Thatcher and John Major. But he failed to notice the growing alienation in working-class communities, reinforced by resentment towards the increase in immigration which took place on his watch. Indeed, in the longer term this helped pave the way for Brexit, rendering the once-feted guru of Labour's miraculous recovery one of its unintended architects by pushing voters towards Nigel Farage and UKIP, or simply into not voting.

One scholar who spotted the growing apathy was Oliver Heath, who noted that whereas in the 1980s the difference in the rate of turnout between workers and the middle class had been under five points, by 2010 it had widened to nearly twenty points. This meant that the gap in turnout was as significant as that between young and old. By 2015, one year before Brexit, more than half of all workers and non-degree holders had stopped voting, a natural response to the alienation and voicelessness that we discussed in Chapter 3. Nearly 40 per cent of workers who ceased to vote felt that Labour no longer represented them. As Heath pointed out, whereas in the past the middle and working classes were divided as to which party to support, now they were divided as to whether to bother to vote at all.[25]

This is not unique to Britain. Across the West, the working class has often been more likely than other groups to abstain. In Germany, since the 1980s there has been a notable decline in the willingness of workers to vote, especially in the former East. Consistent with our discussion in Chapter 3, workers who agreed that 'politicians do not care much about what people like me think' were especially likely to give up on politics.[26] When in 2017 the Alternative for Germany shocked the world by winning more than ninety seats in parliament, its number-one source of votes were people who had generally not voted at past elections.

Interestingly, when the Brexit referendum took place in Britain a significant number of these previous abstainers returned to cast a vote, with many opting to leave the EU. One reason why some of the polls had been off was because around 2 million mainly working-class people showed up to vote who had largely avoided the opinion polls, or whose commitment had been underestimated. While turnout was lower than expected in Millennial bastions, it was higher than expected in working-class districts where people seized the opportunity to push for radical political and social reform with both hands – to demand lower immigration, reclaim powers from the EU and to regain their voice.[27]

A year after the Brexit revolt a 'normal' general election was held. Many on the left argued that the new Bernie Sanders-style radical left-wing leader of the Labour Party,

Jeremy Corbyn, would repair this relationship with workers. But it was not to be: the difference in turnout between the working class and middle class soared to a record thirty-one points.[28] While some workers returned to apathy, others defected to the Conservatives, mainly because their socially conservative values fuelled intense worries over immigration and a desire to ensure that Brexit really happened. They no longer trusted Labour.

These political contests entrenched the values divide in Britain. Though Prime Minister Theresa May and the Conservative Party were widely derided for their failure to win a commanding majority as the polls had suggested, they still enjoyed one of their strongest results for many years among the working class and non-graduates, reflecting a re-alignment of the sort that we have seen elsewhere.[29] While pro-Brexit and anti-immigration voters shifted to the Conservatives, Labour recorded particularly strong gains among Millennial graduates, culturally liberal middle-class professionals and in the big cities and university towns, illustrating how Brexit Britain looks set to witness further polarization.

The Collapse of Social Democracy

The traditional parties have been slow to recognize and respond to the way in which the West is being transformed. Although some mainstream right-wing parties in Europe have adopted national-populist-lite policies, a point we develop in the next chapter, social democrats now face a dilemma. Amid the culture conflict, how can they simultaneously hold support from the college-educated and more liberal middle class and from socially conservative blue-collar workers and traditional conservatives? In most countries, especially in Europe, social democrats have been unable to answer this question. Faced with record losses, the issue is not so much whether social democracy can again compete but rather whether it can actually survive over the longer term.

Had you perused the property magazines in Paris during the winter of 2017, your eyes would have been drawn to a rather impressive property that was up for sale. It was a historic city palace in a prime location, nearly 3,500 square metres on the city's chic Left Bank and within walking distance of the Musée d'Orsay. The price tag was in excess of a cool 30 million Euros. But for seasoned observers of French politics, the ad read more like an obituary. For decades, the grand property had been the headquarters of the French Socialists, who were now forced to sell it due to fears of bankruptcy.

This became a symbol of social democracy's woes, which were long in the making. At the end of the 1990s, social-democratic-dominated governments ruled in eleven out of the EU's then fifteen member states. But even then there were warning signs. Between 1945 and the early 1990s the mean share of the vote going to social-democratic parties in the West had fallen by twelve points. Some parties – like Blair's New Labour – managed to stage a recovery, but in the end it proved to be a temporary blip in the overall trend.

Perhaps the most spectacular decline was that of the Greek PASOK party, a regular governing party since the turn of the 1980s which had introduced reforms of the health service, greater rights for women and initially boosted wages

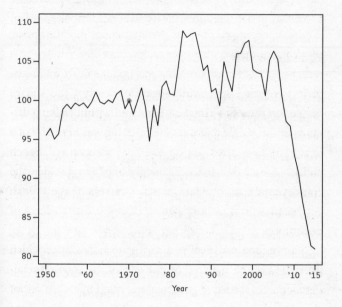

Figure 6.4

Social democratic parties' weighted share of vote

Western Europe, 1970 = 100

and benefits. It came first in national elections as recently as 2009 with almost 44 per cent of the vote, but only six years later it slumped to seventh, with less than 5 per cent. PASOK was undoubtedly affected by specific factors, including a track record of nepotism and corruption, which came to the fore in debates about the harsh conditions imposed on Greece for past 'crimes' following the Great Recession. But its decline is also part of a wider pattern.

In 2009, the Social Democrats in Germany suffered record losses, tumbling to 23 per cent of the vote, losing one-third of their support and experiencing what was then their worst result since the foundation of the Federal Republic in 1949. Some argued that a charismatic leader might have made a difference, but the underlying shifts proved more challenging. At a following election in 2017 the Social Democrats won less than 21 per cent, their worst showing in the post-war era and only slightly ahead of the party's tally during its formative period in 1890. In 2018, the Social Democrats fell to third place in several polls, behind the centre-right and the national-populist Alternative for Germany.

Or look elsewhere. In 2010, social democrats in Sweden suffered their worst result since 1921. Five years later social democrats lost power in Denmark, had their worst-ever results in Finland, Poland and Spain, and were almost subjected to the same fate in Britain. In 2017, the socialists in France, who had ruled the country since 2012, were reduced to barely 6 per cent at the presidential election and 7 per cent at legislative elections, while their number of seats crashed from 280 to just thirty. In the same year, social democrats in the Netherlands and the Czech Republic plunged to single digits and their worst results in history, while in Austria they were turfed out of power and remained on historic lows. In Italy in 2018, the centre-left vote fell below 19 per cent, compared to 34 per cent ten years earlier.

Whereas in the late 1990s social democrats had been the dominant governing force in Europe, today they are in government in only seven of the EU member states. And with the exception of Spain and Germany, where they are the junior partner, these governments are largely on Europe's periphery – Malta, Portugal, Romania, Sweden and Slovakia. Some, like Britain's Labour Party, which moved to the radical left wing, appear to have stalled the decline, but they remain out of power and it is not clear how they can sustain an alliance of groups that think fundamentally differently about the key issues of immigration, European integration and the nation.

What can explain this phenomenon? One answer is that because of the broad social changes we have explored, social democracy has increasingly found itself dependent on irreconcilable groups, some of whom no longer see their concerns as being addressed by the centre-left. Unfortunately, however, many on the left continue to misdiagnose the problem: democrats in America and social democrats in Europe maintain that this divide is really just about racism or objective economic deprivation. They believe that if they can only give workers more jobs, more growth and less austerity, then their supporters will return. They refuse to acknowledge that people's concerns about immigration and rapid ethnic change might be legitimate in their own right and that these are not simply to do with jobs.

There is no doubt that social democracy's failure to halt and reverse rising inequality has eroded its credibility in the eyes of many workers, but the idea that they are merely reacting to their economic circumstances is misleading, as we have seen. Many working-class voters are instinctively socially conservative and will never see eye to eye with the more culturally liberal sections of the centre-left.

Social democrats are now also being outflanked on another front. Unlike other parties, national populists were often the fastest to respond to people's concerns. As we noted in Chapter 1, already in the 1980s the likes of Jean-Marie Le Pen in France were speaking to workers and social conservatives who felt intensely anxious about issues like immigration and were dissatisfied with the distant traditional parties. But now many populists are also talking to these voters about economics, addressing their intense fears over relative deprivation and unbridled neoliberal globalization and demanding that politicians deliver more rights and protections to domestic workers while limiting welfare for 'outsiders' who have not paid into the system. Today, Marine Le Pen portrays herself as a great defender of workers' rights, salaries and standard of living. In Sweden, national populists present their manifestos under the title 'We Choose Welfare', promising to increase unemployment, child and sickness benefits and give the long-term unemployed jobs in municipal authorities or voluntary groups.

A key question going forward, therefore, is whether social democracy will be able to reinvent itself and build a new coalition that gives it a serious chance of returning to its former glories. It seems incredibly unlikely that social democrats will be able to win back workers unless they are prepared to modify their culturally liberal stance on immigration – and so far there is little evidence of that.

Although the Democratic Party in the US has never been social democratic in the European sense, it undoubtedly has similarities and is today facing some similar questions. Many commentators argue that a possible new 'realignment' may be taking place in US politics, one that could lead to a long-term Democratic hegemony.[30] People who are fond of this argument point to the shrinking proportion of white voters in the US, ongoing ethnic change, Millennial voters who have more liberal attitudes on cultural issues, and the rise of secular voters who often oppose the traditional 'family' and religious values that are pushed by conservative Republicans. They also point to the fact that whereas Trump was relatively stronger in rural and small-town America as opposed to the big urban centres, that population is declining – the number of inhabitants of 40 per cent of rural towns has fallen since 1980.[31]

This is certainly a seductive argument and could be taken even further to include potential splits within the Republican movement. Trump carried out a hostile takeover of the party and his (changeable) views are often out of sync with those of important elements of the Republican elite and donor base. Domestically, this includes the major issue of its desire to cut big government, including taxes and welfare. While Trump did enact major tax cuts in 2017, this was largely an existing Republican scheme, and his policies on protectionism, infrastructure spending and (vaguer) views on welfare challenge some of those within the Republican establishment.

But the picture is not quite this clear. As the political scientist Larry Bartels has shown, Trump's views are far from being out of line with those of most Republican voters, who broadly support his economic and nationalist views, especially regarding immigration.[32] Moreover, although cultural issues predominate, many agree with the concept of bigger government to provide a decent standard of living for those unable to work and to ensure access to quality health care, while a substantial minority favour reducing income differentials and helping families pay for childcare and college. For example, the Pew Research Center found in 2016 that 66 per cent of supporters of the main Republican primary candidates and Republican-leaning voters opposed future reductions in social-security benefits, with the figure rising to 73 per cent of Trump supporters (slightly more than among Clinton and Sanders supporters).[33]

Bartels further found that 26 per cent of Democrats had views on cultural issues that were closer to those of Republicans, pointing to possible future losses; he notes too that it is far from clear that Millennials' attitudes will remain unchanged in the longer term, and as we noted in Chapter 1 there remain sizeable pockets of support for national-populist politics among recent generations. Indeed, Bartels challenges the view that the Sanders' vote demonstrates widespread support for more left-wing Democratic policies, arguing that it stemmed more from factors like hostility to Hillary Clinton and the Democratic establishment. Moreover, whereas nearly 90 per cent of the African American vote in presidential elections goes to the Democrats, recent polls have shown that only 59 per cent identify with the

Democrats, and only 26 per cent describe themselves as 'liberal', compared to 27 per cent who answered 'conservative' and 44 per cent 'moderate'.[34]

More specifically, the Census Bureau forecasts that the African American population will only grow from 13 per cent in 2016 to 14 per cent by 2060. The big rise will be in Hispanics, from 17.4 to 28.6 per cent, who, as we have already noted, have a significant minority who voted for Trump (and an increasing number of whom identify as white). This helps explain the optimistic vision of Steve Bannon, Trump's former Chief Strategist, who in 2018 argued that there was much to be learned from European national populists, and that a Trump-transformed Republican Party, aligned to ordinary people's interests and which captured 60 per cent of the white vote and 40 per cent of the Hispanic and African American vote, is on its way to a fifty-year majority. This outcome seems unlikely, but so too does the claim that a new realignment in American politics will automatically benefit the Democrats. As we have seen in this chapter, we are now living in an age of major flux.

Today, a larger number of people in Europe and the US are more de-aligned than ever before; this makes them less loyal to the traditional parties and more open to new challengers such as national populists. These changes have coincided with a new culture conflict in the West, rooted in divides over values, which is unlikely to disappear in the near future. Immigration, European integration, rights for minorities and specific issues like Islam will not only continue to expose these value divides but will also cut across the electorates of the old parties and make it harder for them to cobble together election-winning majorities, which is especially true for traditional social-democratic parties in Europe.

A growing number of people today are searching for new political homes, while others have withdrawn into apathy. This is fuelling the rise of new parties and giving them a durability that many observers, who remain fixated on the short term, continue to underestimate. When seen as a whole, de-alignment represents another significant and long-term challenge to the mainstream.

As Western democracies transitioned into the early years of the twenty-first century, a growing number of voters were turning to parties that had not existed when our political systems were created. The dividing lines of politics are in a process of fundamental transformation and will continue to evolve in the years ahead. The established political class has been far too slow to respond. National populists are a by-product of this change; they were among the first to recognize the backlash and to articulate a response that was, for key groups of voters, both resonant and compelling. Liberals were, in some cases rightly, criticized for having ignored the new reality.

Towards
Post-Populism

National populists are being driven forward by the deep-rooted 'Four Ds' that often lay hidden in our day-to-day debates. In the short term, this will give them an ongoing and large reservoir of potential support. While they might not necessarily win elections, and their following will ebb and flow, 'the fundamentals' behind this phenomenon look set to remain in place for many years to come.

This is not to say that the national populists themselves will be the main beneficiaries, however. Rather, over the longer term, and as the West transitions into an era of 'post-populism', it may be that the real winners will be those we call 'national populist-lite', an argument that we develop in this chapter.

We started the book by noting how, across the West, the rise of controversial populists like Trump, Le Pen, Farage, Wilders or Orbán is routinely traced to short-term factors, for example the post-2008 Great Recession, the post-2014 refugee crisis, or to particular election campaigns. This narrow perspective encourages writers and thinkers to see these revolts as a passing phase in the history of liberal democracy – flash protests that will soon disappear once stability and 'normal' times resume.

This assumption runs through our public debates. Trump voters will drift back to the mainstream once they realize that he is mentally unfit for the highest office, or when his links to Russia are exposed. The Leavers who voted for Brexit will change their minds once Britain's economy takes a tumble, while in Europe national populists will run out of steam as soon as economic growth returns. More broadly, these rebellions will fade once their 'old white men' voters are replaced by cosmopolitan Millennials.

These are comforting narratives, but they are very misleading. We are not denying that recent major shocks in the West, like the Great Recession and the refugee crisis, are important. These seismic events exacerbated the divides between different groups in society, inflaming tensions and encouraging more people to look around the political marketplace. But these divides, as we have seen, opened up long ago, decades before the fall of Lehman Brothers, the arrival of austerity or Angela Merkel's fateful decision to allow more than a million refugees into Germany.

The factors that paved the way for national populism are woven deeply into the fabric of our nations. They are rooted in the contradictions between the functioning of democracy at the national level and an increasingly global economic market, a long and entrenched tradition of elite suspicion of the masses, latent and fairly widespread nationalist sentiment and the long-term erosion of the relationship between citizens and parties. These deep roots are unlikely to be removed by the latest macroeconomic data, or a particular campaign. Rather, the rise of national populism reflects a far more significant shift in the evolution of our (still young) liberal democracies. This is why we asked readers to step back and take in the broad view, to look at how democracy, the nation, the economy and people's feelings about the traditional parties have evolved over a much longer period of time.

The 'Four Ds'

Much of our focus has been on the key 'bottom-up' trends, or what scholars call the 'demand-side'– the fundamental currents that shape the way that people see the world around them. Critics might argue that we have not looked enough at the 'supply side', at how national populists themselves tap into these currents, how charismatic leaders communicate with the people, how they and their opponents navigate specific elections, or how the media – both old and new – cover these issues.

These short-term factors are important and will be looked at by others. But they can also be distractions, leading us away from acknowledging and exploring the more fundamental shifts that are changing the political world around us. Individual elections come and go, as do party leaders and presidents. The national-populist tradition can be traced back to an era long before Trump, Brexit and Marine Le Pen, yet much of the debate would have you believe that what was said on the campaign trail or written on the side of a bus made all the difference in the world.

In terms of these deep roots, we have argued that four broad transformations have been key: people's *distrust* of the increasingly elitist nature of liberal democracy, which has

271

fuelled a feeling among many that they no longer have a voice in the conversation, and which is likely to spur their support for a more 'direct' model of democracy; ongoing anxieties about the *destruction* of the nation that have been sharpened by rapid immigration and a new era of hyper ethnic change, which raise legitimate questions as well as xenophobic fears; strong concerns about relative *deprivation* resulting from the shift towards an increasingly unequal economic settlement, which has stoked the correct belief that some groups are being unfairly left behind relative to others, and fears about the future; and the rise of *de-alignment* from the traditional parties, which has rendered our political systems more volatile and larger numbers of people 'available' to listen to new promises, while others have retreated into apathy.

The 'Four Ds' have left large numbers of people in the West instinctively receptive to the claims being made by national populism: that politicians do not listen to them, even treat them with contempt, that immigrants and ethnic minorities benefit at the expense of 'natives', and that hyper ethnic change and in particular Islam pose a new and major threat to the national group, its culture and way of life.

We have also seen how these are far from fringe concerns. Sometimes more than half of the populations in the West express views that are broadly in line with national populism. But over the past three decades liberal-left politicians and commentators have routinely underestimated the reach and potency of national populism, dismissing it as a narrow refuge for 'old white men', ignorant racists or anti-democrats who, like the inter-war fascists, want to tear down political institutions.

National populists have attracted a relatively broad-based following. These supporters are not 'all the same', even though they are often treated this way. Republicans on above-average incomes who sided with Trump have very different life stories to their struggling blue-collar counter-parts, in some cases former Democrats, who despite previously voting for Barack Obama were attracted to Trump's opposition to immigration and his call to make America great again. Similarly, affluent middle-class Conservatives who voted for Brexit in prosperous areas have led very different lives from the workers who also backed Brexit in left-behind coastal towns like Clacton, Great Yarmouth or Grimsby. The managers and secure professionals who vote for the Swiss People's Party are quite different from the struggling workers who vote for the Sweden Democrats, or the rural and small-town voters who heavily back the Hungarian Fidesz Party.

But there are some common threads. We have looked at the big picture without reducing complex movements to narrow debates that seek out 'one factor', for example by focusing only on the white working class. We have also sought a middle way between simplistic arguments about 'economics versus culture' and narratives that completely ignore the important impact of political factors stemming from public hostility towards liberal elitism.

While the supporters of national populism often have different life experiences, were they to sit down for a beer or glass of wine and discuss politics, they would agree on much. They would share a similar outlook, which has been shaped by their educational experiences, values and worries about social and cultural loss, not only in terms of what this means for themselves but also their wider group. They would no doubt concur about the need to push back against the rise of the New Left and liberal identity politics that began during the 1960s. They would also most likely agree that their wider national group is being left behind relative to others in society, that immigration and rapid ethnic change are damaging the nation, and that untrustworthy elites in the mainstream, who did not respond to these issues or, even worse, actively encouraged them, are too quick to ridicule or dismiss their opponents as 'deplorables', 'fruitcakes', even 'fascists' and/or 'racists'.

They would also feel firmly at odds with the growing number of graduates and more liberal-minded middle-class professionals who hold what they see as self-evident truths about immigration, minority rights, European integration and unrestricted free trade. National populists tend to view their national community from a more restricted perspective, highlighting the critical importance of ethnic ancestry – or at least shared customs and values which can be forged in 'melting pots', as US history shows. In part this reflects a common desire to live among one's own people but, as scholars like David Miller have argued, a strong, shared national identity also lies at the heart of what many see as desirable goals, such as redistributing from the rich to the poor and sustaining the inter-generational contract, whereby people today accept the need to pay tax to help others in society or future generations.[1]

Not all national populists see the world in this way, but many do. And crucially, their values are far more important in explaining their political choices than *objective* economic indicators like how much money they earn or whether they are unemployed – indeed, most of these voters, as we have seen, are working full-time and are often skilled. It is their *subjective* feelings of relative deprivation which are a particularly powerful influence on how they perceive the world, both personally and in terms of groups with whom they identify.

Those with fewer qualifications and more traditionalist values are far more alarmed about how their societies are changing: they fear the eventual destruction of their community and identity, they believe that both they and their group are losing out, and distrust their increasingly distant representatives. National populists spoke to these voters, albeit in ways that many dislike. For the first time in years, their supporters now feel as though they have agency in the debate. Thus we saw past 'non-voters' returning to politics to cast a vote for Brexit or the Alternative for Germany. In the future it may well be that more of these non-voters return to voting, depending on whether populists are able to deliver in office, a point we return to later.

These voters are often misleadingly portrayed as protestors who want to rebel *against* the system. Certainly, this is part of national populism's appeal, especially the way in which many reject post-material concerns which focus on issues such as women's and LGBT rights. But this is only one element of the equation, as most agree with the broadly conservative vision of society that is being promised – although 'conservative' in this context can sometimes be relatively liberal where this feature is seen as part of the national identity:

hence populists like Wilders strongly defend women's and gay rights. They seek to preserve or restore the dominance of the national group, including its customs and traditions, to live in a country which accepts fewer immigrants and has slower rates of ethnic change, and a state which has more power while transnational bodies like the EU have less. But in terms of economics they want changes to be made to the current unfair settlement. And in terms of politics they are more radical, though not extremist, seeking to live in a democratic system but one in which their voice is louder and matters, and in which there are more politicians who look and sound like them – or ones who at least take them seriously.

The last point is an important caveat, as most national-populist leaders do not come from working-class backgrounds. Trump flaunted his wealth during his rise to the White House as proof not only of his celebrity status but also his long-standing business talent, which could be transferred to Washington to 'drain the swamp'. Nigel Farage, though less wealthy, drew attention to his previous career as a trader in the City of London, contrasting himself with 'careerist' politicians who he argued had spent their lives in Westminster. Although some national populists support economic policies which have much in common with the historic left, the vast majority of their voters are not seeking a highly egalitarian society. Rather, they want what they see as a *fair* one, fair in the way in which the national group is prioritized over immigrants in fields like employment and welfare, fair in terms of their economic rewards, and fair in terms of how other countries trade and deal with their nation.

These views are unlikely to disappear or soften. Populists

will continue to enjoy ongoing potential support. Consider some of the strong winds that were sweeping through public opinion as we finished this book. As Democrats in the US debated how to bounce back from their loss to Trump, the polling company Ipsos-MORI surveyed nearly 18,000 adults around the world and found that on average only one in four felt that immigration has had a positive impact on their nation, a figure which tumbled to 14 per cent in France, 10 per cent in Italy and 5 per cent in Hungary. As Britain grappled with the Brexit vote, surveys suggested that more than half of its population felt that the government 'did not care much what people like me think'. As Germany came to terms with the first major national-populist breakthrough in its post-war history, 60 per cent of its people told pollsters that Islam did not belong in their country (a view then publicly endorsed by the country's new Interior Minister).

Supporters of national populism have also been more loyal to the movement than was initially predicted by many columnists, who talked of flash protests. In the shadow of his election, Trump's overall approval ratings soon slumped to some of the lowest levels on record. Yet they concealed big differences: while only 15 per cent of non-white women with a degree approved of their new president, this soared to 67 per cent of white men without a degree. In early 2018, only 4 per cent of Hillary Clinton's voters approved of Trump, compared to 91 per cent of his own voters.[2]

Similarly, after the Brexit vote it was widely predicted that those who had voted to leave the EU would change their minds and begin to voice 'Bregret' – an assumption made on the basis of narrow arguments about economic self-interest. Pundits contended that dissatisfaction with Brexit would be heightened by a sharp decline in the value of the pound, a rise in inflation that would eat into household income and the fact that it was soon clear that there would be no quick and easy exit from the EU.

Yet public opinion has remained remarkably stable. In the spring of 2018 the Brits were asked whether in hindsight the Brexit vote had been 'right or wrong' and they were still split down the middle, as they had been since the referendum (42 per cent said right, 45 per cent said wrong). These figures masked big divides: the percentage that felt Brexit was right ranged from 4 per cent among Remainers and 19 per cent among those aged between eighteen and twenty-four to 61 per cent among pensioners, 64 per cent among Conservatives and 82 per cent among Leavers.[3] There has been no mass 'Bregret'. If anything, most Leavers are singing 'Je ne bregrette rien'. Britain is divided and will remain so for years.

Liberals often respond by arguing that if national populists got what they wanted, then the result would be lower economic growth. But, as we have seen, many of those who turn to national populists would happily be a little poorer if it meant they had more control over their nation and more of a voice. Many voters do not think in transactional terms about costs and benefits, gross domestic product, jobs or growth. If they did, then responding to populism would be much easier. Instead, they attach as much value, if not more, to community, belonging, group identity and the nation – and it is these deeper concerns that will need to be addressed. But so far, very few people on the liberal left seem interested in engaging in these conversations, preferring to dismiss such worries as racism and move quickly on.

We can further explore the space for national populism by considering three points about the future. The first concerns political inequality, which will likely become *more* rather than *less* apparent. Look at the stellar rise of Emmanuel Macron, whom many saw as a counter-punch against populism. Yet Macron's movement reflects the problematic currents that we have explored, including a political elite that looks increasingly insular and detached from the experiences of most people. While the average French household possesses assets worth around 160,000 Euros, one in three of Macron's ministers were millionaires, some of whom held multi-millions worth of assets in shares and properties and were far richer than even the top 10 per cent, a divide that had also been visible in the previous 'socialist' government, which counted fourteen millionaires among thirty-nine ministers.[4] Among his top appointments, several came from the traditional centre-right, including the Prime Minister and Economics Minister. Furthermore, when Macron announced that he would try to fend off populism and revive support for the EU by launching consultations with citizens, observers who went along found an 'empty publicity stunt'; panel discussions replaced citizen-led debate while most of those who attended were students, university faculty members and civil servants working on EU-related issues.[5]

Or consider Britain's Brexit debate and the rise of the radical left-winger Jeremy Corbyn. One obvious reply to the Brexit vote would have been to trigger a national debate about how to radically reform the nation's political, social and economic settlement in order to begin to grapple with some of the underlying grievances. Should the first-past-the-post electoral system, which renders large numbers of votes in safe seats meaningless, be replaced with a more proportional system? Which of the country's major economic, political or civic institutions that are concentrated in London should be moved into other regions in order to try to address people's profound sense that both they and their communities have been cut adrift and to connect them with the broader civic culture? How should the country reform its very unpopular immigration policy? And how can Britain revive the fortunes of incredibly disadvantaged coastal and northern industrial communities where, for obvious reasons, large majorities concluded they would rather roll the dice on a new but unknown settlement than continue with the current one? But instead of asking such questions and triggering some much-needed reform, much of the debate focused on what London wants and what financial institutions in the City want.

Though some have seen Corbyn's revitalization of the Labour Party as a reaction against the way in which politics has become increasingly centralized and careerist, it has proposed little that will promote a broad and genuinely grassroots-led rejuvenation of democracy. Given these examples, it is difficult to avoid the conclusion that a profound sense of political frustration will remain.

The second point is the continuing impact of immigration and hyper ethnic change. We have seen how supporters of national populism are far more likely than others to see the nation as a critical part of who they are. In some cases, especially in Eastern Europe, they feel that membership of their nation should be restricted to those who were born in the country and share its customs and traditions. But elsewhere, this conception of national identity does not always preclude taking in new members who are willing to adapt to what have always in practice been changing conceptions of national identity. For example, British national identity prior to 1945 did not encompass any conception of 'blackness', as there were only a small number of black people in the country. But today you need only look at the composition of national sports teams, pop-music bands or television programmes to see how this has changed, especially for Afro-Caribbeans.

Nevertheless, although such updates to the perception of national identity are widely accepted, many people feel intensely anxious about recent high levels of immigration and ethnic change, which they see as damaging the nation. While many of these fears are exaggerated – especially in the case of Muslims, who as a group are often damned for the sins of a very small minority of Islamists – we need to appreciate how people feel. Given ongoing immigration and rapidly rising rates of ethnic, cultural and religious change, it seems to us unlikely that these anxieties will fade.

It is important to try to engage with their concerns, particularly for those on the centre-left who, to avoid further losses, will need to make short-term concessions. Meeting the demand for tighter borders or modifying the *type* of immigration (i.e. prioritizing high-skilled migrants, international students and people who contribute to public services) is compatible with progressive politics. Simply making the case for open borders and endless low-skilled and non-contributory forms of immigration will only push parties further towards electoral irrelevance, or leave them dependent on only small numbers of New Left true believers. Certainly, this will not be easy given factors such as communal segregation in countries like Britain and France and the tendency among many national-populist voters to resent any form of 'lecturing' by people they see as liberal elites. But unless the mainstream can find a way of sparking a new debate about immigration reform, it will cede even more ground to populists.

The third ongoing factor relates to relative deprivation. In some countries like Britain there are signs that wages are beginning to rise, but in general inequalities remain high and factors like automation and globalization pose serious issues for the future of not only the less skilled but also growing number of middle-class workers. It is also worth reminding ourselves of the importance of the educational divide, one of the key factors in national populism. In many countries in the West non-degree holders remain (and often by far) the largest group, including in key states in the US, which underlines why liberal progressives cannot afford to ignore these voters. In 2014, whereas people aged between twenty-five and sixty-four who had completed higher education numbered 40 per cent in countries like Britain, the figure was only 20 per cent in Italy. While record levels of American students are getting their high-school diplomas, rates of college enrolment have stalled or even decreased, despite increases in federal aid for students who cannot afford tuition.[6] If you accept that the educational divide is key, then when you step back and look at the long-term trends it is clear that not only will there be potential support for national populists going forward but also that the traditional parties will need to work much harder to build new bridges with non-degree holders.

Those with high levels of education tend to be more liberal on cultural issues, but the expansion of higher education potentially has a negative corollary. This is the paradox of equality whereby, for example, as the numbers in British further education move towards 50 per cent, another form of left-behind has been created among the rest. Even where participation in higher education is lower, as in France, there is resentment towards elite academic institutions. In spite of this, in 2017 Macron proposed a new set of European super-universities, where teaching would be in at least two languages and which would create a greater European 'sense of belonging'. The view among much of the educated elite which sees itself as key to driving forward the 'European project' remains strong. Solving the problem of relative deprivation, therefore, is not simply a question of trying to raise wages or employment levels, but relates to much wider issues about social integration and respect – issues which, again, will not be easy to solve in the coming years.

National Populism-Lite

However, the strength and future trajectory of national populism should not only be measured *directly* by counting how many potential supporters it has, or whether it wins elections. This is because national-populist challengers are also having powerful *indirect* effects by pushing many of the West's political systems and the mainstream further to the right, especially as they seek to halt the de-alignment which is taking place and build (sometimes new) support.

While their social-democratic rivals have been troubled by how to respond to national populism, many conservatives in Europe have been willing to adopt aspects of the national-populist agenda. This is partly because they are closer ideologically than the centre-left on key issues and so find it easier to build a bridge to voters who have concerns about law and order or immigration. Social democrats need to come up with an entirely new approach and put themselves in uncomfortable territory. Conservatives, in sharp contrast, can just turn up the volume, adopting varieties of national-populist-lite programmes and rhetoric, though ones that mainly focus on immigration and ethnicity.

This has been a common tactic in Europe for some time. During the 2007 presidential election in France, the first since Jean-Marie Le Pen had stunned the world by finishing second in 2002, the centre-right candidate Nicolas Sarkozy promised a quota system to manage immigration and argued that all immigrants should be required to learn French, stressing he would act rather than just talk. This time, Le Pen did not make it to the final round, when 70 per cent of his voters switched to Sarkozy.

In Britain, the growing support won by Nigel Farage and UKIP, which fused anti-immigration with anti-EU sentiment, had a dramatic effect on both the Conservatives and British political history. The first-past-the-post system meant that winning nearly 13 per cent of the vote translated into just two seats in the House of Commons in 2015, but this support, combined with pressure from anti-EU Conservatives, induced Prime Minister David Cameron to call the Brexit referendum.[7] After the Brexit victory Cameron promptly resigned, and the new Conservative Prime Minister, Theresa May, adopted other Farage policies – stating not only that 'Brexit must mean Brexit', but also that immigration must be reduced and criticizing liberal cosmopolitan 'citizens of nowhere'. The Conservative Party went UKIP-lite. UKIP's vote slumped after Farage stood down as leader, feeling, like many former voters, that the party's main task was complete. Most UKIP voters then started to vote Conservative, which further dragged the working class and non-graduates away from Corbyn's radical left-wing Labour.

In 2017 the people also went to the polls in the Netherlands, where Geert Wilders and his Party for Freedom had long been one of Europe's fiercest critics of Islam (a message he regularly took to the US). Wilders demanded that his country ban further Muslim immigration and sales of the Quran, claimed that 'Moroccan scum' were making Dutch streets unsafe, and contrasted help given to immigrants with the impact of austerity on poorer Dutch people. To restore more say to the people, he also promised a referendum on EU membership. Polls suggested that Wilders was on course to be leader of the largest party, but shortly before the election the mainstream conservative Prime Minister, Mark Rutte, wrote an open letter. In this he talked of a breakdown of social order and stated: 'We are feeling a growing unease when people abuse our freedom . . . [People who] harass gays, howl at women in short skirts or accuse ordinary Dutch of being racists . . . If you reject our country in such a fundamental manner, I'd rather see you leave.' Rutte's party leapfrogged Wilders into first place and he returned as Prime Minister.

The Austrian national-populist Freedom Party began the same year with a double-digit lead over the traditional parties. Its programme included a new law that would prohibit 'fascistic Islam', and called the religion 'misogynistic' and 'anti-liberal'. Against the background of the refugee crisis, which led to the Alpine state receiving the third-highest rate of asylum applications in Europe, the Freedom Party demanded zero immigration. The centre-right People's Party had been taken over by thirty-one-year-old Sebastian Kurz, who styled himself as an outsider, but, unlike the centrist newcomer Emmanuel Macron, he appealed directly to national-populist voters. The conservative Kurz warned that the refugee crisis had brought immigrants whose views 'have no place in our country . . . (including) anti-Semitism . . . who reject our way of living, who are against equality between men and women'.[8] Rather than support the EU plan to distribute the refugees evenly across member states through a quota system, Kurz – like Viktor Orbán in Hungary and others – argued that the EU should strengthen its external borders and focus more energy on stopping refugees and immigrants from coming at all. Against this backdrop Kurz went on to win the election, and subsequently forged a coalition government with the national-populist Freedom Party whose leader, Heinz-Christian Strache, became Deputy Prime Minister.

Further evidence of a rightward drift comes from the

scholars Markus Wagner and Thomas Meyer, who looked at how the rise of national populism has had a broader and more profound impact on political debates in Europe since the 1980s. They expected one of two things to have happened. On the one hand, the quest for success might have led national populists to moderate over time, becoming more like the mainstream. This idea fits with the argument that we do not really need to worry about populists because they will be 'tamed' by liberal democracy and/or splits will emerge over issues such as whether to co-operate with the mainstream. On the other hand, national populists might have stayed true to their principles, while also dragging the entire political system over to the right.

What did they find? After studying more than 500 manifestos from nearly seventy parties in seventeen democracies, and over more than three decades, they found strong evidence that the mainstream in Europe has absorbed the national-populist agenda, moving away from liberal issues and towards more 'authoritarian' social positions, such as adopting a tougher stance on law and order and clamping down on immigration (see Figure 7.1). Facing national populists who in some cases had become *more* radical, the mainstream not only talked more about issues like immigration but moved further to the right.[9]

In America, the situation is different because we have not seen an insurgent national-populist party emerge fully outside of the traditional party system. Nevertheless, there are parallels in the case of the eclectic Tea Party movement, which as we have seen combined conservative, libertarian and populist forms of Republicanism. The movement was

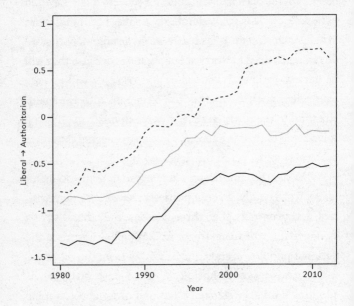

Figure 7.1
Mean positions on liberal–authoritarion issues for
mainstream and national populist parties

----- Radical right
——— Mainstream parties: right
——— Mainstream parties: left

formed in the wake of the financial crisis, but soon broadened its focus on big-government bailouts to 'corrupt' bankers, to staging racist and xenophobic opposition to President Obama and immigration, and a defence of traditional values, including evangelical Christianity. Trump almost certainly learned from the differing appeals of these promises.

His 2016 campaign commitments to 'drain the swamp', cut immigration, spend on infrastructure and attack 'unfair' trade mark him out from the views of almost all the free-market Republican establishment. However, popular support for such policies revealed that there were constituencies which Republicans had previously failed to penetrate, even though the party had been gaining working-class votes since the collapse of the Democratic South in the 1960s and the rise of the 'Reagan coalition' which included workers from well beyond this region by the 1980s.

Nevertheless, most commentators expected Trump to fail on all major fronts, possibly splitting the Republican Party along the way. Robert Reich argues that 'Trump's presidency has been, first and foremost, about marketing Trump' and that he has 'never cared about public policy'.[10] He is widely seen as unlikely to lead to a realignment of Republican politics ideologically, even if he had greater political skills. Critics see him as unable to build another presidential winning coalition that might deliver change, as his core support comes from declining groups such as those in rural areas, while his erratic populist side is alienating major donors. Moreover, strong hostility towards him personally means there is little hope of attracting significant numbers of new voters.

At the same time, powerful forces like ethnic minorities,

women and the more educated are lining up in even greater numbers behind the Democrats, groups which Trump's critics hold will be bolstered by Republican deserters from similar socio-economic milieus. However, as we noted in the last chapter, 26 per cent of Democrat supporters are closer to the Republicans on cultural issues, far more than Republicans who are closer to Democrats. If the Democrats take a stronger line supporting extensive immigration and minority rights, the results could be further significant losses. Indeed, the commentator Fareed Zakaria rightly recommends that the 'party should take a position on immigration that is less absolutist and recognizes both the cultural and economic costs of large-scale immigration'.[11]

And what if Trump does deliver on some of his promises? National Guard troops have already been deployed to patrol America's southern border with Mexico. Certainly, immigration is likely to be reduced, which may harm business and push up prices, but many supporters would accept this unless the impact was major. Moreover, the first year of Trump's presidency witnessed improvements in key economic indicators, including signs of new investment following tax cuts and rising wages. There is a risk that introducing tariffs will create a disastrous trade war with China and others, but it might also trigger a wider surge of patriotism as Trump frames his policy as an attempt to defend precarious workers against unbridled global markets. It could even encourage countries like China to trade more fairly.

In this case, the Trump brand, instead of being toxic, might be an attractive 'franchise' for less abrasive local Republicans competing in areas where there is extensive national-populist potential. There would be a powerful impetus towards a national-populist-lite form of Republicanism, especially as most of its voters care far more about cultural issues than the free-market economic beliefs of the party establishment and its major donors, as we noted in the previous chapter. Indeed, many Republicans support a vision of government that extends well beyond the minimalist views of the libertarians.

Parties in Europe are typically more centralized and controlled by party elites, so they are less open to being captured by outsiders and renegades, but similar dynamics are at play. Leaders and parties that have so far ruled out any form of direct co-operation with national populists may over the coming years shift further towards national-populist territory. Look at the centre-right in France, which in 2017 failed even to make the final round of the presidential election and then suffered a dramatic loss of support in the following legislative elections. At the end of 2017, the Republicans chose as their leader Laurent Wauquiez, whose politics involves a strong national-populist-lite focus on identity, immigration and Islam. This in itself is unlikely to win back all of the lost voters, but it is yet another example of how the rise of Marine Le Pen and national populism, and the shifting political landscape, is pushing parties in the mainstream further to the right.

Certainly, we have shown how national populism is based on deep-rooted factors which are not going to disappear in the near future. Indeed, in some ways they are strengthening the national-populist base. However, in future 'success' might come more in the shape of national-populist-lite parties and politicians, especially if they are willing to adopt a broad swathe of national-populist policies.

By word of final conclusion we will stress just one point. National populism, in whatever form, will have a powerful effect on the politics of many Western countries for many years to come.

Notes

INTRODUCTION

1. CNN/Kaiser Family Foundation poll, September 2016. British data taken from the British Social Attitudes survey.

2. Matthew Karnitschnig, 'Steve Bannon populist roadshow hits Europe', *Politico Europe*, 6 March 2018. Available at: https://www.politico.eu/article/steve-bannon-populism-donald-trump-i-still-love-the-guy/ (accessed 9 March 2018).

3. David Frum, *Trumpocracy: The Corruption of the American Republic* (New York: HarperCollins, 2018).

4. Bandy Lee (ed.), *The Dangerous Case of Donald Trump* (New York: Thomas Dunne Books, 2017); Paul Krugman, 'Trump's deadly narcissism', *The New York Times*, 29 September 2017.

5. Jake Horowitz, 'Bernard-Henri Lévy: Le Pen will not win because: "France is not ready for a fascist regime"', *Mic*, 21 April 2017. Available at: https://mic.com/articles/174291/bernard-henri-levy-marine-le-pen-french-france-election-fascist#.x5Bif18Es (accessed 6 January 2018); Isobel Thompson, 'Can Marine Le Pen make fascism mainstream?', *Vanity Fair*, 25 April 2017. Available at: https://www.vanityfair.com/news/2017/04/can-marine-le-pen-go-mainstream (accessed 6 January 2018).

6. Ruth Ben-Ghiat, 'Donald Trump and Steve Bannon's coup in the making', CNN *Opinion*, 1 February 2017. Available at: http://edition.cnn.com/2017/02/01/opinions/bannon-trump-coup-opinion-ben-ghiat/index.html (accessed 3 February 2017); Timothy Snyder, *On Tyranny: Twenty Lessons from the Twentieth Century* (London: Bodley Head, 2017), p. 45 and p. 71. For a comparative assessment, see Steven Levitsky and Daniel Ziblatt,

How Democracies Die: What History Reveals About Our Future (New York: Viking, 2018).

7. John B. Judis, *The Populist Explosion: How the Great Recession Transformed American and European Politics* (New York: Columbia Global Reports, 2016); Ronald F. Inglehart and Pippa Norris, 'Trump, Brexit, and the rise of populism: economic have-nots and cultural backlash' (2016). Available at: https://papers.ssrn.com/sol3/papers.cfm?abstract_id=2818659 (accessed 23 February 2017).

8. Ipsos-MORI Thinks (2017), 'Millennial. Myths and realities'. Available at: https://www.ipsos.com/sites/default/files/2017-05/ipsos-mori-millennial-myths-realities-full-report.pdf (accessed 20 October 2017).

9. Pew Research Center, 'The generation gap in American politics', 1 March 2018. Available at: http://www.people-press.org/2018/03/01/the-generation-gap-in-american-politics/ (accessed 9 March 2018).

CHAPTER 1: MYTHS

1. Nate Silver, 'The mythology of Trump's "working class support"', FiveThirtyEight, 3 May 2016. Available at: https://fivethirtyeight.com/features/the-mythology-of-trumps-working-class-support/l (accessed 21 October 2017); also Emma Green, 'It was cultural anxiety that drove white, working-class voters to Trump', *The Atlantic*, 9 May 2017.

2. Matt Grossmann, 'Racial attitudes and political correctness in the 2016 presidential election', Niskanen Center, 10 May 2018. Available at: https://niskanencenter.org/blog/racial-attitudes-and-political-correctness-in-the-2016-presidential-election/ (accessed 24 May 2018); also Diana C. Mutz, 'Status threat, not economic hardship, explains the 2016 presidential vote', *Proceedings of the National Academy of Sciences*, published online April 2018. Available at: http://www.pnas.org/content/early/2018/04/18/1718155115 (accessed 24 May 2018).

3. NatCen (2016), 'Understanding the leave vote', National Centre for Social Research, London. NatCen estimates that the average Brexit vote was 66 per cent among those on monthly incomes of less than £1,200, 57 per cent among those on £1,201–£2,200 and 51 per cent among those on £2,201–£3,700. The average income at the time of the referendum was £27,600, or a monthly income of approximately £1,800 after tax.

4. Martin Wolf, 'The economic origins of the populist surge', *Financial Times*, 27 June 2017; Michael Jacobs and Mariana Mazzucato, 'The Brexit-Trump syndrome: it's the economics, stupid', London School of Economics British Politics and Policy Blog, 21 November 2016. Available at: http://blogs.lse. ac.uk/politicsandpolicy/the-brexit-trump-syndrome/ (accessed 1 November 2017).

5. Daniel Stockemer, 'Structural data on immigration or immigration perceptions? What accounts for the electoral success of the radical right in Europe?', *Journal of Common Market Studies*, 54(4) (2016), pp. 999–1016.

6. Janan Ganesh, 'Authenticity is the political snake oil of our age', *Financial Times*, 11 September 2017.

7. Matthew Fowler, Vladimir Medenica and Cathy J. Cohen, 'Why 41 percent of white millennials voted for Trump', *Washington Post*, Monkey Cage blog, 15 December 2017. Available at: https://www.washingtonpost.com/ news/monkey-cage/wp/2017/12/15/racial-resentment-is-why-41-percent-of-white-millennials-voted-for-trump-in-2016/?utm_term=.508ee92e4970 (accessed 5 January 2018).

8. Robert Ford and Matthew Goodwin, *Revolt on the Right: Explaining Support for the Radical Right in Britain* (Abingdon: Routledge, 2014).

9. On France, data taken from the final Ifop-Fiducial polls before the first and second round of voting. On Germany data taken from the Institute for Social Research and Consulting. Available at: http://www.sora. at/fileadmin/downloads/wahlen/2016_BP-Wiederholung_Grafiken-Wahltagsbefragung.pdf.

10. Pew Research Center, 'The generation gap in American politics', 1 March 2018. Available at: http://www.people-press.org/2018/03/01/the-generation-gap-in-american-politics/ (accessed 9 March 2018).

11. Jean Twenge, *iGen: Why Today's Super-connected Kids Are Growing up Less Rebellious, More Tolerant, Less Happy and Completely Unprepared for Adulthood* (New York: Atria Books, 2017). See also YouGov Survey Results (2018). Available at: https://d25d2506sfb94s.cloudfront.net/cumulus_ uploads/document/dqjh8rbx2e/InternalResults_180425_Immigration.pdf (accessed 24 May 2018).

12. James Tilley and Geoffrey Evans, 'Ageing and generational effects on vote choice: Combining cross-sectional and panel data to estimate APC effects', *Electoral Studies*, 33(1) (2014), pp. 19–27.

13. Abdelkarim Amengay, Anja Durovic and Nonna Mayer, 'L'impact du gendre sur le vote Marine Le Pen', *Revue Française de Science Politique*, 67(6) (2017), pp. 1067–87.

14. Stanley B. Greenberg, *America Ascendant: a Revolutionary Nation's Path to Addressing its Deepest Problems and Leading the 21st Century* (New York: Thomas Dunne Books, 2015).

15. J. D. Vance, *Hillbilly Elegy: a Memoir of a Family and Culture in Crisis* (New York: Harper, 2016).

16. Emily Ekins, 'The five types of Trump voters', Voter Study Group, June 2017. Available at: https://www.voterstudygroup.org/publications/2016-elections/the-five-types-trump-voters (accessed 11 December 2017).

17. NatCen (2016), 'Understanding the leave vote', National Centre for Social Research, London.

18. On working-class support for national populism, see Daniel Oesch, 'Explaining workers' support for right-wing populist parties in Western Europe: Evidence from Austria, Belgium, France, Norway, and Switzerland', *International Political Science Review*, 29(3) (2008), pp. 349–73; and Jocelyn A. J. Evans, 'The dynamics of social change in radical right-wing populist party support', *Comparative European Politics*, 3(1) (2005), pp. 76–101; Jens Rydgren (ed.), *Class Politics and the Radical Right* (Abingdon: Routledge, 2012).

19. While Clinton added around nine points to Obama's 2012 vote in the vast majority of the fifty most highly educated counties, she retreated by around eleven points in the vast majority of the least educated ones, many of which were in key states like Ohio and North Carolina. See Rob Griffin, Ruy Texeira and John Halpin, 'Voter trends in 2016: A final examination', Center for American Progress, 1 November 2017. Available at: https://www.americanprogress.org/issues/democracy/reports/2017/11/01/441926/voter-trends-in-2016/ (accessed 22 November 2017); also Nate Silver, 'Education, not income, predicted who would vote for Trump', *FiveThirtyEight*, 22 November 2016. Available at: http://fivethirtyeight.com/features/education-not-income-predicted-who-would-vote-for-trump/ (accessed 12 December 2016).

20. Similarly, while support for Remain reached 70 per cent among degree-holders aged over fifty-five, for people in the same age bracket but who did not have a degree it slumped to 30 per cent. Matthew Goodwin and Oliver Heath, *Brexit Vote Explained: Poverty, Low Skills and Lack of Opportunities* (London: Joseph Rowntree Foundation 2016); see also NatCen, 'The vote to leave the EU: Litmus test or lightning rod?', *British Social Attitudes* 34. Available at: http://www.bsa.natcen.ac.uk/media/39149/bsa34_brexit_final.pdf (accessed 8 January 2018).

21. Data taken from the final Ifop Fiducial poll, 5 May 2017. Available at: http://dataviz.ifop.com:8080/IFOP_ROLLING/IFOP_05-05-2017.pdf (accessed 20 June 2018).

22. Rob Griffin, Ruy Texeira and John Halpin, 'Voter trends in 2016: A final examination', Center for American Progress, 1 November 2017. Available at: https://www.americanprogress.org/issues/democracy/reports/2017/11/01/441926/voter-trends-in-2016/ (accessed 1 December 2018).

23. For evidence of the importance of the socialization experience of education, see Rune Stubager, 'Education effects on authoritarian-libertarian values: a question of socialization', *The British Journal of Sociology*, 59(2) (2008), pp. 327–50; J. Phelan, B. Link, A. Stueve, and R. Moore, 'Education, social liberalism and economic conservatism: Attitudes toward homeless people', *American Sociological Review*, 60(1) (1995), pp. 126–40; Paula Surridge, 'Education and liberalism: pursuing the link', *Oxford Review of Education*, 42(2) (2016), pp. 146–64.

24. NatCen, 'The vote to leave the EU: Litmus test or lightning rod?', *British Social Attitudes* 34. Available at: http://www.bsa.natcen.ac.uk/media/39149/bsa34_brexit_final.pdf (accessed 8 January 2018).

25. Eric Kaufmann, 'Immigration and white identity in the West', *Foreign Affairs*, 8 September 2017; Ariel Edwards-Levy, 'Nearly half of Trump voters think whites face a lot of discrimination', *Huffington Post*, 21 November 2016. Available at: https://www.huffingtonpost.co.uk/entry/discrimination-race-religion_us_5833761ee4b099512f845bba?guccounter=1 (accessed 24 May 2018); Michael Tesler and John Sides, 'How political science helps explain the rise of Trump: the role of white identity and grievances', *Washington Post*, 3 March 2016; see also Michael Tesler, *Post-Racial or Most-Racial?: Race and Politics in the Obama Era* (Chicago: University of Chicago Press, 2016).

26. NatCen (2016), 'Understanding the leave vote', London: National Centre for Social Research.

27. On cultural displacement and Trump, see PRRI, 'Beyond economics: fears of cultural displacement pushed the white working-class to Trump', 5 September 2017. Available at: https://www.prri.org/research/white-working-class-attitudes-economy-trade-immigration-election-donald-trump/ (accessed 15 October 2017). On the study of whites fearing a non-white takeover, see Brenda Major, Alison Blodorn and Gregory Major Blascovich, 'The threat of increasing diversity: why many white Americans support Trump in the 2016 presidential election', *Group Processes &*

Intergroup Relations, published online October 2016. Available at: https://doi.org/10.1177/1368430216677304 (accessed 24 May 2018). There is a growing pile of studies on the Trump electorate, but see notably Michael Tesler and John Sides, 'How political science helps explain the rise of Trump: the role of white identity and grievances,' *Washington Post*, Monkey Cage blog, 3 March 2016. Available at: www.washingtonpost.com/news/monkey-cage/wp/2016/03/03/how-political-science-helps-explain-the-rise-of-trump-the-role-of-white-identity-and-grievances (accessed 10 January 2017); Michael Tesler, 'Trump is the first modern Republican to win the nomination based on racial prejudice,' *Washington Post*, Monkey Cage blog, 1 August 2016. Available at: www.washingtonpost.com/news/monkey-cage/wp/2016/08/01/trump-is-the-first-republican-in-modern-times-to-win-the-partys-nomination-on-anti-minority-sentiments (accessed 10 January 2017); Michael Tesler, 'In a Trump-Clinton match-up, racial prejudice makes a striking difference,' *Washington Post*, Monkey Cage blog, 25 May 2016. Available at: www.washingtonpost.com/news/monkey-cage/wp/2016/05/25/in-a-trump-clinton-match-up-theres-a-striking-effect-of-racial-prejudice (accessed 10 January 2017); Michael Tesler, 'Views about race mattered more in electing Trump than in electing Obama,' *Washington Post*, Monkey Cage blog, 22 November 2016. Available at: www.washingtonpost.com/news/monkey-cage/wp/2016/11/22/peoples-views-about-race-mattered-more-in-electing-trump-than-in-electing-obama (accessed 10 January 2017).

28. Emily Flitter and Chris Kahn, 'Trump supporters more likely to view blacks negatively', Reuters/Ipsos 28 June 2016. Available at: https://www.reuters.com/article/us-usa-election-race/exclusive-trump-supporters-more-likely-to-view-blacks-negatively-reuters-ipsos-poll-IDUSKCN0ZE2SW (accessed 18 August 2016); Bradley Jones and Jocelyn Kiley, 'More warmth for Trump among GOP voters concerned by immigrants, diversity', Pew Research Center, 2 June 2016. Available at: http://www.pewresearch.org/fact-tank/2016/06/02/more-warmth-for-trump-among-gop-voters-concerned-by-immigrants-diversity/ (accessed 15 December 2016).

29. John Sides, Michael Tesler and Lynn Vavreck, 'How Trump lost and won', *Journal of Democracy*, 28(2) (2017), pp. 34–44.

30. On this poll, see YouGov (2017), 'The "extremists" on both sides of the Brexit debate'. Available at: https://yougov.co.uk/news/2017/08/01/britain-nation-brexit-extremists/ (accessed 20 December 2017). On Brexit and the immigration issue, see Harold Clarke, Paul Whiteley and Matthew Goodwin, *Brexit: Why Britain Voted to Leave the European Union*

(Cambridge: Cambridge University Press, 2017); Matthew Goodwin and Caitlin Milazzo, 'Taking back control? Investigating the role of immigration in the 2016 vote for Brexit', *British Journal of Politics and International Relations*, 19(3) (2017), pp. 450–64; Matthew Goodwin and Oliver Heath, 'The 2016 referendum, Brexit and the left behind: an aggregate level analysis of the result', *The Political Quarterly*, 87(3) (2016), pp. 323–32; Ipsos-MORI (2017), *Shifting Ground: Eight Key Findings from a Longitudinal Study on Attitudes Toward Immigration and Brexit*. Available at: https://www.ipsos.com/sites/default/files/ct/news/documents/2017-10/Shifting%20Ground_Unbound.pdf (accessed 24 May 2018).

31. Daniel Oesch, 'Explaining workers' support for right-wing populist parties in Western Europe: evidence from Austria, Belgium, France, Norway, and Switzerland', *International Political Science Review*, 29(3) (2008), pp. 349–73; Han Werts, Peer Scheepers and Marcel Lubbers, 'Euro-scepticism and radical right-wing voting in Europe, 2002–2008: social cleavages, socio-political attitudes and contextual characteristics determining voting for the radical right', *European Union Politics*, 14(2) (2013), pp. 183–205; on the later study, see Marcel Lubbers and Marcel Coenders, 'Nationalistic attitudes and voting for the radical right in Europe', *European Union Politics*, 18(1) (2017), pp. 98–118.

CHAPTER 2: PROMISES

1. Robert Kagan, 'This is how fascism comes to America', *Washington Post*, 18 May 2016. Available at: https://www.washingtonpost.com/opinions/this-is-how-fascism-comes-to-america/2016/05/17/c4e32c58-1c47-11e6-8c7b-6931e66333e7_story.html?utm_term=.bf2a6b503098 (accessed 4 September 2016).

2. Henry Giroux, 'Fascism's return and Trump's war on youth', *The Conversation*, 13 December 2017. Available at: http://theconversation.com/fascisms-return-and-trumps-war-on-youth-88867 (accessed 10 January 2018).

3. Benjamin Moffitt, *The Global Rise of Populism: Performance, Political Style, and Representation* (Stanford: Stanford University Press, 2016).

4. Jana Winter and Elias Groll, 'Here's the memo that blew up the NSC', *Foreign Policy*, 10 August 2017. Available at: http://foreignpolicy.com/2017/08/10/heres-the-memo-that-blew-up-the-nsc/ (accessed 12 January 2018).

5. Richard Hofstadter, 'The paranoid style in American politics', *Harper's Magazine*, November 1964. Available at: https://harpers.org/archive/1964/11/the-paranoid-style-in-american-politics/ (accessed 7 December 2016).

6. Cas Mudde, *Populist Radical Right Parties in Europe* (Cambridge: Cambridge University Press, 2007).

7. For example, Cas Mudde and Cristóbal Rovira Kaltwasser, 'Exclusionary vs. inclusionary populism: comparing contemporary Europe and Latin America', *Government and Opposition*, 48(2) (2012), pp. 147–74.

8. Roger Eatwell, 'Fascism', in Michael Freeden, Lyman Tower Sargent and Marc Stears (eds), *The Oxford Handbook of Political Ideologies* (Oxford: Oxford University Press, 2013); Roger Eatwell, 'Populism and fascism', in Cristóbal Rovira Kaltwasser, Paul Taggart, Pauline Ochoa Espejo and Pierre Ostiguy (eds), *The Oxford Handbook of Populism* (Oxford: Oxford University Press, 2017).

9. Justin Gest, *The New Minority. White Working Class Politics in an Age of Immigration* (New York: Oxford University Press, 2016); Lucian Gideon Conway, Meredith A. Repke and Shannon C. Houck, 'Donald Trump as a cultural revolt against perceived communication restriction: priming political correctness norms causes more Trump support', *Journal of Social and Political Psychology*, 5(1) (2017), pp. 244–59.

10. Margaret Canovan, 'Trust the people: populism and the two faces of Democracy', *Political Studies*, 47(1) (1999), pp. 2–16. See also Margaret Canovan, *The People* (Cambridge: Polity Press, 2005).

11. For example, Jan-Werner Müller, *What Is Populism?* (Philadelphia: University of Pennsylvania Press, 2016); see also Yascha Mounk, 'How populists uprisings could bring down liberal democracy', *The Guardian* 4 March 2018. Available at: s://www.theguardian.com/commentisfree/2018/mar/04/shock-system-liberal-democracy-populism (accessed 25 May 2018).

12. Charles Postel, *The Populist Vision* (Oxford: Oxford University Press, 2007); Walter Nugent, *The Tolerant Populists: Kansas Populism and Nativism* (Chicago: University of Chicago Press, 2013).

13. Dennis W. Johnson, *Democracy for Sale: A History of American Political Consulting* (Oxford: Oxford University Press, 2017).

14. Paul Taggart, *Populism* (Buckingham: Open University Press, 2000).

15. For general surveys, see Roger Eatwell, *Fascism: A History* (London: Pimlico, 2003); Robert Paxton, *The Anatomy of Fascism* (London: Allen Lane, 2004); and Stanley Payne, A *History of Fascism, 1914–45* (Madison: University of Wisconsin Press, 1995).

16. Richard Bessel, *Nazism and War* (London; Phoenix, 2005), p. 3.

17. James Q. Whitman, *Hitler's American Model: the United States and the Making of Nazi Race Law* (Princeton: Princeton University Press, 2017).

18. David Cesarani, *Final Solution: The Fate of the Jews 1933–1949* (Basingstoke: Palgrave Macmillan, 2016); Dan Stone, *Histories of the Holocaust* (Oxford: Oxford University Press, 2010).

19. Victoria De Grazia, *How Fascism Ruled Women Italy, 1922–1945* (Berkeley: University of California Press, 1993); Jill Stephenson, *Women in Nazi Germany* (London: Routledge, 2001).

20. Avraham Barkai, *Nazi Economics: Ideology, Theory and Policy* (New Haven: Yale University Press, 1990); see also David Baker, 'The political economy of fascism: myth or reality or myth and reality?', *New Political Economy*, 11(2) (2006), pp. 227–250.

21. Juan Linz, *Authoritarian and Totalitarian Regimes* (Boulder, CO: Lynne Riener Publishers, 2000); see also Roger Eatwell, 'The nature of "generic fascism": complexity and reflective hybridity', in António Costa Pinto and Aristotle Kallis (eds), *Rethinking Fascism and Dictatorship in Europe* (Basingstoke: Palgrave Macmillan 2014).

22. Robert Gellately, *Backing Hitler: Consent and Coercion in Nazi Germany* (Oxford: Oxford University Press 2001); Ian Kershaw, *The 'Hitler Myth': Image and Reality in The Third Reich* (Oxford: Oxford University Press 1987).

23. Seymour Martin Lipset and Earl Raab, *The Politics of Unreason: Right-wing Extremism in America, 1790–1970* (New York: Harper and Row, 1971).

24. Noberto Bobbio, *Left and Right: The Significance of a Political Distinction* (Cambridge: Polity Press, 1996); Roger Eatwell and Noël O'Sullivan (eds), *The Nature of the Right* (London: Frances Pinter, 1989).

25. Nicholas Vinocaur, 'Marine Le Pen makes globalization the enemy', *Politico Europe*, 2 May 2017. Available at: https://www.politico.eu/article/marine-le-pen-globalization-campaign-launch-french-politics-news-lyon-islam/ (accessed 22 January 2018).

26. On varieties of populism, see Cristóbal Rovira Kaltwasser, Paul Taggart, Pauline Ochoa Espejo and Pierre Ostiguy (eds), *The Oxford Handbook of Populism* (Oxford: Oxford University Press, 2017), and Jens Rydgren (ed.), *The Oxford Handbook of the Radical Right* (Oxford: Oxford University Press, 2018).

27. For a sympathetic point of view, stressing liberalism's failure to understand conservative concerns, see Frank Furedi, *European Culture Wars: The Conflict of Values between Hungary and the EU* (Abingdon: Routledge, 2017).

28. Martin Barker, *The New Racism: Conservatives and the Ideology of the Tribe* (London: Junction Books, 1981). For an academic reader on racism, see Martin Bulmer and John Solomos (eds), *Racism* (Oxford: Oxford University Press, 1999).

29. David Miller, *Strangers in our Midst: The Political Philosophy of Immigration* (Cambridge MA: Harvard University Press, 2016).

30. Ta-Nehisi Coates, 'The first white president. The foundation of Donald Trump's presidency is the negation of Barack Obama's legacy', *The Atlantic*, October 2017. Available at: https://www.theatlantic.com/magazine/archive/2017/10/the-first-white-president-ta-nehisi-coates/537909/ (accessed 30 October 2017).

31. Cas Mudde, *Populist Radical Right Parties in Europe* (Cambridge: Cambridge University Press, 2007). See also Cas Mudde, 'Why nativism not populism should be declared word of the year', *The Guardian*, 7 December 2017. Available at: https://www.theguardian.com/commentisfree/2017/dec/07/cambridge-dictionary-nativism-populism-word-year (accessed 25 May 2018).

32. For an introduction to the varieties of and debates surrounding the nature and causes of nationalism, see John Breuilly (ed.), *The Oxford Handbook of the History of Nationalism* (Oxford: Oxford University Press, 2013); John Hutchinson (ed.), *Nationalism* (Oxford: Oxford University Press, 1995).

CHAPTER 3: DISTRUST

1. Francis Fukuyama, 'The end of history?', *The National Interest*, 16, Summer 1989, pp. 3–18; Francis Fukuyama, *The End of History and the Last Man* (New York: Free Press, 1992).

2. Fareed Zakaria, 'The rise of illiberal democracy', *Foreign Affairs*, 76(6) (1997), pp. 22–43; Colin Crouch, *Post-Democracy* (Cambridge: Polity Press, 2004).

3. *Freedom in the World 2018*. Available at: https://freedomhouse.org/report/freedom-world/freedom-world-2018 (accessed 17 January 2018).

4. Karl Popper, *The Open Society and its Enemies. Volume 1: the Spell of Plato* (London: Routledge & Kegan Paul, 1945).

5. Joseph Schumpeter, *Capitalism, Socialism and Democracy* (New York: Harper and Brothers, 1942); Clinton Rossiter, *The American Presidency* (New York: Harcourt Brace, 1956).

6. Bernard R. Berelson, Paul F. Lazarsfeld and W. N. McPhee, *Voting. A Study of Opinion Formation in a Presidential Campaign* (Chicago: Chicago University Press, 1954); Angus Campbell, Philip E. Converse, Warren E. Mitchell and Donald E. Stokes, *The American Voter* (Chicago: Chicago University Press, 1960).

7. Richard Hofstadter, 'The paranoid style in American politics', *Harper's Magazine*, November 1964. Available at: https://harpers.org/archive/1964/11/the-paranoid-style-in-american-politics/ (accessed 7 December 2016). See also Daniel Bell (ed.), *The Radical Right* (New York: Doubleday, 1963).

8. Gabriel Almond and Sidney Verba, *The Civic Culture: Political Attitudes and Democracy in Five Nations* (Princeton: Princeton University Press, 1963).

9. Hanspeter Kriesi, 'The populist challenge', *West European Politics*, 37(2) (2014), pp. 361–78.

10. Vernon Bogdanor, 'After the referendum, the people, not parliament, are sovereign', *Financial Times*, 9 December 2016.

11. David Butler and Uwe Kitzinger, *The 1975 Referendum* (Basingstoke: Palgrave Macmillan, 2016), p. 280.

12. Cited in Wolfgang Müller, Marcelo Jenny and Alejandro Ecker, 'The elites-masses gap in European integration', in Heinrich Best, György Lengyel and Luca Verzichelli (eds), *The Europe of Elites: A Study into the Europeanness of Political and Economic Elites* (Oxford: Oxford University Press, 2012), p. 167.

13. Max Haller, *European Integration as an Elite Process: The Failure of a Dream?* (London: Routledge, 2008), pp. 16–18.

14. Hermann Schmitt and Jacobus Johannes Adrianus Thomassen (eds), *Political Representation and Legitimacy in the European Union* (Oxford: Oxford University Press, 1999).

15. Lauren McLaren, *Identity, Interests and Attitudes to European Integration* (Basingstoke: Palgrave Macmillan, 2005).

16. 'We're not morons. Brexit divisions harden across Britain', *The Guardian*, 26 January 2018. Available at: https://www.theguardian.com/politics/2018/jan/26/uk-brexit-voters-mansfield-bristol-torbay-leeds-post-referendum (accessed 3 February 2018).

17. OECD Education at a Glance, 12 September 2017. Available at: http://www.oecd.org/education/education-at-a-glance-19991487.htm (accessed 9 December 2017).

18. Ruy Texeira, 'The math is clear: Democrats need to win more working-class white votes', Vox, 29 January 2018. Available at: https://www.vox.com/the-big-idea/2018/1/29/16945106/

democrats-white-working-class-demographics-alabama-clinton-obama-base (accessed 5 February 2018).

19. Geoffrey Evans and James Tilley, *The New Politics of Class: The Political Exclusion of the British Working Class* (Oxford: Oxford University Press, 2017); see also House of Commons Library, *Social Background of Members of Parliament, 1979–2017* (London, 2017). Available at: (http://researchbriefings.parliament.uk/ResearchBriefing/Summary/CBP-7483#fullreport (accessed 7 January 2018).

20. Eric Lipton, 'Half of Congress members are millionaires, report says', *New York Times*, 9 January 2014; '50 richest members of Congress', *Newsweek*, 7 April 2018.

21. Mark Bovens and Anchrit Wille, *Diploma Democracy: The Rise of Political Meritocracy* (Oxford: Oxford University Press, 2017); Larry M. Bartels, *Unequal Democracy: The Political Economy of the New Gilded Age* (Princeton, Princeton University Press, 2016).

22. Social Mobility Commission, *State of the Nation 2017: Social Mobility in Great Britain* (London, 2017). Available at: https://www.gov.uk/government/uploads/system/uploads/attachment_data/file/662744/State_of_the_Nation_2017_-_Social_Mobility_in_Great_Britain.pdf (accessed 7 January 2018).

23. Elmer E. Schattschneider, *The Semisovereign People: A Realist's View of Democracy in America* (Chicago: Holt, Rinehart and Winston, 1960).

24. Nicholas Carnes, *White Collar Government: The Hidden Role of Class in Economic Policy Marking* (Chicago: University of Chicago Press, 2013).

25. Nancy MacLean, *Democracy in Chains: The Radical Right's Stealth Plan for America* (New York: Viking, 2017); Jane Mayer, *Dark Money: How a Secretive Group of Billionaires Is Trying to Buy Political Control in the US* (New York: Doubleday, 2016).

26. Benjamin R. Barber, *Strong Democracy: Participatory Politics for a New Age* (Berkeley: University of California Press, 1984); James S. Fishkin, *When the People Speak: Deliberative Democracy and Public Consultation* (Oxford: Oxford University Press, 2009).

27. Karl Vick, 'The digital divide: a quarter of the nation without broadband', *Time*, 30 March 2017. Available at: http://time.com/4718032/the-digital-divide/ (accessed 17 March 2018).

28. Cass R. Sunstein, *#Republic: Divided Democracy in the Age of Social Media* (Princeton: Princeton University Press, 2017).

29. Mark Lilla, *The Once and Future Liberal: After Identity Politics* (New York: HarperCollins, 2017).

30. Baxter Oliphant, 'Views about whether whites benefit from societal advantages split sharply along racial and partisan lines', Pew Research Center, 28 September 2017. Available at: http://www.pewresearch.org/fact-tank/2017/09/28/views-about-whether-whites-benefit-from-societal-advantages-split-sharply-along-racial-and-partisan-lines/ (accessed 8 March 2018).

31. Charles Murray, *Coming Apart: The State of White America, 1960–2010* (New York: Crown Forum, 2012).

32. Mitchell Langbert, Anthony J. Quain and Daniel B. Klein, 'Faculty voter registration in economics, history, journalism, law and psychology', *Econ Journal Watch* 13(3), (2016) pp. 422–51.

33. 2018 Edelman Trust Barometer. Available at: http://cms.edelman.com/sites/default/files/2018-01/2018_Edelman_Trust_Barometer_Global_Report_Jan.PDF (accessed 22 January 2018). Pew data on colleges and universities. Available at: http://www.pewresearch.org/fact-tank/2017/07/20/republicans-skeptical-of-colleges-impact-on-u-s-but-most-see-benefits-for-workforce-preparation/ft_17-07-20_collegessince2015/ (accessed 13 March 2018).

34. Lucian Gideon Conway, Meredith A. Repke and Shannon C. Houck, 'Donald Trump as a cultural revolt against perceived communication restriction: priming political correctness norms causes more Trump support', *Journal of Social and Political Psychology*, 5(1), (2017) pp. 244–59.

35. Lee Drutman, Larry Diamond and Joe Goldman, 'Follow the leader: exploring American support for democracy and authoritarianism', March 2018. Available at: https://www.voterstudygroup.org/publications/2017-voter-survey/follow-the-leader (accessed 4 April 2018).

36. 'Globally, broad support for representative and direct democracy', Pew Research Center, 16 October 2017. Available at: http://www.pewglobal.org/2017/10/16/globally-broad-support-for-representative-and-direct-democracy/ (accessed 8 January 2018).

37. Nick Clarke, Will Jennings, Jonathan Moss and Gerry Stoker, *The Rise of Anti-politics in Britain* (Southampton: University of Southampton, 2016). Available at: https://eprints.soton.ac.uk/394835/ (accessed 26 May 2018).

38. Gabriela Catterberg and Alejandro Moreno, 'The individual bases of political trust: trends in new and established democracies', *International Journal of Public Opinion Research*, 18(1) (2006), pp. 31–48.

39. Ipsos (2017), 'The Rise of Populism: A Global Approach. Entering a New Supercyle of Uncertainty'. Available at: https://www.ipsos.com/sites/

default/files/2017-07/IpsosPA_TheRiseOfPopulism.pdf (accessed 24 January 2018).

40. Richard Wike, Katie Simmons, Bruce Stokes and Janell Fetterolf, 'Globally, broad support for representative and direct democracy', Pew Research Centre, 16 October 2017. Available at: http://www.pewglobal. org/2017/10/16/globally-broad-support-for-representative-and-direct-democracy/ (accessed 16 October 2017).

41. For example, John P. McCormick, 'Contain the wealthy and patrol the magistrates: restoring elite accountability to popular government', *American Political Science Review*, 100(2) (2006), pp. 159 and 160.

CHAPTER 4: DESTRUCTION

1. Noah Y. Harari, *Sapiens. A Brief History of Humankind* (New York: HarperCollins, 2015), p. 231.

2. James Q. Whitman, *Hitler's American Model. The United States and the Making of Nazi Race Law* (Princeton: Princeton University Press, 2017).

3. 'Immigration's impact on past and future U.S. population change', Pew Research Center, 28 September 2015. Available at: http://www.pewhispanic. org/2015/09/28/chapter-2-immigrations-impact-on-past-and-future-u-s-population-change/ (accessed 8 February 2018); 'Key findings about U.S. immigrants', Pew Research Center, 3 May 2017. Available at: http:// www.pewresearch.org/fact-tank/2017/05/03/key-findings-about-u-s-immigrants/ (accessed 20 May 2017).

4. 'From Ireland to Germany to Italy to Mexico: how America's source of immigrants has changed in the states, 1850–2013', Pew Research Center, 28 September 2015. Available at: http://www.pewhispanic.org/2015/09/28/ from-ireland-to-germany-to-italy-to-mexico-how-americas-source-of-immigrants-has-changed-in-the-states-1850-to-2013/ (accessed 12 November 2017).

5. Peter Morici, 'Opinion: immigration reform could be the win that Trump and the economy need', MarketWatch, 28 March 2017. Available at: https:// www.marketwatch.com/story/immigration-reform-could-be-the-win-that-trump-and-the-economy-need-2017-03-27 (accessed 24 May 2018).

6. United States Census Bureau, 'Quick Facts' (2016). Available at: https:// www.census.gov/quickfacts/fact/table/US/PST045216 (accessed 23 May 2018); Mohamed Besheer, 'A new estimate of the US Muslim

population', 6 January 2016. Available at: http://www.pewresearch.org/fact-tank/2016/01/06/a-new-estimate-of-the-u-s-muslim-population/ (accessed 22 December 2017).

7. Kuang Keng Kuek Ser, 'After the UK, which nations are more vulnerable to an anti-EU revolt? These 5 charts may tell you,' PRI, 11 July 2016. Available at: https://www.pri.org/stories/2016-07-11/after-uk-which-nations-are-more-vulnerable-anti-eu-revolt-these-5-charts-may-tell (accessed 24 May 2018).

8. Maurice Crul, 'Super-diversity vs. assimilation: how complex diversity in majority-minority cities challenges the assumptions of assimilation', *Journal of Ethnic and Migration Studies*, 42(1) (2016), pp. 54–68.

9. Tim Immerzeel, Eva Jaspers and Marcel Lubbers, 'Religion as catalyst or restraint of radical right voting?', *West European Politics*, 36(5) (2013), pp. 946–68.

10. Giulio Meotti, 'Christianity is rattling: "Lights out in Germany"', 12 October 2016. Available at: https://www.gatestoneinstitute.org/9072/germany-christianity (accessed 13 October 2016).

11. Alexander Betts and Paul Collier, *Refuge: Transforming a Broken Refugee System* (London: Allen Lane, 2017).

12. Cited in Angelique Chrisafis, 'Marine Le Pen not guilty of inciting religious hatred', *The Guardian*, 15 December 2015.

13. Bat Ye'Or, *Eurabia: The Euro-Arab Axis* (Madison, NJ: Fairleigh Dickinson Press, 2005); Samuel P. Huntington, *The Clash of Civilizations and the Remaking of World Order* (New York: Simon and Schuster, 1996).

14. Bruce Bawer, *While Europe Slept. How Radical Islam Is Destroying Europe from Within* (New York: Doubleday, 2006), p. 25.

15. John Tirman, *Immigration and the American Backlash* (Cambridge MA: MIT Press, 2016).

16. Data taken from 2010–2014 World Values Survey. Average for all European nations in sample and US (Estonia, Germany, Netherlands, Poland, Romania, Slovenia, Spain, Sweden). Available at: http://www.worldvaluessurvey.org/wvs.jsp (accessed 9 February 2018).

17. Gallup data. 'In US, 87% approve of black–white marriage, vs. 4% in 1958', 25 July 2013. Available at: http://news.gallup.com/poll/163697/approve-marriage-blacks-whites.aspx (accessed 5 December 2017); Rob Ford, 'The decline of racial prejudice in Britain', Manchester Policy Blogs, 21 August 2014. Available at: http://blog.policy.manchester.ac.uk/featured/2014/08/the-decline-of-racial-prejudice-in-britain/ (accessed 5 July 2017).

18. Elisabeth Carter, *The Extreme Right in Western Europe: Success or Failure?* (Manchester: University of Manchester Press, 2005).

19. Jack Citrin and John Sides, 'Immigration and the imagined community in Europe and the United States', *Political Studies*, 56(1) (2008), pp. 33–56; Lauren M. McLaren, 'Public support for the European Union: cost/benefit analysis or perceived cultural threat?', *The Journal of Politics*, 64(2) (2002), pp. 551–66; Lauren M. McLaren, 'Explaining opposition to Turkish membership of the EU', *European Union Politics*, 8(2) (2007), pp. 251–78; Jens Hainmueller and Daniel J. Hopkins, 'Public attitudes toward immigration', *Annual Review of Political Science*, 17 (2014), pp. 225–49.

20. Robert Ford, 'Acceptable and unacceptable immigrants: how opposition to immigration in Britain is affected by migrants' region of origin', *Journal of Ethnic and Migration Studies*, 37(7) (2011), pp. 1017–37; Elizabeth Ivarsflaten, 'Threatened by diversity: why restrictive asylum and immigration policies appeal to Western Europeans', *Journal of Elections, Public Opinion and Parties*, 15(1) (2005), pp. 21–45; Lauren McLaren and Mark Johnson, 'Resources, group conflict and symbols: explaining anti-immigration hostility in Britain', *Political Studies*, 55(4) (2007), pp. 709–32; John Sides and Jack Citrin, 'European opinion about immigration: the role of identities, interests and information', *British Journal of Political Science*, 37(3) (2007), pp. 477–504.

21. Jacob Poushter, 'European opinions of the refugee crisis in five charts', 16 September 2016. Available at: http://www.pewresearch.org/fact-tank/2016/09/16/european-opinions-of-the-refugee-crisis-in-5-charts/ (accessed 9 August 2017).

22. Matthew Goodwin, Tom Raines and David Cutts, 'What do Europeans think about Muslim immigration', 7 February 2017. Available at: https://www.chathamhouse.org/expert/comment/what-do-europeans-think-about-muslim-immigration (accessed 29 December 2017); Forschungsgruppe Wahlen: Politbarometer, Mai 2018. Available at: http://www.forschungsgruppe.de/Aktuelles/Politbarometer/ (accessed 26 May 2018).

23. Steven Levitsky and Daniel Ziblatt, *How Democracies Die: What History Tells Us about Our Future* (New York: Viking, 2018).

24. Bruce Stokes, 'What it takes to truly be one of us', 1 February 2017. Available at: http://www.pewglobal.org/2017/02/01/what-it-takes-to-truly-be-one-of-us/ (accessed 12 December 2017).

25. On support for UKIP, see Robert Ford and Matthew Goodwin, *Revolt on the Right: Explaining Public Support for the Radical Right in Britain* (Abingdon: Routledge, 2014); Matthew Goodwin and Caitlin Milazzo, *UKIP: Inside the Campaign to Redraw the Map of British Politics* (Oxford: Oxford

University Press, 2015); Robert Ford, Matthew J. Goodwin and David Cutts, 'Strategic Eurosceptics and polite xenophobes: support for the United Kingdom Independence Party (UKIP) in the 2009 European Parliament elections', *European Journal of Political Research*, 51(2) (2012), pp. 204–34; Paul Webb and Tim Bale, 'Why do Tories defect to UKIP? Conservative Party members and the temptations of the populist radical right', *Political Studies*, 62(4) (2014), pp. 961–70.

26. Jens Rydgren, 'Immigration sceptics, xenophobes or racists? Radical right-wing voting in six West European countries', *European Journal of Political Research*, 47(6) (2008), pp. 737–65.

27. Gordon Allport, *The Nature of Prejudice* (Cambridge, MA: Perseus Books,1954).

28. Robert D. Putnam, 'E pluribus unum: diversity and community in the twenty-first century – the 2006 Johan Skytte Prize Lecture', *Scandinavian Political Studies*, 30(2) (2007), pp. 137–74; Paul Collier, *Exodus: Immigration and Multiculturalism in the 21st Century* (London: Allen Lane, 2013).

29. Samuel P. Huntington, *Who Are We? The Challenges to America's National Identity* (New York: Simon and Schuster, 2004).

30. D. J. Hopkins, 'Politicized places: explaining where and when immigrants provoke local opposition', *American Political Science Review*, 104 (1) (2010), pp. 40–60; B. J. Newman, (2013) 'Acculturating contexts and anglo opposition to immigration in the United States', *American Journal of Political Science*, 57(2) (2013), pp. 374–90; M. Abrajano and Z. Hajnal, *White Backlash: Immigration, Race and American Politics* (Princeton: Princeton University Press, 2015).

31. Janet Adamy and Paul Overberg, 'Places most unsettled by rapid demographic change are drawn to Donald Trump', *Wall Street Journal*, 1 November 2016. Available at: https://www.wsj.com/articles/places-most-unsettled-by-rapid-demographic-change-go-for-donald-trump-1478010940?mod=e2fb (accessed on 15 December 2016).

32. Benjamin J. Newman, Sino Shah and Loren Collingwood, 'Race, place, and building a base: Latino population growth and the nascent Trump campaign for president', *Public Opinion Quarterly* 82(1) (2018), pp. 122–134.

33. Chris Lawton and Robert Ackrill, 'Hard evidence: how areas with low immigration voted mainly for Brexit', *The Conversation*, 8 July 2016. Available at: https://theconversation.com/hard-evidence-how-areas-with-low-immigration-voted-mainly-for-brexit-62138 (accessed on 29 August 2016).

34. For this research, see B. Bowyer, 'Local context and extreme right support in England: the British National Party in the 2002 and 2003

local elections', *Electoral Studies*, 27(4) (2008), pp. 611–20; Robert Ford and Matthew J. Goodwin, 'Angry white men: individual and contextual predictors of support for the British National Party', *Political Studies*, 58(1) (2010), pp. 1–25; Marcel Lubbers and Peer Scheepers, 'French Front National voting: a micro and macro perspective', *Ethnic and Racial Studies*, 25(1) (2002), pp. 120–49; Elias Dinas and Joost van Spanje, 'Crime story: the role of crime and immigration in the anti-immigration vote', *Electoral Studies*, 30(4) (2011), pp. 658–71; H. Coffé, B. Heyndels and J. Vermeir, J. 'Fertile grounds for extreme right-wing parties: explaining the Vlaams Blok's electoral success', *Electoral Studies*, 26 (1) (2007), pp. 142–55; M. Lubbers and P. Scheepers, 'Explaining the trend in extreme right-wing voting: Germany 1989–1998', *European Sociological Review*, 17(4) (2001), pp. 431–49; M. Golder, 'Explaining variation in the success of anti-immigrant parties in Western Europe', *Comparative Political Studies*, 36(4) (2003), pp. 432–66; P. Knigge, 'The ecological correlates of right-wing extremism in Western Europe', *European Journal of Political Research* 34(2) (1998), pp. 249–79; Jens Rydgren and Patrick Ruth, 'Contextual explanations of radical right-wing support in Sweden: socioeconomic marginalization, group threat, and the halo effect', *Ethnic and Racial Studies*, 36(4) (2013), pp. 711–28; Michael Savelkoul, Joran Laméris and Jochem Tolsma, 'Neighbourhood ethnic composition and voting for the Radical Right in the Netherlands. The role of perceived neighbourhood threat and interethnic neighbourhood contact', *European Sociological Review*, 33(2) (2017), pp. 209–24; Sarah Valdez, 'Visibility and votes: a spatial analysis of anti-immigrant voting in Sweden', *Migration Studies*, 2(2) (2014), pp. 162–88; Eva G. T. Green et al., 'From stigmatized immigrants to radical right voting: a multilevel study on the role of threat and contact', *Political Psychology*, 37(4) (2016), pp. 465–80; N. Mayer, *Ces Français qui votent Le Pen* (Paris: Flammarion, 2002).

35. David Goodhart, 'White self-interest is not the same thing as racism', *Financial Times*, 2 March 2017.

36. Eric J. Hobsbawm, *Nations and Nationalism since 1789: Programme, Myth, Reality* (Cambridge: Cambridge University Press, 2012), p. 12.

37. David Miller, *On Nationality* (Oxford: Clarendon Press, 1995).

38. Jonathan Haidt, *The Righteousness Mind. Why Good People Are Divided by Politics and Religion* (New York: Pantheon Books, 2012); and 'When and why nationalism beats globalism', *The American Interest*, 12(1) (2016).

39. Yomi Kazeem, 'More than half of the world's population growth will be in Africa by 2050', *Quartz Africa*, 29 June 2017. Available at: https://qz.com/1016790/more-than-half-of-the-worlds-population-growth-will-be-in-africa-by-2050/ (accessed 3 February 2018).

40. Yemsi Adegoke, 'UN: half of world's population growth is likely to occur in Africa', CNN 26 June 2017. Available at: https://edition.cnn.com/2017/06/25/africa/africa-population-growth-un/index.html?no-st=1527359812 (accessed 26 May 2018).

41. David Coleman, 'Projections of the ethnic minority populations of the United Kingdom 2006–2056', *Population and Development Review*, 36(3) (2010), pp. 441–86.

42. Michael Lipka, 'Europe's Muslim population will continue to grow – but how much depends on migration', 4 December 2017. Available at: http://www.pewresearch.org/fact-tank/2017/12/04/europes-muslim-population-will-continue-to-grow-but-how-much-depends-on-migration/ (accessed on 12 February 2018).

43. 'US Muslims concerned about their place in society, but continue to believe in the American Dream', Pew Research Center, 26 July 2017. Available at: http://www.pewforum.org/2017/07/26/findings-from-pew-research-centers-2017-survey-of-us-muslims/ (accessed 6 April 2018).

44. For example, see Frank Van Tubergen, 'Religious affiliation and attendance among immigrants in eight Western countries: individual and contextual effects', *Journal for the Scientific Study of Religion*, 45(1) (2006), pp. 1–22; Frank Van Tubergen, 'Religious affiliation and participation among immigrants in a secular society: a study of immigrants in the Netherlands', *Journal of Ethnic and Migration Studies*, 33(5) (2007), pp. 747–65.

45. Eric Kaufmann, Anne Goujon and Vegard Skirbekk. 'The end of secularization in Europe?: a socio-demographic perspective', *Sociology of Religion*, 73(1) (2012), pp. 69–91.

46. Frank Van Tubergen and Jorunn I. Sindradottir, 'The religiosity of immigrants in Europe: a cross-national study', *Journal for the Scientific Study of Religion*, 50(2) (2011), pp. 272–88; also see evidence summarized by David Voas and Fenella Fleischmann, 'Islam moves west: religious change in the first and second generations', *Annual Review of Sociology*, 38 (2012), pp. 525–45. On Pew, see 'Being Christian in Western Europe', Pew Research Center, 29 May 2018. Available at: http://www.pewforum.org/2018/05/29/being-christian-in-western-europe/ (accessed 1 June 2018).

CHAPTER 5: DEPRIVATION

1. Thomas Piketty, *Capital in the 21st Century* (Cambridge, MA: Belknap Press, 2014).

2. Kara Scannell and Richard Milne, 'Who was convicted because of the global financial crisis?' *Financial Times*, 9 August 2017.

3. Deidre McCloskey, *Bourgeois Equality: How Ideas, not Capital or Institutions, Enriched the World* (Chicago: University of Chicago Press, 2016); Joel Mokyr, *A Culture of Growth: The Origins of the Modern Economy* (Princeton: Princeton University Press, 2016).

4. Gary King et al., 'Ordinary economic voting behavior in the extraordinary election of Adolf Hitler', *The Journal of Economic History*, 68(4) (2008), pp. 951–96.

5. Chris Renwick, *Bread for All. The Origins of the Welfare State* (London: Allen Lane, 2017).

6. Peter A. Hall, *The Political Power of Economic Ideas: Keynesianism Across Nations* (Princeton: Princeton University Press, 1989); Robert Skidelsky (ed.), *The Essential Keynes* (London: Penguin Books, 2015).

7. Mariana Mazzucato, *The Entrepreneurial State: Debunking Public vs Private Sector Myths* (London: Anthem Press, 2013).

8. David Green, *The New Right: The Counter Revolution in Political, Economic and Social Thought* (Brighton: Harvester Wheatsheaf, 1987); cf. Desmond S. King, *The New Right: Politics, Markets and Citizenship* (Basingstoke: Macmillan, 1987).

9. Nancy MacLean, *Democracy in Chains: The Radical Right's Plans for America* (New York: Viking, 2017); Jane Mayer, *Dark Money: How a Secretive Group of Billionaires Is Trying to Buy Political Control in the US* (New York: Doubleday, 2016).

10. Murray Rothbard, *For a New Liberty: The Libertarian Manifesto* (New York: Macmillan, 1973); cf. Charles Murray, *Losing Ground* (New York: Basic Books, 1984).

11. David Harvey, *A Brief History of Neoliberalism* (Oxford: Oxford University Press, 2005).

12. Angus Deaton, 'How inequality works', Project Syndicate, *OnPoint*, 21 December 2017. Available at: https://www.project-syndicate.org/onpoint/ anatomy-of-inequality-2017-by-angus-deaton-2017-12 ?barrier=accesspaylog (accessed 14 January 2018).

13. Jeffrey M. Jones, 'In U.S. positive attitudes toward foreign trade stay high', 1 March 2018. Available at: http://news.gallup.com/poll/228317/positive-attitudes-toward-foreign-trade-stay-high.aspx (accessed 31 March 2018).

14. Alec Tyson, 'Americans generally positive about NAFTA, but most Republicans say it benefits Mexico more than US', 13 November 2017. Available at: http://www.pewresearch.org/fact-tank/2017/11/13/

americans-generally-positive-about-nafta-but-most-republicans-say-it-benefits-mexico-more-than-u-s/ (accessed 27 January 2018).

15. Dani Rodrik, 'Populism and the economics of globalization' (2017). Available at: https://drodrik.scholar.harvard.edu/files/dani-rodrik/files/populism_and_the_economics_of_globalization.pdf (accessed 4 April 2018).

16. Data taken from Eurobarometer.

17. John Rapley, *Twilight of the Money Gods: Economics as a Religion and How It All Went Wrong* (London: Simon and Schuster, 2017).

18. Emily Ekins, 'Today's bailout anniversary reminds us that the Tea Party is more than anti-Obama', Reason.com, 3 October 2014. Available at: http://reason.com/archives/2014/10/03/the-birth-of-the-tea-party-movement-bega/ (accessed 13 November 2017).

19. Matthew Cooper, 'Poll: most Americans support Occupy Wall Street', *The Atlantic*, 19 October 2011. Available at: https://www.theatlantic.com/politics/archive/2011/10/poll-most-americans-support-occupy-wall-street/246963/ (accessed 30 January 2016).

20. Markus Wagner, 'Fear and anger in Great Britain: blame assignment and emotional reactions to the financial crisis', *Political Behavior*, 36(3) (2014), pp. 683–703.

21. Paul Krugman, *End This Depression Now* (New York: W.W. Norton and Company, 2012); Joseph Stiglitz, *The Euro: And Its Threat to the Future of Europe* (London: Allen Lane, 2016).

22. Johan Norberg, *Progress: Ten Reasons to Look Forward to the Future* (London: Oneworld, 2016).

23. OECD, 'Understanding the socio-economic divide in Europe', 26 January 2017. Available at: https://www.oecd.org/els/soc/cope-divide-europe-2017-background-report.pdf (accessed 15 January 2018).

24. Jeremy Greenwood, Nezih Guner, Georgi Kocharkov and Cezar Santos, 'Marry your like: assortative mating and income inequality' (Philadelphia, 2014). Available at: https://repository.upenn.edu/cgi/viewcontent.cgi?article=1052&context=psc_working_papers (accessed 5 March 2018).

25. Table in Martin Wolf, 'The long and painful journey to world disorder', *Financial Times*, 5 January 2017. Available at: https://www.ft.com/content/ef13e61a-ccec-11e6-b8ce-b9c03770f8b1 (accessed 7 July 2017).

26. Peter Temin, *The Vanishing Middle Class: Prejudice and Power in a Dual Economy* (Cambridge MA: MIT Press, 2017).

27. Mai Chi Dao, Mitali Das, Zsoka Koczan and Weicheng Lian, 'Drivers of declining labor share of income', IMF Blog, 12 April 2017. Available at:

https://blogs.imf.org/2017/04/12/drivers-of-declining-labor-share-of-income/ (accessed 12 November 2017).

28. Brenna Hoban, 'Robots aren't taking the jobs, just the paychecks', *Brookings*, 8 March 2018. Available at: https://www.brookings.edu/blog/brookings-now/2018/03/08/robots-arent-taking-the-jobs-just-the-paychecks-and-other-new-findings-in-economics/ (accessed 11 March 2019).

29. IMF Fiscal Monitor, 'Tacking Inequality', October 2017. Available at: https://www.imf.org/en/Publications/FM/Issues/2017/10/05/fiscal-monitor-october-2017 (accessed 30 January 2018).

30. Noam Gidron and Peter Hall, 'The politics of social status: economic and cultural roots of the populist right', *British Journal of Sociology*, 68(Special Issue) (2017), pp. 57–84. Available at: https://doi.org/10.1111/1468-4446.12319 (accessed 26 May 2018); see also J. Gest, T. Reny and J. Mayer, 'Roots of the Radical Right: nostalgic deprivation in the United States and Britain', *Comparative Political Studies*, published online July 2017.

31. Christopher J. Anderson and Matthew M. Singer, 'The sensitive left and the impervious right: multilevel models and the politics of inequality, ideology, and legitimacy in Europe', *Comparative Political Studies*, 41(4–5) (2008), pp. 564–99; see also Robert Andersen, 'Support for democracy in cross-national perspective: the detrimental effect of economic inequality', *Research in Social Stratification and Mobility*, 30(4) (2012), pp. 389–402.

32. Teresa Kuhn, Erika van Elsas, Armen Hakhverdian and Wouter van der Brug, 'An ever wider gap in an ever closer union: rising inequalities and euroscepticism in 12 West European democracies, 1975–2009', *Socio-Economic Review*, 14(1) (2014), pp. 27–45.

33. Justin Gest, *The New Minority: White Working-class Politics in an Age of Immigration and Inequality* (New York: Oxford University Press, 2016).

34. YouGov/Legatum Institute Survey Results, 14–15 October 2015. Available at: https://d25d2506sfb94s.cloudfront.net/cumulus_uploads/document/ghloropd9r/Summary_Table.pdf (accessed 15 January 2018).

35. Robert Griffin and Ruy Teixeira, 'The story of Trump's appeal', Voter Study Group, June 2017. Available at: https://www.voterstudygroup.org/publications/2016-elections/story-of-trumps-appeal (accessed April 4 2018).

36. Brian Rathbun, Evgenia Iakhnis and Kathleen E. Powers, 'This new poll shows that populism doesn't stem from people's economic distress', *Washington Post*, 19 October 2017.

37. Herbert Kitschelt, *The Radical Right in Western Europe: A Comparative Analysis* (Ann Arbor: University of Michigan Press, 1995).

38. Matthew Holehouse, 'I'd rather be poorer with fewer migrants, Farage says', *Daily Telegraph*, 7 January 2014.

CHAPTER 6: DE-ALIGNMENT

1. Philip E. Converse and Georges Dupeux, 'Politicization of the electorate in France and the United States', *Public Opinion Quarterly*, 26(1) (1962), pp. 1–23.

2. Seymour Martin Lipset and Stein Rokkan, 'Cleavage structures, party systems and voter alignments: an introduction', in Lipset and Rokkan (eds), *Party Systems and Voter Alignments* (Glencoe: Free Press, 1967), pp. 1–64.

3. For example, Agnieszka Walczak, Wouter van der Brug and Catherine Eunice de Vries, 'Long- and short-term determinants of party preferences: inter-generational differences in Western and East Central Europe', *Electoral Studies*, 31(2) (2012), pp. 273–84.

4. Ronald Inglehart, *The Silent Revolution: Changing Values and Political Styles Among Western Publics* (Princeton: Princeton University Press, 1977).

5. Piero Ignazi, 'The silent counter-revolution', *European Journal of Political Research*, 2(1) (1992), pp. 3–34.

6. Hanspeter Kriesi, E. Grande, R. Lachat, M. Dolezal, S. Bornschier and T. Frey, *West European Politics in the Age of Globalisation* (Cambridge: Cambridge University Press, 2008).

7. Russell J. Dalton, Scott C. Flanagan and Paul Beck, *Electoral Change in Advanced Industrial Democracies* (Princeton: Princeton University Press, 1984); Russell J. Dalton and Mark P. Wattenberg, *Parties Without Partisans: Political Change in Advanced Industrial Democracies: Realignment or Dealignment?* (Oxford: Oxford University Press, 2002); Russell J. Dalton, *The Apartisan American: Dealignment and Changing Electoral Politics* (Washington DC: CQ Press, 2013).

8. Gallup party images data. Available at: http://news.gallup.com/poll/24655/party-images.aspx (accessed 25 April 2018).

9. Jeffrey M. Jones, 'Democratic, Republican identification near historical lows', 11 January 2016. Available at: http://news.gallup.com/poll/188096/democratic-republican-identification-near-historical-lows.aspx (accessed

11 November 2017); 'Trends in party identification, 1939–2014', Pew Research Center, 7 April 2015. Available at: http://www.people-press.org/interactives/party-id-trend/ (accessed 12 January 2018). See also Russell J. Dalton and Mark P. Wattenberg, *Parties without Partisans: Political Change in Advanced Industrial Democracies* (Oxford: Oxford University Press, 2002); 'The generation gap in American politics', Pew Research Center, 1 March 2018. Available at: http://www.people-press.org/2018/03/01/the-generation-gap-in-american-politics/ (accessed 20 April 2018).

10. Data on party affiliation from Gallup. Available at: http://news.gallup.com/poll/15370/party-affiliation.aspx. (accessed 20 April 2018). Russell J. Dalton, *The Apartisan American: Dealignment and Changing Electoral Politics* (Washington DC: CQ Press, 2013).

11. Data from German election studies. See also Russell J. Dalton, 'Interpreting partisan dealignment in Germany', *German Politics*, 23(1–2) (2014), pp. 134–44.

12. Peter Mair and Ingrid Van Biezen, 'Party membership in twenty European democracies, 1980–2000', *Party Politics*, 7(1) (2001), pp. 5–21; Ingrid Van Biezen, Peter Mair and Thomas Poguntke, 'Going, going . . . gone? The decline of party membership in contemporary Europe', *European Journal of Political Research*, 51(1) (2012), pp. 24–56. On the general decline of membership across the West, see also Susan Scarrow, 'Parties without members? Party organization in a changing electoral environment', in Russell J. Dalton and Mark P. Wattenberg, *Parties Without Partisans: Political Change in Advanced Industrial Democracies* (Oxford: Oxford University Press, 2002).

13. Richard S. Katz and Peter Mair, 'Changing models of party organization and party democracy: the emergence of the cartel party', *Party Politics*, 1(1) (1995), pp. 2–28.

14. Tim Bale, 'Inside Labour's massive membership base', Labour List, 6 October 2017. Available at: https://labourlist.org/2017/10/tim-bale-inside-labours-massive-membership-base/ (accessed 12 January 2018).

15. These are estimates compiled by Ipsos-MORI, 'How Britain voted in the 2016 EU referendum'. Available at: https://www.ipsos.com/ipsos-mori/en-uk/how-britain-voted-2016-eu-referendum (accessed 16 January 2018).

16. Russell Dalton, 'Why don't millennials vote?', *Washington Post*, Monkey Cage blog, 22 March 2016. Available at: https://www.washingtonpost.com/news/monkey-cage/wp/2016/03/22/why-don't-millennials-vote/ (accessed 26 May 2018).

17. It is calculated by adding up the absolute values of all gains and losses for the parties and dividing the total by two. M. N. Pedersen, 'The dynamics of European party systems: changing patterns of electoral volatility', *European Journal of Political Research*, 7(1) (1979), pp. 1–26. For instance, at elections in the Netherlands the volatility score jumped more than fourfold, from five in the 1950s to twenty-two in the 2000s; in Austria it jumped more than threefold, from four to almost fourteen, while in Germany it jumped from nearly eight in the 1990s to over fourteen in 2017. See also evidence in Russell J. Dalton, *The Apartisan American: Dealignment and Changing Electoral Politics* (Washington DC: CQ Press, 2013), Chapter 9.

18. Sara B. Hobolt and James Tilley, 'Fleeing the centre: the rise of challenger parties in the aftermath of the euro crisis', *West European Politics*, 39(5) (2016), pp. 971–91.

19. Jeff Manza and Clem Brooks, *Social Cleavages and Political Change. Voter Alignments and U.S. Party Coalitions* (Oxford: Oxford University Press, 1999); also Michael Hout, Clem Brooks and Jeff Manza, 'The democratic class struggle in the United States, 1948–1992', *American Sociological Review*, 60(6) (1995), pp. 805–28.

20. Geoffrey Skelley, 'Just how many Obama 2012-Trump 2016 voters were there?', Center for Politics/Sabato's Crystal Ball, 1 June 2017. Available at: http://www.centerforpolitics.org/crystalball/articles/just-how-many-obama-2012-trump-2016-voters-were-there/#_edn1 (accessed 17 March 2018).

21. John Sides, 'Race, religion, and immigration in 2016. How the debate over American identity shaped the election and what it means for a Trump presidency', Democracy Fund Voter Study Group, June 2017. Available at: https://www.voterstudygroup.org/publications/2016-elections/race-religion-immigration-2016 (accessed 4 April 2018).

22. Enrique Hernández and Hanspeter Kriesi , 'The electoral consequences of the financial and economic crisis in Europe', *European Journal of Political Research*, 55(2) (2016), pp. 203–24.

23. Henrik Oscarsson and Sören Holmberg, 'Swedish voting behaviour' (2010). Available at: https://www.valforskning.pol.gu.se/digitalAssets/1309/1309446_swedish-voting-behavior-juni-2010.pdf (accessed 20 January 2018).

24. Jonathan Mellon, 'Party attachment in Great Britain: Five Decades of Dealignment', SSRN Papers, 10 August 2017, pp. 1–4. Available at: https://papers.ssrn.com/sol3/papers.cfm?abstract_id=2745654 (accessed 26 May 2018).

25. Oliver Heath, 'Policy alienation, social alienation and working-class abstention in Britain, 1964–2010', *British Journal of Political Science*,

published online September 2016. Available at: https://doi.org/10.1017/S0007123416000272 (accessed 26 May 2018). See also Geoff Evans and James Tilley, *The New Politics of Class: The Political Exclusion of the British Working Class* (Oxford: Oxford University Press, 2017); Robert Ford and Matthew Goodwin, *Revolt on the Right: Explaining Support for the Radical Right in Britain* (Abingdon: Routledge, 2014).

26. Martin Elff, 'Disenchanted Workers, Selective Abstention and the Electoral Defeat of Social Democracy in Germany', paper at the 106th Annual Meeting of the American Political Science Association, 2–5 September 2010, Washington, DC. Available at: https://papers.ssrn.com/sol3/papers.cfm?abstract_id=1644676## (accessed 25 May 2018).

27. Matthew J. Goodwin and Oliver Heath, 'The 2016 referendum, Brexit and the left behind: an aggregate-level analysis of the result', *The Political Quarterly*, 8(3) (2016), pp. 323–32.

28. James Tilley and Geoffrey Evans, 'The new politics of class after the 2017 general election', *Political Quarterly*, 88(4) (2017), pp. 710–15.

29. On the 2017 general election and these divides, see Oliver Heath and Matthew J. Goodwin, 'The 2017 general election, Brexit and the return to two-party politics: an aggregate-level analysis of the result', *The Political Quarterly*, 88(3) (2017), pp. 345–58; Matthew J. Goodwin and Oliver Heath, *The UK 2017 General Election Examined: Income, Poverty and Brexit* (London: Joseph Rowntree Foundation, 2017).

30. For example, Stan Greenberg, *America Ascendant: A Revolutionary Nation's Path to Addressing its Deepest Problems and Leading the 21st Century* (New York: Thomas Dunne Books, 2015); Mark Siegel, 'A new political era: the 2016–2020 realignment is under way', *Huffpost*, 8 August 2016. Available at: https://www.huffingtonpost.com/mark-siegel/a-new-political-era-the-2_b_11392304.html (accessed 12 March 2018).

31. Justin Fox, 'Rural America is aging and shrinking', *Bloomberg View*, 20 June 2017. Available at: https://www.bloomberg.com/view/articles/2017-06-20/rural-america-is-aging-and-shrinking (accessed 18 March 2018).

32. Larry M. Bartels, 'Partisanship in the Trump era', Vanderbilt Center for the Study of Democratic Institutions Working Paper (2018). Available at: https://www.vanderbilt.edu/csdi/includes/Workingpaper2_2108.pdf (accessed 4 April 2018).

33. 'Campaign exposes fissures over issues, values and how life has changed in the US', Pew Research Center, 31 March 2016. Available at: http://www.people-press.org/2016/03/31/campaign-exposes-fissures-over-issues-values-and-how-life-has-changed-in-the-u-s/ (accessed 4 April 2018).

34. Perry Bacon Jr and Dhrumil Mehta, 'The diversity of black political views', *FiveThirtyEight*, 6 April 2019. Available at: https://fivethirtyeight.com/features/the-diversity-of-black-political-views/ (accessed 7 April 2018).

CONCLUSIONS: TOWARDS POST-POPULISM

1. David Miller, *On Nationality* (Oxford: Clarendon Press, 1995).

2. Gallup US Daily, 20 January–8 March 2017. Available at: http://news.gallup.com/poll/205832/race-education-gender-key-factors-trump-job-approval.aspx (accessed 30 November 2017).

3. YouGov/*The Times* Survey results, 28–29 January 2018. Available at: https://d25d2506sfb94s.cloudfront.net/cumulus_uploads/document/yzgd1a3wr0/TimesResults_180129_Trackers_VI.pdf (accessed 31 January 2018).

4. Tony Cross, 'One-third of Macron's ministers are millionaires', RFI English, 16 December 2017. Available at: http://en.rfi.fr/france/20171216-one-third-macrons-ministers-are-millionaires (accessed 5 March 2018).

5. Mario Munta, 'The empty taste of Macron's citizens' consultations', Euractiv, 11 April 2018. Available at: https://www.euractiv.com/section/future-eu/opinion/the-empty-taste-of-macrons-citizens-consultations/?utm_term=Autofeed&utm_campaign=Echobox&utm_medium=Social&utm_source=Twitter#link_time=1523446555 (accessed 11 April 2018).

6. Rob Griffin, Ruy Texeira and John Halpin, 'Voter trends in 2016: a final examination', Center for American Progress, 2017. Available at: https://www.americanprogress.org/issues/democracy/reports/2017/11/01/441926/voter-trends-in-2016/ (accessed 12 January 2018); Alia Wong, 'Where are all the high-school grads going?' *The Atlantic*, 11 January 2016; Derek Thompson, 'This is the way the college "Bubble" ends', *The Atlantic*, 26 July 2017.

7. At its peak in 2014 UKIP held two seats in the House of Commons that had been won through two parliamentary by-elections, but only one of these was retained at the 2015 general election. Matthew Goodwin and Caitlin Milazzo, *UKIP: Inside the Campaign to Redraw the Map of British Politics* (Oxford: Oxford University Press, 2015).

8. Ralph Atkins, 'Austria's Sebastian Kurz leans towards tougher line on migrants', *Financial Times*, 18 October 2017.

9. See Markus Wagner and Thomas M. Meyer, 'The Radical Right as niche parties? The ideological landscape of party systems in Western Europe, 1980–2014', *Political Studies*, 65(1 Supplement) (2017), pp. 84–107. Available at: https://doi.org/10.1177/0032321716639065 (accessed 26 May 2018). Certainly, they were not the first to explore this question. For similar studies and evidence, see also Tarik Abou-Chadi, 'Niche party success and mainstream party policy shifts – How green and radical right parties differ in their impact', *British Journal of Political Science*, 46(2) (2016), pp. 417–36; Michael Minkenberg, 'The new radical right in the political process: interaction effects in France and Germany', in Martin Schain, A. Zolberg and P. Hossay (eds), *Shadows Over Europe: The Development and Impact of the Extreme Right in Western Europe* (Basingstoke: Palgrave Macmillan, 2002), pp. 245–68; J. Van Spanje, 'Contagious parties. Anti-immigration parties and their impact on other parties' immigration stances in contemporary Western Europe', *Party Politics*, 16(5) (2010), pp. 563–86; Tim Bale, 'Cinderella and her ugly sisters: the mainstream and extreme right in Europe's bipolarising party systems', *West European Politics*, 26(3) (2003), pp. 67–90.

10. Robert Reich, 'Trump is using Fox News to prepare for battle', *Newsweek*, 28 March 2018. Available at: http://www.newsweek.com/robert-reich-trump-using-fox-news-prepare-battle-861725 (accessed 28 March 2018).

11. Fareed Zakaria, 'The Democrats' problem not the economy, stupid', *Washington Post*, 29 June 2017. Available at: https://www.washingtonpost.com/opinions/the-democrats-problem-is-not-the-economy-stupid/2017/06/29/50fb7988-5d07-11e7-9fc6-c7ef4bc58d13_story.html?utm_term=.6fa52bd70847 (accessed 8 April 2018).

Further Reading

The following list is intended to guide the general reader towards mainly scholarly studies in English that offer (relatively) accessible accounts of key topics. In the interest of provoking further thought about these controversial and important topics, we include works that give different points of view, highlighting authors' broad positions in brief annotations on many of them. Some of the works included in the two opening general lists are also relevant to the later Brexit/UKIP and Trump cases. As this guide is aimed at the general reader, it omits articles in academic journals that typically do not allow free online access – though many are listed in the Notes, as the book is based on the very latest research of others, as well as our own.

GENERAL WORKS RELATING TO POPULISM AND NATIONALISM

John Breuilly (ed.), *The Oxford Handbook of the History of Nationalism* (Oxford: Oxford University Press, 2013). Highlights the variety of forms of nationalism and includes a chapter by Roger Eatwell on fascism and racism.

Margaret Canovan, *The People* (Cambridge: Polity, 2005). Political philosopher who argues that populism is a response to the tensions in liberal democracy.

Eric J. Hobsbawm, *Nations and Nationalism since 1789: Programme, Myth, Reality* (Cambridge: Cambridge University Press, 2012). Left-wing attack on the irrationality of nationalism.

Cristóbal Rovira Kaltwasser, Paul Taggart, Pauline Ochoa Espejo and Pierre Ostiguy (eds), *The Oxford Handbook of Populism* (Oxford: Oxford University Press, 2017). Broad survey of mainly recent movements and issues, including a chapter by Roger Eatwell on populism and fascism.

David Miller, *On Nationality* (Oxford: Clarendon Press, 1995). Political philosopher defends moderate nationalism as important to social solidarity and redistribution.

Cas Mudde and Cristóbal Rovira Kaltwasser, *Populism: A Very Short Introduction* (Oxford: Oxford University Press, 2017).

Jan-Werner Müller, *What Is Populism?* (Philadelphia: University of Pennsylvania Press, 2016). Critical account from a liberal political philosopher who sees populism as a threat to democratic pluralism and tolerance.

Paul Taggart, *Populism* (Buckingham: Open University Press, 2000).

GENERAL WORKS RELATING TO CONTEMPORARY NATIONAL POPULISM

Andrew Geddes and Peter Scholten, *The Politics of Migration and Immigration in Europe* (London: Sage, 2016).

Justin Gest, *The New Minority: White Working Class Politics in an Age of Immigration* (New York: Oxford University Press, 2016). Empathetic account of British and US sociological change.

Jonathan Haidt, 'When nationalism beats globalism', *The American Interest*, July 2016. Available at: https://www.the-american-interest.com/2016/07/10/when-and-why-nationalism-beats-globalism/. Leading American social psychologist defends moderate nationalism.

John B. Judis, *The Populist Explosion: How the Great Recession Transformed American and European Politics* (New York: Columbia Global Reports, 2016).

Paul Krugman, *End this Depression Now* (New York: W.W. Norton and Company, 2012).

Steven Levitsky and Daniel Ziblatt, *How Democracies Die: What History Reveals About our Future* (New York: Viking, 2018).

Benjamin Moffitt, *The Global Rise of Populism: Performance, Political Style and Representation* (Stanford: Stanford University Press, 2016). Populism as 'style'.

Cas Mudde (ed.), *The Populist Radical Right: A Reader* (Abingdon: Routledge, 2016). Good selection of classic academic articles, including two by Roger Eatwell.

Sasha Polakow-Suransky, *Go Back to Where You Came From: The Backlash Against Immigration and the Fate of Western Democracy* (London: Hurst Publishers, 2017). Liberal journalist's critique of the far right.

Dani Rodrik, *The Globalization Paradox: Why Global Markets, States and Democracy Can't Coexist* (Oxford: Oxford University Press, 2012).

Jens Rydgren (ed.), *The Oxford Handbook of the Radical Right* (Oxford: Oxford University Press, 2018). Contains a good range of national and thematic studies, including a chapter by Roger Eatwell on charismatic leaders.

Joseph E. Stiglitz, *The Euro: And Its Threat to the Future of Europe* (London: Allen Lane, 2016).

BREXIT, UKIP AND BRITISH POLITICS

Harold Clarke, Paul Whiteley and Matthew J. Goodwin, *Brexit: Why Britain Voted to Leave the European Union* (Cambridge: Cambridge University Press, 2017).

Geoffrey Evans and Anand Menon, *Brexit and British Politics* (Cambridge: Polity, 2017). Short book on the Brexit vote.

Robert Ford and Matthew Goodwin, *Revolt on the Right: Explaining Support for the Radical Right in Britain* (Abingdon: Routledge, 2014). Award-winning book on UKIP.

David Goodhart, *The Road to Somewhere: The Populist Revolt and the Future of Politics* (London: C. Hurst & Co., 2017).

Matthew J. Goodwin and Caitlin Milazzo, *UKIP: Inside the Campaign to Redraw the Map of British Politics* (Oxford: Oxford University Press, 2015).

DONALD TRUMP AND US POLITICS

Emily Ekins, 'The five types of Trump voters', Voter Study Group paper, 2017. Available at: https://www.voterstudygroup.org/publications/2016-elections/the-five-types-trump-voters

David Frum, *Trumpocracy: The Corruption of the American Republic* (New York: Harper Collins, 2018). Best-selling attack on Trump and his threat to democracy.

Arlie Russell Hochschild, *Strangers in Their Own Land: Anger and Mourning on the American Right* (New York: The New Press, 2016). Sociological study of the Tea Party and the prelude to Trump's victory.

Mark Lilla, *The Once and Future Liberal: After Identity Politics* (New York: HarperCollins, 2017). A self-described liberal sets out the problems with current 'identity' liberalism which has moved away from classic working-class concerns.

John Sides, 'Race, religion and immigration in 2016', 2017. Available at: https://www.voterstudygroup.org/publications/2016-elections/race-religion-immigration-2016. A look at long-term trends in the US.

Michael Tesler and David O. Sears, *Obama's Race: The 2008 Election and the Dream of a Post-Racial America* (Chicago: University of Chicago Press, 2010). A look at the role of race in America and the effects of the Obama presidency.

John Tirman, *Immigration and the American Backlash* (Cambridge, MA: MIT Press, 2016).

Leonard Weinberg, *Fascism, Populism and American Democracy* (Abingdon: Routledge, 2018).

Michael Wolff, *The Fire and Fury: Inside the Trump White House* (New York: Henry Holt and Company, 2018). Best-selling account of the workings of the Trump administration.

Index

(Italic indicates a reference to the subject matter in a Figure)

H

I

U